PENGUIN BOOKS

THE ESSENTIAL GESTURE

Nadine Gordimer was born and lives in South Africa. Her collections of short stories include *The Soft Voice of the Serpent*, *Friday's Footprint*, *Livingstone's Companions*, *No Place Like: Selected Stories*, *A Soldier's Embrace* and *Something Out There*. Among her novels are *A World of Strangers*, *A Guest of Honour*, *The Conservationist*, joint winner of the Booker Prize, *Burger's Daughter*, *The Late Bourgeois World*, *July's People* and *A Sport of Nature*, all published by Penguin. She has also collaborated with the photographer David Goldblatt on two books, *On the Mines* and *Lifetimes: Under Apartheid*. She has received numerous literary awards, including the Malaparte Prize from Italy, the Nelly Sachs Prize from West Germany, the Scottish Arts Council's Neil Gunn Fellowship and the French International award, the Grand Aigle d'Or.

Stephen Clingman was born and educated in South Africa. He received his doctorate in English Literature from Oxford University in 1983. Since then he has held fellowships at Yale University, the University of Witwatersrand and the Society for the Humanities at Cornell University. He is the author of *The Novels of Nadine Gordimer: History from the Inside* (1986).

NADINE GORDIMER

The Essential Gesture: Writing, Politics and Places

Edited and introduced by Stephen Clingman

Penguin Books

PENGUIN BOOKS

Published by the Penguin Group
27 Wrights Lane, London W8 5TZ, England
Viking Penguin Inc., 40 West 23rd Street, New York, New York 10010, USA
Penguin Books Australia Ltd, Ringwood, Victoria, Australia
Penguin Books Canada Ltd, 2801 John Street, Markham, Ontario, Canada L3R 1B4
Penguin Books (NZ) Ltd, 182–190 Wairau Road, Auckland 10, New Zealand

Penguin Books Ltd, Registered Offices: Harmondsworth, Middlesex, England

First published by Jonathan Cape 1988
Published in Penguin Books 1989
1 3 5 7 9 10 8 6 4 2

Printed and bound in Great Britain by
Cox & Wyman Ltd, Reading

Contents

Acknowledgments

Compiling this volume has involved intensive as well as pleasurable work and in this regard I must acknowledge my gratitude to Nadine Gordimer who not only gave me the free run of her personal material, but was always at hand to help with the tracking of elusive references to sources she might have used. This was service above and beyond the call of duty, and I could not have done without it. Others who helped me trace particularly intractable references, or else provided invaluable background information, include colleagues at the University of the Witwatersrand: Gilbert Marcus and Laura Mangan of the Centre for Applied Legal Studies, Tim Couzens, Kelwyn Sole and Paul la Hausse of the African Studies Institute, Philip Bonner, Department of History, Henrietta Mondry, Department of Russian Studies, and Reingard Nethersole, Department of Comparative Literature. Andrea van Niekerk assisted with aspects of translation; Reeva Borowsky helped me find an important clue in the pursuit of Turgenev; Tamsin Donaldson (later) provided advice and words of wisdom. I am especially grateful to Professors Charles van Onselen and Tim Couzens of the African Studies Institute for providing such a congenial setting in which to carry out this work, and to the Society for the Humanities, Cornell University, where the book was completed. One acknowledgment is a close and heartfelt one: my wife Moira not only helped with references and proof-reading, but once again was the reservoir of serenity from which I continue to draw strength. Needless to say, whatever deficiencies remain in the editing of this volume are the fault of none of the people mentioned here.

Ithaca, *May 1988*   Stephen Clingman

Introduction

In June 1937, at the age of thirteen, Nadine Gordimer's first published fiction appeared.[1] In the fifty-one years since then people the world over have become familiar with the career of a major writer. Since 1949 Gordimer has published seven volumes of short stories and nine novels; her work has been translated into some twenty languages; she has won several of the most important literary prizes in Europe, the United States and South Africa. To many she has, through her fiction, become the *interpreter* of South Africa as, over the years, her country has marched down its doom-ridden slope of apartheid. Inside that tragedy Gordimer's has been a voice of conscience, of moral rigour, and of a clarified hope – the kind of hope that writing of brilliance can bring with it, no matter what kind of social distortions it is forced to survey.

What not many readers are aware of, however, is that for much of that period Gordimer's fiction has been accompanied by a remarkable output and array of non-fictional writing. Essays on writing and other writers, on South African politics, on censorship; biographical and autobiographical pieces; reviews and travelogues: these have been a consistent accompaniment to her fiction, echoing its concerns, providing a picture of South Africa in transition, and an inner account of an equivalent set of changes in Gordimer's life, experience and thoughts. Of a comprehensive catalogue of nearly 160 titles – some originally appearing in major international publications, some in small, out-of-the-way magazines, some relatively minor or never published at all – this is a selection of essays on writing, politics and places.[2]

In some respects the categorisations are broad ones. Thus, the essays on 'writing' and 'politics' include biographical pieces on literary and political figures, while Gordimer's articles on censorship cover both literary and political ground. Similarly, the idea of 'places' alludes to Gordimer's continuing attention to her South African world — a world which emerges in some breadth and depth through these essays — as well as those pieces of a specifically geographical alignment — her travel essays on Africa. What then are some of the issues which arise through a volume such as this? What are the thematic continuities which bind it together? This introduction cannot answer these questions at any length, but it can open up some avenues of thought.

'I remain a writer, not a public speaker: nothing I say here will be as true as my fiction.' Gordimer's pronouncement, from her essay 'Living in the Interregnum',[3] stands as a kind of judgment on her non-fiction as a whole. One can readily understand why she makes it. Beyond the mere conventionality of a belief in the essential mystique of fiction, there is the formulation she offers elsewhere in this volume, in 'Selecting My Stories': 'fiction is a way of exploring possibilities present but undreamt of in the living of a single life.' Here we do begin to see how fiction may represent social truths more searching and comprehensive than strict limitation to the 'facts' would allow. But is it necessarily so that Gordimer's fiction is 'truer' than her non-fiction? Is there such a radical gap between the two? Are there perhaps other kinds of truths which emerge from a collection such as this?

One kind of truth evident here is an obvious and immediately compelling one: Nadine Gordimer is a most extraordinary observer of her society. Through her essays the reader will gain an intricate and intimate view of what life in South Africa is like; even the South African reader is likely to be taken aback, perhaps recognising for the first time an aspect of the familiar or everyday world because Nadine Gordimer has *noticed* it. The quality of her writing has everything to do with this. On occasion here, as elsewhere, she has been dismissive of journalism in general because of its supposed superficiality. Yet these essays show what a superb journalist Gordimer might have been, because her insight is inseparable from her literary skills: one might say she is able *to see* in these words. Thus, in describing Albert Luthuli, or Bram Fischer, or Nat

Nakasa, suddenly the factual account deepens. By means of a word or a gesture characterisation comes through; a story envelops the characters; we are in the midst of a narrative, and the narrative adds substantially to our understanding. This is not very different from the skills with which Gordimer's fiction is imprinted, and indeed it would be surprising if this were not the case. Because of the skills, however, we are getting a highly privileged factual account.

In the same way that journalism takes on the proclivities of narrative in her hands, over the course of the essays – considering now the South African essays primarily – Gordimer's social depiction deepens into an implicit history. Nowhere in this volume is there a comprehensive survey of South African society or politics over the last forty or so years (any such overview is beyond the scope of this introduction as well). Yet, through these essays a history emerges none the less, one which the reader can follow. The rise to power of the National Party in 1948, and life under apartheid; the political, social and cultural world of the 1950s; the sabotage and resistance of the 1960s, as well as their defeat by the state; the rise of the Black Consciousness movement in the 1970s and the Soweto Revolt; the revolution which seemed to have begun by the 1980s: a cumulative picture builds up not only of these events and movements themselves, but also of what it has been like to live *through* them. This is a further kind of truth which emerges from these essays; in much the same way as in Gordimer's fiction, there is a 'history from the inside' [4] presented here, in which social change is described while it is occurring by one of its most perspicacious observers.

One must be clear as to what this history means. On the one hand, as just mentioned, it refers to the fact that Gordimer is describing change in South Africa from the midst of those changes, and relaying her vision of them to us. On the other hand, the searching reader will realise that there is here an inner history which relates to Gordimer *herself*, and to the substance and form of her vision. One is talking of a transformation of Gordimer's consciousness. For cognate to an outer change is an inner change whereby Gordimer matches up to it. This is what enables her *to see change in a particular way*; we watch the transformation of her perceptions and apprehensions, her very sense of moral and political obligation, in response to external events. The fact of this transformation will be apparent from even the most cursory glance: one need only compare the blithe innocence and gaiety of 'A Bolter and the Invincible Summer' to the studied seriousness and sense of responsibility of the essays of the 1980s to see how profound a change in Gordimer's awareness the pressure of political events in South Africa has provoked. Both kinds of change — inner and outer — it must be left to the reader to trace; above and beyond the excellence of the essays in themselves, this is part of their interest overall. However, it may be appropriate to suggest some of the significant dimensions in which these developments are to be found.

One of the most unusual areas of transformation in these essays concerns nothing less than Gordimer's sense of *identity*. This is perhaps best understood as a series of transgressions, an overstepping of successive boundaries. We see it begin as a young girl: the daughter of immigrant parents in a new country, in a sense for Gordimer the question of identity was already open, as to what life would become. Yet here, in a small mining-town, there was another set of social conventions belonging to the late-colonial world: school, tea-parties, office typing; love, marriage and motherhood. In this context, from early on *reading* was Gordimer's first transgression, introducing her to an alternative world. Still, there was the pull of the known and local setting: Gordimer records her lingering at home, her dallying before confessing that writing was her only vocation. But if reading was the first activity to free her, there is no doubt that writing was the second. For this was what made her scrutinise her accustomed world. Led by doubt, led 'by Kafka rather than Marx', Gordimer went falling through the surface, as she puts it, of the South African way of life.[5] Thereafter we watch the struggles waged within, and by, her sense of identity: her contradictory feelings of alienation and belonging in the 1950s, her politicisation in the 1960s, the radical challenge to her identity from the Black Consciousness movement in the 1970s, and a process of reconstruction in the 1980s whereby a new set of inner definitions comes to match vastly changed external circumstances. At each stage there is an opening out to new possibilities, a willingness to be exposed to new demands, no matter how difficult these may be for the inner life.

Transformation, then, is the motif. If this is so, however, it is only because it is based on a constancy: the constancy of Gordimer's approach, already implicit in what has been said. For underlying all Gordimer's changes, the flexibility of a mind growing stronger and more radical as it grows older, is the firmness of conviction. In politics, as in writing, Gordimer's sustained attempt, following her great example, Turgenev, is to see and then to relay 'life as it happens to be'.[6] There are to be no lies, no party line, no propaganda for the sake of a good cause. If anything is to help a good cause, it can only be the truth. 'We are here to challenge ourselves, without cant ... that is why I have agreed to speak on this platform,' she remarks at a conference in 1979.[7] The attitude and tone are characteristic: neither society nor the self is to be left immune from her uncompromising scrutiny. For this is Gordimer's central understanding: anything less than the truth is by definition complicit in the perpetuation of obfuscation and inequality; nothing can be too good for its demands. This is what has prompted her, with such verve and vitality, to inveigh against the evils of apartheid. This provides the resilience with which she has resisted and attacked the system of censorship. This same ethic is what underlies both her fiction and non-fiction, in a commitment to see neither more nor less than what there *is*. And this is the kernel of inner conviction that has allowed her to transform her social identity in response to the demands of the truth, to discard what is no longer viable, to take on the tasks of new obligations.

These are personal qualities, and no doubt wherever Gordimer had been active as a writer they would have come to the fore. Yet if there is a special intensity to them in South Africa, it has come about through a single sociological fact: the reality of Gordimer's marginality. This perhaps is a matter of some surprise, that the world-famous writer should yet be a figure on the margins. But this is how the matter stands: in South Africa Gordimer belongs, as she says, to a minority within the minority.[8] Out there is the world of apartheid. The majority – mostly black – suffers under one of the most elaborate systems of racial oppression and economic exploitation ever devised. The minority − by and large, the whites − are the ones to exercise that oppression and exploitation for their own supposed benefit. Within that world is yet a further group − of whites who are opposed to this system, who, somehow, wish to link up with the country's real majority. But how to do it remains the question, and it becomes particularly intense in the 1970s when the Black Consciousness movement begins to reject any form of affiliation with whites altogether.

What reservoirs of intellectual and emotional strength are required to confront the facts of one's own privilege while seeking ways to undo it? How does one deal with the daily compromises and contradictions explicit and implicit in one's situation? These problems are nothing as compared to the suffering experienced by starving children in South Africa's 'homelands', or families divided and kept in wretched poverty by the social and economic exactions of the migrant labour system; and this too is something the white in Gordimer's situation must recognise. But these are the problems she deals with, and there is perhaps a particular heroism in doing so; more than that, in continuing to attempt, despite these odds, to make one's way towards circumstances in which these realities will no longer apply. For there is a *solitude* here, an existential loneliness which accompanies commitment.

It is partly out of this solitude that Gordimer's scrutiny emerges. She is by nature an analytical thinker, looking at things, round them, viewing them from all angles; this flows in the first instance, one suspects, from the closeness of her visual inspection. In South Africa, however, it takes on special features, and what is induced is, simultaneously, a heightened social sensitivity and self-consciousness (understood here as a matter of both weakness and strength). For Gordimer's home territory is the world of irony and ambiguity, related to the ambiguity of her position. Even 'knowing where one belongs' can in this respect be highly ironical and ambiguous. In her essay 'Where Do Whites Fit In?' we watch Gordimer toiling honestly and with some anguish at the end of the 1950s to decide that Africa is indeed her 'place'. But later, partly under the impact of Black Consciousness in the 1970s, we see the other side of what 'knowing one's place' can mean:

> Although I am white and fully aware that my conscious-
> ness inevitably has the same tint as my face, when I have
> spoken of white attitudes and opinions I have not taken it
> upon myself to speak for whites, but have quoted attitudes
> and opinions expressed by whites themselves, or manifest
> (in my opinion) in their work. When I have spoken of
> black attitudes and opinions, I have not taken it upon
> myself to speak for blacks, but have quoted attitudes and
> opinions expressed by blacks themselves or (in my
> opinion) manifest in their work.[9]

This is a statement of extraordinary vulnerability and
toughness; the experience which has produced it speaks
through it; but it matches up to the experience. Here, in a few
lines, is the tremendous honing of political and literary
consciousness in South Africa. It is a statement unlikely to
come from anywhere else in the world, and there not quite in
this form from any other writer.

Evident here is Gordimer's sense of *limitation*, and also her
self-reflexivity. For where individuals, communities, classes
are living in such radically different social and existential
circumstances, it soon becomes clear that no vantage point is
neutral, that every observation reflects on the observer as
much as the observed. Because objective reality is out of kilter,
the self who is a part of it must be inspected as well, and cannot
be taken for granted. Every gaze at society is thus accompanied
by a look in the mirror to check that the eyes are not partially
closed, or that some distortion even in that glass has not by
chance intervened. 'I have to offer you myself as my most
closely observed specimen.'[10] This has a significance for Gordimer in South Africa beyond mere familiarity with an
identity, albeit a changing one; this self-inspection, growing in
intensity as time goes on, is part of the force of these essays.

Other dichotomies follow from the ambiguity of Gordimer's
position; specifically, they have to do with her being as a
writer. Again, the patterns we see may have occurred anywhere: there is always the tension Gordimer posits for the
writer between 'standing apart and being fully involved'.[11]
Again, however, in South Africa the pattern takes on especial
emphasis. For in a country suffering under apartheid, where

one's social and political commitments are fundamental, a
central question remains: how is one to fulfil those commitments as a writer? How far should one's writing be put at the
service of a cause; or, how far can 'good' writing be morally and
politically useful? Good writing, Gordimer tells us, requires
solitude. But is this solitude merely a reinforcement of a social
alienation which already exists – a virtue perhaps made of
necessity? Or is there some way in which the product of that
solitude – writing – may none the less be profoundly social,
rejoining the commonalty of society, and through its indirec-
tions and specificities being the most authentic contribution
the writer can offer? How far is one committed to history? How
far can one retain any sense of transcendent value in writing?
What – in essence – is the relationship between creativity and
responsibility? These questions have absorbed other writers
and societies in times of political upheaval. There can be no
doubt that they are central ones in South Africa, and central to
the life of Nadine Gordimer. In these pages the reader will
follow a continuing debate – of the greatest significance for her
fiction – which she wages with herself on these points.

Through all this, however, the underlying trend of Gordimer's development is plain. Beyond division and dichotomy
hers is a quest for wholeness, the vision of which imaginative
writing can offer, and which remains a political ideal. In her
life this has also been a quest in practical terms. It takes
tremendous courage to realise the full enormity of one's own
alienation, and in the 1970s the Black Consciousness movement pushed that recognition home to whites in Gordimer's
situation with a vengeance. After this, however, there was
resilience. In the wake of the Soweto Revolt we see Gordimer
taking up the mental struggle again: given the fact of social
fragmentation, a rupture which feels so deep it can hardly be
measured, how can whites and blacks make their ways separately and together towards a common future? And specifically:
how can white and black *writers* do this? For this is one of
Gordimer's primary commitments: towards a community of
writers. It started early on in her career, through her friendships with the black writers of the 1950s. Then this community
was destroyed, and Gordimer's piece in memory of Nat
Nakasa, 'One Man Living Through It', is almost a requiem for

the era. In the 1970s it was the black writers who rejected common action with the whites. In the 1980s, however, there is again something to be won, and Gordimer's latest essays record the minutiae of the battle, fending off attacks by the state on the one hand, jousting with black separatism on the other. Interestingly, one of the key measures of Gordimer's commitment becomes a willingness to *criticise* black writers and assess them, to assume that she has a place in the formation of a common future. This is an act of assertion, the obligation of an equal among equals. In making this assertion is the finding of a place, and in finding a place the formation of an identity.

At its widest, then, what defines these essays is a notion of *cultural* change, a word seen to run across a spectrum of meanings. The literary side of things is clear enough: Gordimer considers the essence of culture in South Africa and the writer's 'essential gesture' in these circumstances. But it is also a deeply personal and psychological issue. For, where the legacy of apartheid has been one of domination, a sense of self is bound up with cultural patterns at the broadest level. Similarly, where black and white identities have been ravaged through the false definitions imposed and fixed by systematic racial obsession, another sense of self is critical to the notion of an alternative future. At the social level identity *is* culture, and this is why politics and culture are so deeply intertwined in South Africa. One can see it in these essays: the tremulous feeling that literature – the condensation of all these issues – has an importance way beyond its own specific or autonomous interest. The extent to which this is the case is reminiscent of other societies in a state of political turmoil – a prime example being pre-revolutionary Russia, where politics and culture could similarly not be divorced.

It is the setting for the drama of these essays. As the work in this volume shows, over the last three decades Nadine Gordimer has been at the centre of developments in South Africa, a writer working through the political implications of her writing, writing about the implications of politics. Can it be entirely coincidental that over the years her political powers and her powers as a writer have grown concomitantly? In the 1980s, in her most deeply considered essays, the growing strength and vitality of her politics is expressed in the tensions and torsions of a newly poeticised and similarly strengthened language. One thing at any rate is clear: whatever future culture develops in South Africa, it could do far worse than to be based on the kind of rigorous, questioning independence of mind that we see in these essays, and that continues to grow in agility and strength.

As far as the South African essays are concerned then, we have arrived at a provisional understanding of what links them together, despite their diversity. If they resolve themselves in general into pieces on 'writing' and 'politics', this is also a distinction which breaks down and overflows its boundaries. For in a country such as South Africa there is no aspect of writing which is not deeply infused with political issues; similarly, when Gordimer deals with political or other social matters, she is always responding *as a writer*. For this reason, if there is an issue at the core of this volume, it is also the one closest to Gordimer's heart, even when not explicitly being discussed. It is what it *means* to be a writer in South Africa; how one writes in response to its politics.

Yet these essays are not only about South Africa, or the literary–political nexus within that setting. Almost of equal importance to Gordimer from the start of her writing career has been her sense of place. Indeed, perhaps it was of greater importance at the beginning since, as we have seen, it was through her feel for place – her particular place in the world – that Gordimer first came to political consciousness. It was, then, something of a natural and logical extension that when Gordimer began to travel in Africa she should proceed from local observation of her own world to travel descriptions, producing the kind of essay found in the third section of this book, 'A Writer in Africa'.

By and large their qualities speak for themselves. There is Gordimer's wry, amused and intrigued eye in her essay on Madagascar; there is her political independence of mind in her account of Ghana and the Ivory Coast. One quality of all the essays also extends directly from her South African work. Gordimer remarks that her preoccupation as a writer has always lain in 'seeing the link or finding the link between people and the place that has bred them'.[12] Consequently, people are seldom out of the picture in these travel accounts, whether in Gordimer's concern for the relationship between rulers and ruled in Egypt, or, in all her descriptions, the way that the figures she comes across meld into and emerge out of their physical environment. Gordimer has a particularly acute eye for incongruous juxtapositions, at the same time understanding their naturalness in their own settings: in Botswana she encounters Herero women in Victorian dress; in the Transkei she finds Pondo youths adorned in the eclectic paraphernalia of a rural–urban, peasant–industrial, migrant economy and culture. Always she has a feel for total beauty, as in the young Mbukushu woman in Botswana, sparse and functional in her presence, though equally complicated in her dress, who seems to embody the spirit of her time and place. Indeed, at times dress tells its own kind of history: as the colourful Pondo youths reel off the names of the mines they have worked in, Gordimer imagines 'their steel-helmeted heads' in another, more sombre context.

Perhaps it is Gordimer's natural descriptions, however, which readers will find most compelling. The sensuousness of Gordimer's response to her physical environment has always been a feature of her writing, and those searching for it here will find no lack. Travelling up the length of the Congo River or descending from one of the Ruwenzori peaks in East Africa, Gordimer shows an extraordinary ability to capture shape, form, colour, smell, feel, particularity and general impression. In towns she has the bustle of markets; in the desert the spareness of absence. In Botswana she writes of a day at Lake Ngami, and the virtuosity of her apt impressionism, as colours and shapes shift and merge through the shimmering hours, is quite dazzling. Above all here we see Gordimer's enthralment by, and her extraordinary response to, Africa. There are moments of writing whose movement and imagery are those of the continent itself, deeply moved by it, moving into it, standing apart and watching it with that piercing, receptive perception. Again there is the question: would we be able to see it, were it not described in this way?

Gordimer's presence and separateness as an observer raise an earlier issue in a different form, having to do with her status as a traveller in Africa. The presupposition of the travelogue as a genre is that the writer is an *outsider* – transient and standing apart from the world which is visited. Yet Gordimer's position is obviously more complex than this. Thus, despite her sense of strangeness in the Congo, she remarks, she was not 'the same kind of stranger as a European from Europe'.[13] Because of having been born in Africa, amongst black people, and in the midst of that strange relationship between black and white, there are levels of original understanding that cannot come easily to a complete outsider. Similarly, among the Pondo mineworkers in the Transkei, she had been seeing such people, she says, since she was five or six years old.[14] Yet – and the Transkei essay is a good example – it is also clear that to some extent, because of the enormous disparity in living conditions, Gordimer is also a foreigner in regions of her own country. The alienness of the interiors of huts, where grandmothers have to bring up young children in the absence of their fathers and mothers, is something implicitly conceded.

If Gordimer is both insider and outsider, the question becomes: what is her status as an African writer? Writing travelogues may, paradoxically, be the sign of a fundamental estrangement. If so, it is no more than anyone else faces; the paradox swiftly dissolves. Which African writer is at home in *all* of Africa? Gordimer is no less African for this problem. Indeed, on the contrary, these essays become evidence of a different commitment: to *be* an African writer. In much the same way as in her novels *A Guest of Honour*[15] and *A Sport of Nature*[16] – the one set wholly in Africa, the other partly so – the essays indicate Gordimer's continuing endeavour to extend her sense of self-definition, as not only South African, but African. This is part of her sense of obligation; this is part of her sense of curiosity; this is part of what she has to offer, as a reporter of what is happening both above and below the surface, from her continent in this time. Again we meet the theme of cultural engagement in these essays, especially in so far as it involves an idea of social identity: Gordimer's travel writing embodies her being as an African writer. This is true for all the duality of her familiarity and estrangement in the continent. If her other essays are about the meaning of being a writer in South Africa, these are, in part, about the meaning of being a writer in Africa.

These are some of the issues raised by this volume. As far as this introduction is concerned, however, it should be read less as an explication than an encouragement – for the reader to go directly to the essays themselves. Yet at least one question has been answered: there is no radical gap between Gordimer's fiction and non-fiction. Indeed, those who know both will find many echoes running between them. For these essays must not simply be understood as *background*. It is true that they will deepen and enrich any understanding of Gordimer's short stories and novels (for instance her latest novel, *A Sport of Nature*, has drawn on some of the experiences that led to her travel essays here); but also they exist in their own right. Here we see Gordimer living through in real life what she lives through in her imagination in her fiction. The two – her fiction and non-fiction – are best thought of not as two separate entities, but as two different modes revolving around a single process. If this collection will encourage further exploration of Gordimer's fiction and non-fiction alike, it will have more than succeeded in its purpose.

It remains only to remark on the organisational principles of the book. Within its different sections the layout of the volume is chronological (in the first section there is only one essay, but it deals with Gordimer's early life). The reasons for this temporal fidelity are simple. Apart from the fact that the essays are often responses to particular moments, if readers are to follow some of the developments mentioned in this intro-duction, or fashion their own appreciation of changes both within South Africa and in Gordimer's perceptions of them, then the chronological procedure is necessary. Without labouring the point, even the relationship between the different sections bears this dimension. These correspond to different phases and movements in Gordimer's life, from the 'begin-nings' of her career, through her respective explorations as a writer in South Africa and in Africa from the late 1950s to the 1970s, to the period of 'interregnum' of the 1980s, when, surveying a world of great conflict and moment in South Africa, Gordimer looks also towards the future.

A primary intention here is to provide a sense of context.

Just as Gordimer has been concerned to explore her own space and time, in the same way, it is felt, readers may wish to follow her on that journey. The idea has been, besides the attraction of the essays themselves, to provide a feel for the world, the figures, the places Gordimer has moved through and among. Consequently, a series of short introductions to the essays sets each in its particular context, and draws the most significant lines of development between them (in 'A Writer in Africa' there is one introduction to the section as a whole). Editorial annotation has followed the same rationale. Thus, for those readers (professional or otherwise) who require it, editorial notes enlarge upon the world Gordimer has lived through, or provide sources unreferenced by her which may also be of interest.

Editorial notes are numbered in the text and may be found at the back of the book. Yet there is another set of notes in the volume – Gordimer's own; these will be asterisked in the text, and found as footnotes at the bottom of the page. The only point worth mentioning here is that Gordimer's independence of mind carries over to her scholarly pursuits: her annotation of sources is endearingly erratic as she transfers striking or illuminating quotations from her sources to her notebooks to her essays. All I have attempted to do, wherever possible, is trace them again, verify them, and standardise them. For all notes – Gordimer's and my own – I have attempted, where applicable, to provide American, English and South African publication details for sources, except where a particular edition and page reference are given. Only where it seemed necessary have I intervened to draw attention to a specific edition Gordimer may have been using as a source, or a particular translation. Editorial interventions throughout are shown by square brackets – '[ ]' – while Gordimer's own interpolations within quotations are indicated thus: '{ }'. In general, through the short introductions, Gordimer's notes and the editorial notes, information will be regarded as cumulative. This should enable those readers who wish to to construct much of what they need to know around and about the essays; but for all there is the central experience of the essays themselves.

Finally, a comment on the status of the essays: the procedure here has operated between two principles – that of historical accuracy, and that of the need to produce a definitive edition. These principles are not always easy to reconcile, but readers may be assured that where necessary and where possible an attempt has been made to retain Gordimer's original versions; there has been little change of substance in these essays.[17] As regards terminology this procedure has been exact: Gordimer's terminology, especially on racial matters, has been retained in its original form through the essays; as she remarks herself in 'Selecting My Stories', this provides its own inner history of a changing social consciousness in South Africa. Current terminology should be self-explanatory, except in the case of one group. The so-called 'coloureds' or 'mixed-race' people of South Africa do not necessarily accept their categorisation as a separate race. This is strictly a legislative and administrative term, and this is the reason for the quotation marks; other spurious creations of the apartheid system will also appear in such marks.

Beginnings

A Bolter
and the Invincible Summer

(1963)[1]

*Including youthful work, by 1963 Nadine Gordimer had published
in South Africa for nearly twenty-five years and internationally for
over ten. Here she recalls how her writing career began.*

My writing life began long before I left school, and I began to
leave school (frequently) long before the recognised time came,
so there is no real demarcation, for me, between school and
'professional' life. The quotes are there because I think of
professional life as something one enters by way of an examination, not as an obsessional occupation like writing for which
you provide your own, often extraordinary or eccentric, qualifications as you go along. And I'm not flattered by the idea of
being presented with a 'profession', *honoris causa*; every honest
writer or painter wants to achieve the impossible and needs no
minimum standard laid down by an establishment such as a
profession.

This doesn't mean that I think a writer doesn't need a good
education in general, and that I don't wish I had had a better
one. But maybe my own regrets arise out of the common
impulse to find a justification, outside the limits of one's own
talent, for the limits of one's achievement.

I was a bolter, from kindergarten age, but unlike most small
children rapidly accustoming their soft, round selves to the
sharp angles of desks and discipline, I went on running away
from school, year after year. I was a day scholar at a convent in
Springs, the Transvaal gold-mining town where we lived, and
when I was little I used to hide until I heard the hive of voices
start up 'Our Father' at prayers, and then I would walk out of
the ugly iron gates and spend the morning on the strip of open
veld that lay between the township where the school was and

19

the township where my home was. I remember catching white butterflies there, all one summer morning, until, in the quiet when I had no shadow, I heard the school bell, far away, clearly, and I knew I could safely appear at home for lunch. When I was older I used to take refuge for hours in the lavatory block, waiting in the atmosphere of Jeyes' Fluid for my opportunity to escape. By then I no longer lived from moment to moment, and could not enjoy the butterflies; the past, with the act of running away contained in it, and the future, containing discovery and punishment, made freedom impossible; the act of seizing it was merely a desperate gesture.

What the gesture meant, I don't know. I managed my school work easily, and among the girls of the class I had the sort of bossy vitality that makes for popularity; yet I was overcome, from time to time, by what I now can at least label as anxiety states. Speculation about their cause hasn't much place here, which is lucky, for the people who were around me then are still alive. Autobiography can't be written until one is old, can't hurt anyone's feelings, can't be sued for libel, or, worse, contradicted.

There is just one curious aspect of my bolting that seems worth mentioning because it reveals a device of the personality that, beginning at that very time, perhaps, as a dream-defence, an escape, later became the practical sub-conscious cunning that enabled me to survive and grow in secret while projecting a totally different, camouflage image of myself. I ran away from school; yet there was another school, the jolly, competitive, thrillingly loyal, close-knit world of schoolgirl books, to which I felt that I longed to belong. (At one time I begged to go to boarding school, believing, no doubt, that I should find it there.) Of course, even had it existed, that *School Friend* world would have been the last place on earth for me. I should have found there, far more insistently, the walls, the smell of serge and floor polish, the pressure of uniformity and the tyranny of bell-regulated time that set off revolt and revulsion in me. What I did not know — and what a child never knows — is that there is more to the world than what is offered to him; more choices than those presented to him; more kinds of people than those (the only ones he knows) to which he feels but dares not admit he does not belong. I thought I *had* to accept school and all the attitudes there that reflected the attitudes of home; therefore, in order to be a person I had to have *some* sort of picture of a school that would be acceptable to me; it didn't seem possible to live without it. Stevie Smith once wrote that all children should be told of the possibility of committing suicide, to console them in case they believed there was no way out of the unbearable; it would be less dramatic but far more consoling if a child could be told that there is an aspect of himself he *does not know is permissible*.

The conclusion my bolting school drew from the grown-ups around me was that I was not the studious type and simply should be persuaded to reconcile myself to the minimum of learning. In our small town many girls left school at fifteen or even before. Then, after a six-week course at the local commercial college, a girl was ready for a job as a clerk in a shop or in the offices of one of the gold mines which had brought the town into being. And the typewriter itself merely tapped a marktime for the brief season of glory, self-assertion and importance that came with the engagement party, the pre-nuptial linen 'shower', and culminated not so much in the wedding itself as in the birth, not a day sooner than nine months and three weeks later, of the baby. There wasn't much point in a girl keeping her head stuck in books anyway; even if she chose to fill the interim with one of the occupations that carried a slightly higher prestige, and were vaguely thought of as artistic — teaching tap-dancing, the piano, or 'elocution'.

I suppose I must have been marked out for one of these, because, although I had neither talent nor serious interest in drumming my toes, playing Czerny, or rounding my vowels, I enjoyed using them all as material in my talent for showing off. As I grew toward adolescence I stopped the home concerts and contented myself with mimicking, for the entertainment of one group of my parents' friends, other friends who were not present. It did not seem to strike those who were that, in their absence, they would change places with the people they were laughing at; or perhaps it did, I do them an injustice, and they didn't mind.

All the time it was accepted that I was a candidate for home-dressmaking or elocution whom there was no point in keeping at school too long, I was reading and writing not in secret, but as one does, openly, something that is not taken into account. It didn't occur to anyone else that these activities were connected with learning, so why should it have occurred to me? And although I fed on the attention my efforts at impersonation brought me, I felt quite differently about any praise or comment that came when my stories were published in the children's section of a Sunday paper.[2] While I was terribly proud to see my story in print — for only in print did it become 'real', did I have proof of the miracle whereby the thing created has an existence of its own — I had a jealous instinct to keep this activity of mine from the handling that would pronounce it 'clever' along with the mimicry and the home concerts. It was the beginning of the humble arrogance that writers and painters have, knowing that it is hardly likely that they will ever do anything really good, and not wanting to be judged by standards that will accept anything less. Is this too high-falutin' a motive to attribute to a twelve-year-old child? I don't think so. One can have a generalised instinct toward the unattainable long before one has actually met with it. When, not many years later, I read *Un Cœur simple* or *War and Peace* — O, I knew this was it, without any guidance from the list of the World's Hundred Best Books that I once tried to read through!

I started writing at nine, because I was surprised by a poem I produced as a school exercise. The subject prescribed was 'Paul Kruger',[3] and although an item of earliest juvenilia, in view of what has happened between people like myself and our country since then, I can't resist quoting, just for the long-untasted patriotic flavour:

> Noble in heart,
> Noble in mind,
> Never deceitful,
> Never unkind . . .

It was the dum-de-de-dum that delighted me rather than the sentiments or the subject. But soon I found that what I really enjoyed was making up a story, and that this was more easily done without the restrictions of dum-de-de-dum. After that I was always writing something, and from the age of twelve or thirteen, often publishing. My children's stories were anthropomorphic, with a dash of the Edwardian writers' Pan-cult paganism as it had been shipped out to South Africa in Kenneth Grahame's books, though already I used the background of mine dumps and veld animals that was familiar to me, and not the European one that provided my literary background, since there were no books about the world I knew. I wrote my elder sister's essays when she was a student at the Witwatersrand University, and kept up a fair average for her. I entered an essay in the literary section of the Eisteddfod run by the Welsh community in Johannesburg and bought with the prize chit *War and Peace*, *Gone with the Wind*, and an Arthur Ransome.

I was about fourteen then, and a happy unawareness of the strange combination of this choice is an indication of my reading. It was appetite rather than taste, that I had; yet while it took in indiscriminately things that were too much for me, the trash tended to be crowded out and fall away. Some of the books I read in my early teens puzzle me, though. Why Pepys's *Diary*? And what made me plod through *The Anatomy of Melancholy*? Where did I hear of the existence of these books? (That list of the World's One Hundred Best, maybe.) And once I'd got hold of something like Burton, what made me go on from page to page? I think it must have been because although I didn't understand all that I was reading, and what I did understand was remote from my experience in the way that easily-assimilable romance was not, the half-grasped words dealt with the world of ideas, and so confirmed the recognition, somewhere, of that part of myself that I did not know was permissible.

All the circumstances and ingredients were there for a small-town prodigy, but, thank God, by missing the encouragement and practical help usually offered to 'talented' children, I also escaped the dwarf status that is clapped upon the poor little devils before their time (if it ever comes). It did not occur to anyone that if I wanted to try to write I ought to be given a wide education in order to develop my powers and to give me some cultural background. But this neglect at least meant that I was left alone. Nobody came gawping into the private domain that was no dream-world, but, as I grew up, the scene of my greatest activity and my only disciplines. When school-days finally petered out (I had stopped running away, but various other factors had continued to make attendance sketchy) I did have some sort of show of activity that passed for my life in the small town. It was so trivial that I wonder how it can have passed, how family or friends can have accepted that any young person could expend vitality at such a low hum. It was never decided what I should 'take up' and so I didn't have a job. Until, at twenty-two, I went to the University, I led an outward life of sybaritic meagreness that I am ashamed of. In it I did not one thing that I wanted wholeheartedly to do; in it I attempted or gratified nothing (outside sex) to try out my reach, the measure of aliveness in me. My existential self was breathing but inert, like one of those unfortunate people who has had a brain injury in a motor accident and lies unhearing and unseeing, though he will eat when food comes and open his eyes to a light. I played golf, learnt to drink gin with the RAF pupil pilots from the nearby air station, and took part in amateur theatricals to show recognisable signs of life to the people around me. I even went to first aid and nursing classes because this was suggested as an 'interest' for me; it did not matter to me what I did, since I could not admit that there was nothing, in the occupations and diversions offered to me, that really did interest me, and I was not sure — the only evidence was in books — that anything else was possible.

I am ashamed of this torpor nevertheless, setting aside what I can now see as probable reasons for it, the careful preparation for it that my childhood constituted. I cannot understand why I did not free myself in the most obvious way, leave home and small town and get myself a job somewhere. No conditioning can excuse the absence of the simple act of courage that would resist it. My only overt rejection of my match-box life was the fact that, without the slightest embarrassment or conscience, I let my father keep me. Though the needs provided for were modest, he was not a rich man. One thing at least I would not do, apparently — I would not work for the things I did not want. And the camouflage image of myself as a dilettantish girl, content with playing grown-up games at the end of my mother's apron strings — at most a Bovary in the making — made this possible for me.

When I was fifteen I had written my first story about adults and had sent it off to a liberal weekly that was flourishing in South Africa at the time. They published it.[4] It was about an old man who is out of touch with the smart, prosperous life he has secured for his sons, and who experiences a moment of human recognition where he least expects it — with one of their brisk young wives who is so unlike the wife he remembers. Not a bad theme, but expressed with the respectable bourgeois sentiment which one would expect. That was in 1939, two months after the war had broken out, but in the years that followed the stories that I was writing were not much influenced by the war. It occupied the news bulletins on the radio, taking place a long way off, in countries I had never seen; later, when I was seventeen or eighteen, there were various boy-friends who went away to Egypt and Italy and sent back coral jewellery and leather bags stamped with a sphinx.

Oddly enough, as I became engaged with the real business of learning how to write, I became less prompt about sending my efforts off to papers and magazines. I was reading Maupassant, Chekhov, Maugham and Lawrence, now, also discovering O. Henry, Katherine Anne Porter and Eudora Welty, and the stories in *Partisan Review*, *New Writing* and *Horizon*. Katherine Mansfield and Pauline Smith,[5] although one was a New Zealander, confirmed for me that my own 'colonial' background provided an experience that had scarcely been looked at, let alone thought about, except as a source of adventure stories. I had read 'The Death of Ivan Ilyich'[6] and 'The Child of Queen Victoria';[7] the whole idea of what a story could do, be, swept aside the satisfaction of producing something that found its small validity in print. From time to time I sent off an attempt to one of the short-lived local politico-literary magazines — meant chiefly as platforms for liberal politics, they were the only publications that published poetry and stories outside the true romance category — but these published stories were the easy ones. For the other I had no facility whatever, and they took months, even years, to cease changing shape before I found a way of getting hold of them in my mind, let alone nailing the words down around them. And then most of them were too long, or too outspoken (not always in the sexual sense) for these magazines. In a fumbling way that sometimes slid home in an unexpected strike, I was looking for what people meant but didn't say, not only about sex, but also about politics and their relationship with the black people among whom we lived as people live in a forest among trees. So it was that I didn't wake up to Africans and the shameful enormity of the colour bar through a youthful spell in the Communist Party, as did some of my contemporaries with whom I share the rejection of white supremacy, but through the apparently esoteric speleology of doubt, led by Kafka rather than Marx. And the 'problems' of my country did not set me writing; on the contrary, it was learning to write that sent me falling, falling through the surface of 'the South African way of life'.

It was about this time, during a rare foray into the nursery bohemia of university students in Johannesburg, that I met a boy who believed I was a writer. Just that; I don't mean he saw me as Chosen for the Holy Temple of Art, or any presumptuous mumbo-jumbo of that kind. The cosmetic-counter sophistication that I hopefully wore to disguise my stasis in the world I knew and my uncertainty of the possibility of any other, he ignored as so much rubbish. This aspect of myself, that everyone else knew, he did not; what he recognised was my ignorance, my clumsy battle to chip my way out of shell after shell of ready-made concepts and make my own sense of life. He was often full of scorn, and jeered at the way I was going about it; but he *recognised the necessity*. It was through him, too, that I roused myself sufficiently to insist on going to the University; not surprisingly, there was opposition to this at home, since it had been accepted so long that I was not the studious type, as the phrase went. It seemed a waste, spending money on a university at twenty-two (surely I should be married soon?); it was suggested that (as distinct from the honourable quest for a husband) the real reason why I wanted to go was to look for men. It seems to me now that this would have been as good a reason as any. My one preoccupation outside the world of ideas was men, and I should have been prepared to claim my right to the one as valid as the other.

But my freedom did not come from my new life at university; I was too old, in many ways, had already gone too far, on my own scratched tracks, for what I might once have gained along the tarmac. One day a poet asked me to lunch. He was co-editor of yet another little magazine that was then halfway through the dozen issues that would measure its life. He had just published a story of mine and, like many editors when the contributor is known to be a young girl, was curious to meet its author. He was the Afrikaans poet and playwright Uys Krige, who wrote in English as well, had lived in France and Spain, spoke five languages, was familiar with their literature, and translated from three. He had been a swimming instructor on the Riviera, a football coach somewhere else, and a war correspondent with the International Brigade in Spain.

When the boy (that same boy) heard that I was taking the train into Johannesburg for this invitation — I still lived in Springs — he said: 'I wouldn't go, if I were you, Nadine.'

'For Pete's sake, why not?'

'Not unless you're prepared to change a lot of things. You may not feel the same, afterwards. You may never be able to go back.'

'What on *earth* are you talking about?' I made fun of him: 'I'll take the train back.'

'No, once you see what a person like that is like, you won't be able to stand your ordinary life. You'll be miserable. So don't go unless you're prepared for this.'

The poet was a small, sun-burned, blond man. While he joked, enjoyed his food, had an animated discussion with the African waiter about the origin of the name of a fruit, and said for me some translations of Lorca and Eluard, first in Afrikaans and then, because I couldn't follow too well, in English, he had the physical brightness of a fisherman. It was true; I had never met anyone like this being before. I have met many poets and writers since, sick, tortured, pompous, mousy; I know the morning-after face of Apollo. But that day I had a glimpse of — not some spurious 'artist's life', but, through the poet's person, the glint of his purpose — what we are all getting at, Camus's 'invincible summer'[8] that is there to be dug for in man beneath the grey of suburban life, the numbness of repetitive labour, and the sucking mud of politics.

Oh yes — not long after, a story of mine was published in an anthology,[9] and a second publisher approached me with the offer to publish a collection.[10] The following year I at last sent my stories where I had never been – across the seas to England and America. They came back to me in due course, in hard covers with my name printed on the coloured jacket.[11] There were reviews, and, even more astonishing, there was money. I was living alone in Johannesburg by then, and was able to pay the rent and feed both myself and the baby daughter I had acquired. These things are a convenient marker for the beginning of a working life. But mine really began that day at lunch. I see the poet occasionally. He's older now, of course; a bit seamed with disappointments, something of a political victim, since he doesn't celebrate his people's politics or the white man's colour bar in general. The truth isn't always beauty, but the hunger for it is.

A Writer
in South Africa

Where Do Whites Fit In?

Nadine Gordimer's second novel, A World of Strangers,[2] was published in 1958. Drawing its inspiration from the middle years of that decade, it is in part a celebration of its era. For this was the time of the movement of 'multi-racialism' in response to the policies of the National Party government. Politically, under the Congress Alliance, and socially, in Johannesburg particularly, members of the different races were coming together as if to prove, almost by force of their example, that the precept of inter-racial solidarity must vanquish the divisiveness of apartheid. There was a tremendous optimism too. As Africa's decade of independence from the colonial powers approached (Ghana was the first country to gain its independence, in 1957), it seemed to many that liberation in South Africa could not be far distant. Yet there were at least two forces which undermined this optimism by the end of the 1950s. One was the renewed onslaught by the government against any inter-racial cooperation or mixing, whether politically, socially or culturally. The other was the rise of 'Africanism', a movement linking itself to Pan-Africanism throughout the continent, and dedicated less to a 'multi-racial' opposition against apartheid than to a purer form of African nationalism as such. To those dedicated, as Gordimer was at that stage, to the principles of liberal humanism, and opposed to any form of racial or nationalist categorisation, the overall effects may have been dismaying. It was under these circumstances that she considered the future of whites in Africa.

Where do whites fit in in the New Africa? *Nowhere*, I'm inclined to say, in my gloomier and least courageous moods; and I do believe that it is true that even the gentlest and most western-ised Africans would like the emotional idea of the continent entirely without the complication of the presence of the white

31

man for a generation or two. But *nowhere*, as an answer for us whites, is in the same category as remarks like *What's the use of living?* in the face of the threat of atomic radiation. We are living; we are in Africa. *Nowhere* is the desire to avoid painful processes and accept an ultimate and final solution (which doesn't exist in the continuous process that is life itself); the desire to have over and done with; the death wish, if not of the body, at least of the spirit.

For if we're going to fit in at all in the new Africa, it's going to be sideways, where-we-can, wherever-they'll-shift-up-for-us. This will not be comfortable; indeed, it will be hardest of all for those of us (I am one myself) who want to belong in the new Africa as we never could in the old, where our skin-colour labelled us as oppressors to the blacks and our views labelled us as traitors to the whites. We want merely to be ordinary members of a multi-coloured, any-coloured society, freed both of the privileges and the guilt of the white sins of our fathers. This seems to us perfectly reasonable and possible and, in terms of reason, it is. But belonging to a society implies two factors which are outside reason: the desire to belong, on the one part, and acceptance, on the other part. The new Africa may, with luck, grant us our legal rights, full citizenship and the vote, but I don't think it will accept us in the way we're hankering after. If ever, it will take the confidence of several generations of jealous independence before Africa will feel that she can let us belong.

There is nothing so damaging to the ego as an emotional rebuff of this kind. (More bearable by far the hate-engendered hate that the apartheiders must expect.) And you don't have to be particularly thin-skinned in order to feel this rebuff coming in Africa. Africans are prickling with the desire to be off on their own; the very fact that you welcome the new Africa almost as fervently as they do seems an intrusion in itself. They have had so much of us — let's not go through the whole list again, from tear-gas and taxes to brotherly advice — that all they crave is to have no part of us.

You'll understand that I'm not speaking in economic or even political, but purely in human or, if you prefer it, psychological terms. For the purposes of what I have to say it may be true that in South Africa, for example, foreign capital and skills would have to be retained, in order to keep the mines and industry going, by wide concessions given by any black independent government with its head screwed on the right way. But the fact that we might go on living in our comfortable houses in the suburbs of Johannesburg under a black republic just as we do under a white near-republic, does not mean that we should feel ourselves accepted as part of the homogeneous society of the new Africa. For a long time to come any white South African must expect to find any black man, from any African territory, considered by the black South African as more of a brother than the white South African himself. No personal bonds of loyalty, friendship or even love will change this; it is a nationalism of the heart that has been brought about by suffering. There is no share in it we can hope to have. I for one can read this already in the faces, voices and eloquently regretful but firm handclasps of my own African friends.

Make no mistake, those moderate African political leaders who offer us whites – with sincerity, I believe – full participation in the new life of Africa offer us only the tangibles of existence. The intangibles that make up emotional participation and the sense of belonging cannot be legislated for.

What are we to do? Shall we go? Shall we leave Africa? For those small white communities who are truly foreign to the African territories in which they live, 'sent out' from a homeland in Europe for a spell of duty on administrative jobs or as representatives of commercial firms, there can't be much question of staying on. But in those territories, such as South Africa and the Rhodesias, where there is a sizeable and settled white population whose *home* is Africa, there is no easy answer; sometimes, it seems no answer at all. I do not attempt to speak, of course, for the stubborn mass that will continue, like a Napoleon in a mad house, to see itself as the undisputed master and make no attempt to consider the reality of living another role. I do not even try to guess what will happen to them; what *can* happen to them in a situation that they find unthinkable. I can only fear that events will deal with them grimly, as events usually do with people who refuse to think. I speak for people like myself, who think almost too much about the whole business and hope to arrive at an honest answer, without self-pity for the whites or sentiment about the blacks.

Some of us in South Africa want to leave; a few of us have gone already. And certainly, when one comes to Europe on a visit, one becomes a little uneasy at the number of friends (well-informed friends with a good perspective on the swerves and lurches of the way the world is going) who take one aside and ask whether one isn't planning to leave Africa? Which brings me to the reasons why some people have left and why these friends in Europe think one should pack up, too. A few have left because they cannot bear the guilt and ugliness of the white man's easy lot here; a few have left because they are afraid of the black man; and most, I should say, have left because of a combination of the two. I doubt if any consciously have left for the long-term reason I have elaborated here — the growing unwelcomeness of the white man in Africa. Yet I feel that if the white man's lot were to become no better and no worse than anyone else's tomorrow and the fear of violence at the hands of the black man (which we all have) were to have been brought to the test and disproved, unwelcomeness might still remain as the factor that would, in the end, decide many of us to give up our home and quit Africa.

I myself fluctuate between the desire to be gone — to find a society for myself where my white skin will have no bearing on my place in the community — and a terrible, obstinate and fearful desire to stay. I feel the one desire with my head and the other with my guts. I know that there must be many others who feel as I do, and who realise that generally the head is the more sensible guide of the two. Those of us who stay will need to have the use of our heads in order to sustain the emotional decision that home is not necessarily where you belong ethnogenically, but rather the place you were born to, the faces you first saw around you, and the elements of the situation among your fellow men in which you found yourself and with which you have been struggling, politically, personally or artistically, all your life.

The white man who wants to fit in in the new Africa must learn a number of hard things. He'd do well to regard himself as an immigrant to a new country; somewhere he has never lived before, but to whose life he has committed himself. He'll have to forget the old impulses to leadership, and the temptation to give advice backed by the experience and culture of

Western civilisation — Africa is going through a stage when it passionately prefers its own mistakes to successes (or mistakes) that are not its own. This is an absolutely necessary stage in all political, sociological and spiritual growth, but it is an uncomfortable and disillusioning one to live through. And giving up the impulse to advise and interfere and offer to resume responsibility may not be as easy as we whites think. Even those of us who don't want to be boss (or *baas*, rather) have become used to being bossy. We've been used to assuming leadership or at least tutorship, even if it's only been in liberal campaigns to secure the rights of the Africans to vote and speak for themselves. Out of our very concern to see Africans make a go of the new Africa, we may — indeed, I know we shall — be tempted to offer guidance when we haven't been consulted. The facts that we'll be well-meaning and that the advice may be good and badly-needed do not count; the sooner we drum that into our egos the better. What counts is the need of Africa to acquire confidence through the experience of picking itself up, dusting itself down, and starting all over again; and the quickening marvel of often getting things right into the bargain.

It's hard to sit quiet when you think you can tell how a problem may be solved or a goal accomplished, but it may be even harder to give help without recriminations or, worse, smugness when it is sought. If we want to fit in anywhere in Africa, that is what we'll have to teach ourselves to do; answer up, cheerfully and willingly, when we're called upon and shut up when we're not. Already I notice that the only really happy whites I know in Africa — the only ones who are at peace with themselves over their place in the community — are some South African friends of mine who have gone to live in Ghana, and who have an educational job to do on contract from the Government. They are living as equals among the Africans, they have no say in the affairs of the country for the Africans to resent and they are contributing something useful and welcome to the development of Africa. In other words, they are in the position of foreign experts, employed at the Government's pleasure. I can positively feel my fellow-whites in Africa swelling with indignation at this extreme picture of the white man's future life on the continent; and it makes me feel rather indignant myself. But I think we've got to accept the home truth of the picture, whether we like it or not, and whether or not what we see there seems fair. All that the new Africa will really want from us will be what we can give as 'foreign experts' – the technical, scientific and cultural knowledge that white civilisation has acquired many hundreds of years before black civilisation, and on which, whether the Africans like it or not, their own aspirations are based.

I suppose we may get over being a minority minority instead of the majority minority we've been used to being all these past years, but I don't know whether that valuable change of attitude will actually bring us much nearer the integration we seek. Will intermarriage help us? It would, of course, on a large scale, but personally I don't believe that it will happen on a large scale in Africa. Intermarriage has always been regarded as a social stigma by whites, even in those territories where, unlike South Africa, it is not actually a crime, but I have never been able to find out whether, among blacks, it is regarded as a stigma or a step up in the world. (Most whites assume it is regarded as a deeply-desired privilege, of course.) I know that, for example, in South Africa many Africans who are not Bechuanas, and have nothing whatever to do with the people of Bechuanaland, have on their walls a picture of Ruth and Seretse Khama.[3] It is difficult to say whether this means that they take pride in the fact that a white woman chose to marry an important African, or whether the picture simply gives them a chance to identify themselves with the ex-chief's successful defiance of white taboo and authority.

Once the social stigma is removed – in the new Africa marriage with an African will be marrying into the ruling class, remember, and no one can measure how much of colour-prejudice is purely class-prejudice, in a country where there has been a great gap between the living standards of black and white – and once (in the case of South Africa) there are no legal disabilities in mixed marriages, I think that inter-marriage will increase at two extreme levels of the social scale, but scarcely at all in between. Intellectuals will intermarry because they feel closer to intellectuals, whatever their race or colour, than to the mass, and the humbler and poorly-adjusted fringes of both the black and white masses, who have not found acceptance in their own societies, will intermarry in order to find a home somewhere — if not within the confines of their own background, then in someone else's. But I don't think we can hope for intermarriage on an effective scale between ordinary people, and I shouldn't be surprised if independent black Africa frowned upon it, in an unofficial but firm way. Especially in a country like South Africa, where there might remain whites in sufficiently large numbers to create an unease at the possibility that they might try to close their hands once again on those possessions of power from which their fingers had been prised back one by one. It is quite likely that there will be a social stigma, among ordinary people whose sense of nationalism is well stoked up, attached to marrying whites; it may be considered un-African. (Nkrumah has set the official precedent already, by choosing not a Ruth Williams, but a girl who 'belongs' to the continent — a bride from Nasser's Egypt.) If white numbers do not dwindle in those areas of the continent which are heavily white-populated, and there is integration in schools and universities and no discrimination against white children, the picture will change in a few generations, of course. I do not see those young people as likely to regard parental race prejudice on either side as anything but fuddy-duddy. But will the whites remain, stick it out anywhere in Africa in sufficient numbers for this to come about? Isn't it much more likely that they will dwindle to small, socially isolated communities, whites in the diaspora?

If one will always have to feel white first, and African second, it would be better not to stay on in Africa. It would not be worth it for this. Yet, although I claim no mystique about Africa, I fear that like one of those oxen I sometimes read about in the Sunday papers, I might, dumped somewhere else and kindly treated, continually plod blindly back to where I came from.

Chief Luthuli

(1959)[1]

If anything – or anyone – were to have convinced Nadine Gordimer that her more pessimistic prognostications on the future of whites in Africa were not necessarily correct, it might well have been Albert Luthuli, and everything he stood for. President-General of the African National Congress in the 1950s, Luthuli seemed to embody the commitment of his movement to a democratic and inter-racial future in South Africa. In 1957 he was one of the initial accused in the now famous Treason Trial – an event which Gordimer discusses in this essay, and for reasons over and above its political importance. For it was while Luthuli was on bail in Johannesburg that Gordimer met him. Indeed, he stayed for a while in her house, and this is how she collected the material for the following biographical essay. In 1960 Luthuli was the first South African to be awarded the Nobel Prize for Peace.

There are three million white people and more than nine million black people in the Union of South Africa. Only a handful of the whites have ever met Albert John Luthuli. He has never been invited to speak over the radio, and his picture rarely appears in the white daily press in South Africa. Yet this government-deposed African chief – who, far from losing his honourable title since he was officially deprived of it, is generally known simply as 'Chief' – is the only man to whom the nine million Africans ('African' is becoming the accepted term for a South African black) give any sort of wide allegiance as a popular leader. He is the one man in black politics in South Africa whose personality is a symbol of human dignity which Africans as a whole, no matter what their individual or political affiliations are and no matter what state of enlightenment or ignorance they may be in, recognise as *their* dignity.

Luthuli is a sixty-year-old Zulu and an African aristocrat. His mother was a Gumede — one of the most honoured of Zulu clans — and his grandmother was given, as was the custom with the daughter of a prominent tribal chief, to the court of the famous paramount chief of unconquered Zululand in the 1870s, Cetshwayo. Luthuli has a number of those physical characteristics which are regarded as typical of the warrior Zulu and to which even the most ardent supporter of apartheid would pay grudging admiration. His head is large and set majestically back on a strong neck; he has a deep, soft voice; and although he is not a tall man he seems always to look as big an anyone else in the room.

Among his less obvious characteristics is a sense of repose; sometimes a monumental quiet. If more white South Africans could meet him, or even hear him speak on a public platform, they would be astonished (and perhaps even a little ashamed — he makes that sort of impression) to measure the real man against the bloodthirsty demagogue that is the African leader as they imagine him. Apart from anything else, he speaks English with a distinct American intonation, acquired along with his education at schools run by American missionaries.

Luthuli's ancestral home is Groutville Mission, in the Umvoti Mission Reserve on the coast of Natal, near Durban, and his personality stands sturdily upon this little corner of Africa. He has never, even as a child, lived in the collection of thatched mud huts in which tribal Africans usually live because Reverend Grout, an American missionary who came to South Africa in 1835, had planned his mission village on the European pattern, with houses; and if as a child the young Luthuli did his share of herding cattle, he did it after school hours, because Grout had seen to it that there was fenced common that would free the children to attend school. As the Umvoti Reserve is a mission and not a tribal reserve, the chiefs are elected, and there is no dynasty in the hereditary sense. Yet ability has tended to create a dynasty of its own; a number of the elected chiefs have been members of the Luthuli family. When Luthuli was a child, his uncle was chief, but after 1921 the chieftainship went out of the hands of the family until 1936, when Luthuli himself, then a teacher at Adams College (one of the most respected of mission educational establishments for Africans) was elected.

Luthuli was educated at various mission schools and at Adams College, and in 1921 he qualified as an instructor in the teachers' training course and joined the staff of Adams. He could look back on a gentle, almost sheltered childhood in the protective shadow of his uncle's house and the mission at Groutville. The one had given him the confidence that comes to children who belong to an honoured family; the other, which provided his first contact with the world of whites, did not impose the harsh impact of the colour bar too early on his young mind. Perhaps as a result of this, even today, when the white government of South Africa has deposed him as chief of his people, several times banned him from free movement about the country, and arrested him – as President-General of the African National Congress and a leader of the liberation movement of Africans in South Africa – on a charge of treason that kept him in court through almost a year of inquiry, he has no hate in him. He has never been anti-white and believes he never will be. He started off his life by seeing human beings, not colours. It is a very different matter today for the urban African child who is born and grows up in the slum areas of big cities in South Africa, cheek by jowl with the whites in the paradox of the colour bar; he is made aware, from the start, that his blackness is a shroud, cutting him off, preparing him to be – as the Africans often describe themselves as feeling – 'half a man'.

Luthuli seems to have come to politics through an ideal of service fostered by religion rather than by way of any strong ambition. As early as his primary school days, what he calls the 'Christian ideal' of service captured his faith and his imagination. Many politically-minded Africans deplore the influence the missions – which brought education to Africa and which have continued, because of government neglect of its obligation, to dominate African education – have had among their people in the past. The cry is that the missions have used their influence to reconcile the people to white domination rather than to encourage them to demand their birthright as free human beings. But Luthuli's experience has been that mission teaching gave him a sense of the dignity of man, in the sight of

God, that he wants to see made a reality for all colours and creeds.

The truth probably lies somewhere in the fact that for those, like Luthuli, who had eyes for it, there was a glimpse of freedom in the gospel of humble submission to a discipline greater than man-devised. Out of that glimpse, more than any reasoning of politics and experience, a man may come to say, as Luthuli did when he gave up his chieftainship under government pressure in 1952, 'Laws and conditions that tend to debase human personality – a God-given force – be they brought about by the State or any other individuals, must be relentlessly opposed in the spirit of defiance shown by Saint Peter when he said to the rulers of his day, "Shall we obey God or man?"'

Luthuli's consciousness of the disabilities of the African people awoke as soon as he began to teach. 'Before that,' he explains, 'when men like myself were children at school and college students, we didn't have much chance to compare our lot with that of white people. Living in a reserve and going to a mission school or college, far away from the big white cities, our only real contact with white people was with the school principal and the missionary, and so if we suffered in any way from discriminatory treatment by white men, we tended to confuse our resentment with the natural resentment of the schoolboy toward those in authority who abuse him.' But the moment he was adult and a teacher, the normal disabilities of being a black man in South Africa, plus the disabilities of being a black teacher, plus the special sensitivity to both that comes about through being an educated and enlightened person, hit home. Through church work and the activities of the teachers' association, he busied himself with trying to improve the world of his people within the existing framework that the white world imposed upon it; he was too young and, in a sense, too ignorant to understand then, as he came to later, that the desire and the context in which it existed were contradictory.

In 1936, after some deliberation and misgiving, for he loved to teach, Luthuli left Adams College and teaching forever and went home to Groutville as chief. The duties and responsibilities of chieftainship were in his blood and his family tradition, so from one point of view the change was not a dramatic one. But from another aspect the change was to be total and drastic. His thirty-eight years as a non-political man were over; he found himself, as he puts it, 'plunged right into South African politics – and by the South African government itself'.

The year of the Hertzog Bills[2] was 1936. They were two: the Representation of Natives Bill and the Native Trust and Land Bill. The Representation of Natives Bill took away from all non-whites in South Africa the hope of an eventual universal franchise that they had been told since 1853 they would someday attain.[3] It offered Africans in the Cape Province representation through the election, on a separate voters' roll, of three white members of Parliament. It offered Africans in the rest of the Union the opportunity to elect – not by individual vote but by means of chiefs, local councils, and advisory boards, all acting as electoral colleges – four white senators. Finally, a Natives' Representative Council was to be instituted, to consist of twelve elected African representatives, four government-nominated African representatives, and five white officials, with the Secretary for Native Affairs as chairman. Its function was to be purely advisory, to keep the government acquainted with the wants and views of the African people.

The Native Trust and Land Bill tightened once and for all the Natives' Land Act of 1913,[4] whereby Africans were prohibited from owning land except in reserves. The new bill provided 7.25 million morgen of land to be made available for African occupation and a trust fund to finance land purchase. (Twenty-two years later, this provision has not yet been completely fulfilled.)

Once the bills were law, Luthuli had vested in his authority as chief of the Umvoti Mission Reserve the collective vote of his five thousand people. White men and black canvassed him eagerly. He, who had scarcely talked politics at all, found himself talking scarcely anything else. For him, the reserve and its troubles had come into focus with the whole South African political scene. At the same time, he took up his traditional duties as chief – that combination of administrator, lawgiver, father-confessor, and figurehead. He found his chief's court or *ibandla*, held under a shady tree, 'a fine exercise in logical thinking', and the cases on which he gave judgment, according to a nice balance of tribal lore and the official Code of Native Law, varied from boundary disputes to wrangles over the payment of *lobolo* (bride price). He could not make the land go around among his people – not even the uneconomic five-acre units without freehold which were all that Groutville, a better reserve than most, had to offer – but he tried to help them make the best of what they had: he even formed a Bantu cane growers' association to protect those among his tribesmen who were small growers of sugar. 'The real meaning of our poverty was brought home to me,' he says. 'I could see that the African people had no means of making a living according to civilised standards, even if they belonged, as we did in Groutville, to a civilised Christian community, so far as African communities go.'

From 1945 until 1948, Luthuli himself sat on the Natives' Representative Council. The Council proved to be a 'toy telephone' (in the phrase most tellingly used at the time) and no one regretted its passing when the Nationalist government of Dr Malan abolished it when it came into power in 1948. No one was much surprised, either, when it was not replaced by something more effective, for this was the first government actually dedicated to *apartheid* instead of merely committed to the bogus paternalism of Smuts.[5] What the Africans got in place of the Council was yet another act – the Bantu Authorities Act,[6] which, like many others affecting his people, Luthuli knows almost by heart and can reel off clause by clause. 'It was a velvet-glove act,' he says, 'designed to give Africans in the reserves some feeling of autonomy, of a direct hand in their own affairs, while in fact using the decoy of their own chiefs to attract them to accept whatever the *apartheid* government decided was good for them. Under the Act, the chief becomes a sort of civil servant and must cooperate with the government in selling the government's wishes to the people.'

In the late forties, Luthuli went to the United States at the invitation of the American Missionary Board to lecture on Christian missions in Africa. (The church had provided him with a chance to get to know other countries and peoples once before, when in 1938 he had gone to Madras as the Christian Council delegate to an International Missionary Council meeting.) He spent nine months in the United States, and he enjoyed his visit tremendously despite one or two incidents, those moments – a door closed in one's face, a restaurant where a cup of coffee has been refused – that jolt the black man back to the realisation that, almost everywhere he travels, race prejudice will not let him be at home in the world.

The same year in which Luthuli took up his seat on the Natives' Representative Council, he had joined an organisation to which, in time, no government was to be able to turn a deaf ear. This was the African National Congress. The Congress Movement began in 1912, just after the Act of Union that made the four provinces of South Africa into one country, when the Africans realised that the union's motto, 'Unity is Strength', was to refer strictly to the whites. 'When the ANC started,' Luthuli says, 'it had no idea of fighting for a change in fundamentals. It was concerned with the African's immediate disabilities – passes, not issues. The question of the fight for political rights may have been implied, but was not on the platform at all.'

Other Africans would not agree with him about this. Be that as it may – the history of Congress, a movement shrinking and spawning, according to the times, over the years, is not very well documented except perhaps in the secret files of the Special Branch of the South African Police – the first meeting of Congress laid down at least one principle that has characterised the movement to this day: it was to be 'a greater political and national body, uniting all small bodies and the different tribes in South Africa.' It has since pledged itself to the goal of a multi-racial society in South Africa with equal rights for all colours. 'But it was only after 1936,' says Luthuli, 'when the Hertzog Bills acted as a terrific spur, that Congress began to show signs of becoming a movement that aimed at getting the government to bring about changes in policy that would give equal rights to non-whites in all fields.' At the same time, Luthuli's new responsibility as chief was proving to him the futility of any attempt to secure human rights without political rights; experience was shaping him for Congress, as it was shaping Congress for its historic role to come.

When he joined Congress in 1945, he was elected to the executive of the Natal Branch at once, and he remained on it continuously for the six years during which the movement felt its way to effectiveness, leaving behind the old methods – deputations, petitions, conferences that enabled the government to 'keep in touch with the people' without having to take their views into account – that had failed to achieve anything for the Africans. Finally, in 1949 Congress drafted a Programme of Action that was based on the premise that in South Africa freedom can come to the non-white only through extra-parliamentary methods. A year later, when Luthuli had just been elected Provincial President of Natal, Congress decided to launch a full-scale passive resistance campaign in defiance of unjust, colour-bar laws. 'This decision,' he comments, 'had my full approval.'

The official-sounding, platitudinous remark covers what was the result of considerable heart-searching on Luthuli's part. Luthuli sees it and, for himself, used it as Gandhi conceived it – not only as a technique but as a soul force, *Satyagraha*.

In 1952 the African National Congress, the South African Indian Congress, and other related associations organised defiance groups all over the country.[7] Thousands of Africans and, in lesser numbers, Indians, and even some whites, defied the colour-bar laws and invited arrest. Africans and Indians entered libraries reserved for white people, sat on railway benches reserved for white people, used post office counters reserved for white people, and camped out in open ground in the middle of the white city of Durban. Black and white, they went to prison. Luthuli was everywhere in Natal, addressing meetings, encouraging individuals, carrying with him in the most delicate situations, under the nose of government ire and police hostility, an extraordinary core of confidence and warmth. All his natural abilities of leadership came up simply and strongly.

The Defiance Campaign went on successfully for some months before it was crushed by the heavy sentences imposed upon defiers under new legislation specially devised by the government, which fixed the high penalties (up to three years' imprisonment or a fine of £300) that may be applied to anyone protesting against any of the racial laws or inciting others to do so.

Luthuli had gone into the Campaign a country chief; he came out a public figure. In September 1952, while Defiance was still on, he was given an ultimatum by the Native Affairs Department: he must resign from Congress and the Defiance Campaign or give up his chieftainship. 'I don't see the contradiction between my office as chief and my work in Congress,' he answered, courteously but bluntly. 'In the one I work in the interests of my people within tribal limits, and in the other I work for them on a national level, that's all. I will not resign from either.'

On Wednesday, November 12, 1952, the Native Commissioner announced that Chief A. J. Luthuli was dismissed by the government from his position as chief of the Umvoti Mission Reserve. In reply to this, the African National Congress issued a statement by Luthuli under the title 'Our Chief Speaks'. It is a statement that has been much quoted, in and out of South Africa, both in support of those who believe that right is on the side of the Africans in their struggle against racial discrimination and in support of those who regard the black man's claim to equality of opportunity with the white man as a fearful black nationalism that aims – to quote, in turn, one of the favourite bogies of white South Africa – 'to drive the white man into the sea'.

The lengthy statement is written in the formal, rather Victorian English, laced with biblical cadence and officialese, that Luthuli uses – the English of a man to whom it is a foreign or at best a second language, but impressive, for all that. 'In these past thirty years or so,' he said,

> I have striven with tremendous zeal and patience to work for the progress and welfare of my people and for their harmonious relations with other sections of our multi-racial society in the Union of South Africa. In this effort I have always pursued what liberal-minded people rightly regarded as the path of moderation ...
> In so far as gaining citizenship rights and opportunities for the unfettered development of the African people, who

will deny that thirty years of my life have been spent knocking in vain, patiently, moderately, and modestly at a closed and barred door?

... Has there been any reciprocal tolerance or moderation from the Government, be it Nationalist or United Party? No! On the contrary, the past thirty years have seen the greatest number of Laws restricting our rights and progress until today we have reached a stage where we have almost no rights at all: no adequate land for our occupation, our only asset — cattle — dwindling, no security of homes, no decent and remunerative employment, more restrictions to freedom of movement through passes, curfew regulations, influx control measures; in short we have witnessed in these years an intensification of our subjection to ensure and protect white supremacy.

It is with this background and with a full sense of responsibility that ... I have joined my people in ... the spirit that revolts openly and boldly against injustice and expresses itself in a determined and non-violent manner ... Viewing Non-Violent Passive Resistance as a non-revolutionary and, therefore, a most legitimate and humane political pressure technique for a people denied all effective forms of constitutional striving, I saw no real conflict in my dual leadership of my people.[8]

A month after his deposition as chief, Luthuli was elected President-General of the African National Congress and became leader of the entire Congress movement in South Africa. Wherever he went, he was greeted by cheering crowds of Africans; at last they had a leader who had shown himself a leader in places less comfortable and closer to their lives than conferences and conventions.

The government found that ex-Chief Luthuli seemed to be more of a chief than ever. A ban was served on him under one of those new powers that had been legislated to deal with the Defiance Campaign, a ban which debarred him for a year from all the important cities and towns in South Africa. The day it expired, Luthuli opened the South African Indian Congress in Durban and, guessing that his time was short, left at once by

air for Johannesburg to attend a protest meeting about Sophiatown removals.[9] It was his first visit to Johannesburg since he
had become President-General, and the people of Sophiatown,
under arbitrary orders to quit their homes and move to a
settlement farther away from the white city, were heartened at
the idea of having him among them as champion of their
protest.

As he stepped off the plane at Johannesburg, the Special
Branch police served him with a second ban. And what a ban!
This time he was to be confined for two years to a radius of
about twenty miles around his home in Groutville village.
During the long period of confinement he suffered a slight
stroke, and while he lay ill in his house in Groutville, his wife
had to beg permission from the police to let him be taken to a
hospital in Durban, sixty miles away. Permission was granted,
and he was rushed to Durban. There he spent two months in
the hospital, and from the second day Special Branch men
hung about his ward in constant attendance. Despite these
unwelcome presences, who, he says, day after day used to
inquire sheepishly after his health, Chief made a complete
recovery except for a barely perceptible droop that shows itself
in his left eyelid when he is tired.

His ban expired in July 1956. He was free to move about the
country again: but not for long. About four in the morning of
December 5, there was a loud knocking at the door of the
Luthulis' house in Groutville. The Luthulis struggled out of
sleep. Four white Special Branch men were at the door; they
had come to arrest Chief on a charge of treason. He was flown
to Johannesburg and taken straight to prison at the Johannesburg Fort. And there he found himself accused of treason with
one hundred and fifty-five others. Some were his respected
colleagues over many years; some represented ideologies that
were largely or partly distasteful to him; some he had never
heard of before.

The preliminary hearing of the Treason Trial (the first in the
history of peacetime South Africa) began in January 1957, and
the trial has been in progress, in one form and another — nine
months of preliminary hearing, several sessions of the trial
itself, with a number of adjournments — for two years.[10]
'Treason' is a word with ugly associations. They have become

uglier still during the years since the war, now that the word has become part of the vocabulary of the witch hunters of the world. Like 'Communist', 'treason' may be used, in certain countries and circumstances, to blot out the name of any-one who puts up any sort of opposition to race discrimination and the denial of freedom of movement, opportunity, and education.

Among the hundred and fifty-six of the original accused, there was a sprinkling of ex-Communists and fellow travellers – almost exclusively among the twenty-three whites – but the great majority were simply people who abhor the injustice and misery of apartheid and want all races in South Africa to share freely in the life of the country. At various stages in the trial, the number of accused has been reduced, and the government has not yet succeeded in formulating a satisfactory statement of the charge against them; but the trial drags on and, at the time of writing, the Attorney General has just made a statement that he intends to draw up a fresh indictment against the remaining accused.

The first list of those against whom charges had been withdrawn was announced in December 1957, when the preliminary inquiry was in recess. Among the names was that of Chief A. J. Luthuli, President-General of the African National Congress. Chief was at home in Groutville after the nine-month ordeal in court, preparing for the wedding of his medical-student daughter, when the news came, followed by a paper storm of congratulatory telegrams. His feelings were mixed: he could not see why he should be freed while his colleagues in the liberation movement were held; on the other hand, he was glad to be able to get on with Congress work outside the Drill Hall. A few weeks later, charges were withdrawn against some more accused, bringing down to ninety-one the number of those who were committed for trial for high treason in January 1958.

The particulars of the 'hostile acts' which were read under the charge of high treason included 'the hampering or hindering of the said Government {of the Union of South Africa} in its lawful administration by organising or taking part in campaigns against existing laws'. The laws named included the Natives Resettlement Act and the Group Areas

Act, which involve the uprooting of African, Indian, and coloured communities in order to move them out of white areas; the Bantu Education Act, which has lowered the standard of education available to African children; and the Bantu Authorities Act.

The defence applied for the discharge of the ninety-one, saying that the Crown, by the way it had formulated the charges, had established 'nothing other than a desire to put an end to any form of effective opposition to the Government of this country – a desire to outlaw free expression of thought and ideas which people in all democratic countries of the West assert the right to hold and utter.' The application for discharge was refused. In the public gallery of the Drill Hall (divided down the middle by a token barrier of low chains and posts to ensure that whites sat on one side and blacks on the other) Luthuli heard the magistrate's decision. Why he was not still among the accused in the dock was as much of a mystery to him as to anyone else. Whatever the reason, Chief sat in the Drill Hall as a spectator and a free man that day, and many heads, black and white, turned to look at him. When the court adjourned, he walked out among the free men, too; free to travel about the country and address meetings and attend gatherings where he pleased. For how long, of course, he could not guess.

So far – a year later – he has not been served with a ban again, though he has not minced words, whether addressing the small Liberal Party[11] or Congress. At a meeting before a white audience he was beaten up by white hooligans. At angry meetings of the Transvaal Branch of Congress in Johannesburg Africanists[12] attempted to oust Chief and his kind from leadership and commit the African National Congress to what he calls 'a dangerously narrow African nationalism'. In April 1959 this group broke away to form the Pan-Africanist Congress.

But that day at the beginning of 1958, when he walked out of the Drill Hall, the sudden release of his freedom was fresh upon him, lightheaded, like a weakness, though the weight of the ordeal of trial to which his colleagues were committed oppressed him, and he even looked a little lonely. And such are the paradoxes of human behaviour that, as Luthuli crossed the street, two of the white police officers who had become familiar figures on duty in the Drill Hall all through the preparatory examination came around the corner and called out, forgetful, across the barrier of apartheid that seeks to legislate against all human contact between black and white and across the barrier of hate that the pass and the baton have built between the police and the black man in South Africa, 'Well, hullo! You look fine! What are you doing around here? Can't you keep away from the old Drill Hall, after all?' And rather gingerly, Chief was amiable in reply.

Great Problems in the Street

*If Albert Luthuli embodied the optimism of the 1950s and the belief
in steady progress towards a democratic and enlightened South
Africa, then as the new decade turned South Africa entered an
unprecedented and darker phase of its modern history. In an
atmosphere of heightening political activity both the African
National Congress and the Pan-Africanist Congress announced
campaigns against the pass laws – the most hated of laws in South
Africa, severely restricting the free movement, settlement and
economic rights of blacks. On 21 March 1960, however, there was
disaster: at Sharpeville (a black township of Vereeniging, near
Johannesburg) 67 people at an anti-pass demonstration called by the
Pan-Africanist Congress were killed in police shooting, and 187
wounded. On 30 March a State of Emergency was declared. On 8
April both the African National Congress and the Pan-Africanist
Congress were made illegal and driven underground; mass arrests
took place throughout the country. The government stepped up its
crackdown on all political opposition; but the opposition
movements, believing peaceful methods of organisation and campaign were now futile, turned to new ones. Before South Africa
became a republic and left the Commonwealth in 1961, a wave of
sabotage had begun. By the time Gordimer wrote the following
short essay, she was in a new world.*

People who don't live in South Africa find it difficult to hold in
their minds at once an image of the life lived by the banished,
banned, harried and spied-upon active opponents of
apartheid, and the juxtaposed image of life in the sun lived by a
prosperous white population that does not care what happens
so long as it goes on living pleasantly. Even those of us who do
live here – once out of the country, the situation we have just

left and to which we are about to return seems improbable. For the gap between the committed and the indifferent is a Sahara whose faint trails, followed by the mind's eye only, fade out in sand. The place is not on the map of human relations; but, like most unmapped areas, there is a coming and going that goes unrecorded; there is a meeting of eyes at points without a name; there is an exchange of silences between strangers crossing one another far from the witness of their own kind – once you are down there on your own two feet you find the ancient caravan trails connecting human destiny no matter how much distance a man tries to put between himself and the next man.

Of course, the committed know this – it is at the base of liberal and progressive politics, and most philosophies – but the indifferent don't, or won't. To them the desert seems absolutely foolproof, reassuringly impassable. Nothing can get to me through *that*, they are saying, when they turn to the sports page after a glance at the latest list of house arrests or banning orders. Those sort of people are black, or communist or something – they have nothing whatever to do with *me*, though I may be jostled among them in the street every day. If it happens to be a white person who has been arrested, the indifference may be enlivened by a spark of resentment – 'people like that, ratting on their own kind, they deserve all that's coming to them'.

Kindly and decent, within the strict limits of their 'own kind' (white, good Christians, good Jews, members of the country clubs – all upholders of the colour bar though not necessarily supporters of the Nationalist government), the indifferent do not want to extend that limit by so much as one human pulse reaching out beyond it. Where the pretty suburban garden ends, the desert begins. This 'security' measure brings about some queer situations when the indifferent stray into the company of a committed person, as it were by mistake. During the State of Emergency after Sharpeville, a friend who is a frequent visitor to my house was among those imprisoned without trial. A couple who had met him when dining with us, and had found him amusing and charming, heard about his arrest. (Newspapers were forbidden to publish the names of people taken into custody in this way.)

'Is it true that D—— B—— is in prison?'

'Yes, he was picked up last Thursday night.'

'But *why*? He seems such a fine person. I mean I couldn't imagine him doing anything wrong – '

'Do you think it's wrong for Africans to demonstrate against the pass laws?'

'Well, I mean, that's got to be put down, that's political agitation – '

'Yes, exactly. Well, D—— B—— thinks the pass laws are wrong and so, quite logically, since he is a fine person, he's prepared to do what he can to help Africans protest against them.'

How could the indifferent keep at a safe distance this man whom they had accepted and who was at once the same man who sat in prison, *nothing whatever to do with them*? The subject was dropped into the dark cupboard of questions that are not dealt with.

But it is not in private, drawing-room encounters that indifference meets commitment most openly. Nietzsche said, 'Great problems are in the street.'[2] South Africa's problems are there, in the streets, in the tens of thousands of Africans going about their city work but not recognised as citizens, in the theatres and libraries and hotels into which the white people may turn, but the black people must pass by; in the countless laws, prejudices, 'traditions', fallacies, fears that regulate every move and glance where white and black move together through the city. The great problems are alive in the street, and it is in the street, too, that (until now) they have always been debated. The street has held both the flesh and the word. For the meeting-halls of African political movements have been the open spaces in the streets, in the townships and on the city's fringe, and progressive movements in general have used the City Hall steps in Johannesburg as a platform, and also as a final rallying-point in protest marches. In the townships or down in Fordsburg the supporters gathered close to hear Mandela[3] or Tambo[4] or Naicker[5] speak, while the Special Branch took notes, and idlers and children hung about; in times of a campaign the crowd of supporters swelled enormously. At the City Hall steps at lunch time speakers from the Congress of Democrats,[6] the Liberal Party, or some other liberatory or progressive movement would stand among their placards with a small band of supporters. Slowly their numbers would grow; the pavements thicken with silent faces, black and white, office cleaners and executives, young students from the University and old bums from the Library Gardens. The antenna of an attendant police car would poke a shining whisker out of the traffic.

Probably the meetings in the townships will prove to have been the decisive ones in the future of this country, in the long run. But the meetings on the City Hall steps made the flesh and word of great problems curiously manifest because these meetings took place in the one place where black and white participated in them together. And they happened right in the middle of the daily life of the city, under the eyes of all those people who were going about their own business – which excluded, of course, things like the Extension of University Education Act (it provided the exact opposite; not extension but restriction of the universities, formerly part 'open', to whites only) or the Group Areas Act (it has enabled the government to move Africans, coloureds and Indians living or trading in areas declared white). Their children were white and would have no difficulty in getting into a university; they did not fall into any racial category affected by removals; these things had nothing to do with them. Yet they were confronted with them in the street, they read the posters on the way to pick up the latest kitchen gadget at the bargain basement, they paused a moment (another face showing among the dark and light faces in the crowd) or walked quickly past to the business lunch, carrying with them a snatch of the speaker's words like a torn streamer.

The atmosphere of these meetings hung about the city, an unease, after two o'clock. Like the more formal mass meetings called from time to time in the City Hall itself, at night, they sometimes ended in an ill-defined scuffle on the edge of the melting crowd: hooligans, in their blind and violent way giving vent to the resentment the city feels at being forced to admit the guilt and fear that lie under indifference.

The march through Johannesburg last year when the Sabotage Bill[7] was introduced was the last for no one can say how long, since one of the restrictions imposed by the Bill itself was an end to gatherings on the City Hall steps and to protest demonstrations generally. The march was also one of the biggest there has ever been, and it drew a tension between marchers and onlookers that was an extraordinary experience. Assembling for a demonstration of this kind is always a rather foolish-making business: the individuals coming up awkwardly, craning about for the sight of friends; the shuffling and coming and going; the detachment of a figure from the watching crowd, and his sudden appearance beside you in the ranks – has a longing for freedom burst in him like a blood-vessel? Is he a paid rowdy muscling in to break up the ranks? Is he merely one of those nameless, placeless pieces of city driftwood that are attracted to any stream of humanity going anywhere? Behind these nervous speculations is a fierce longing to seize the tendrils of impulse which are running, in spite of themselves, from the watchers; the desire of those within the ranks to pull on those feelers of awareness – insults, laughter, embarrassment – *anything* that offers a hold, a sign of life by which the onlookers might be drawn in to speak up for it.

On the day of that last march, as on other occasions, the onlookers let the hooligans speak for them. And this time, the last time before their mouths were stopped up once and for all by the accumulation of public safety bills, press bills, censorship bills, they let the hooligans speak in word and deed more uninhibitedly and wildly than ever. All the white man's battened-down fear of the consequences of the 'South African way of life' he has chosen poured out in a mess of infantile regression – senseless blows, rotten eggs, foul words. As the marchers went through the city – filling the width of the street, several thousand strong – these fell upon them at intervals. In between, there was the gaze of flat-dwellers and office workers looking down silently on the passing backs. When the procession passed an elegant first-floor restaurant, five well-dressed men came out on to the balcony, whiskies in hand, to watch. An equally well-dressed man walking near me broke the ranks. The five waved to him, but he stood there in the street, legs apart, palms up, and called: 'Why don't you come down here with us?' They laughed, and one of them called back, 'You always were crazy, Reg.' For a moment the eyes of the procession were on that balcony where the five men stood glass in hand; then the five turned and went in.

And so the last march came to its end. The meetings on Freedom Square ended long ago, with the banning of the African National Congress and subsequently the Pan-Africanist Congress. The Congress of Democrats is banned, too. The Federation of South African Women,[8] the Liberal Party and others are refused the special permission necessary, now, to hold meetings at the City Hall steps or at any other rallying point in the streets. The speakers who defended human rights against the attrition of one repressive apartheid measure after another, all committed to this over and above their varying political standpoints in the opposition – all are banned, in exile, or under house arrest. Even the posters of the newspapers will soon no longer provide any unwelcome reminders; those that are not closed down by the censorship bill will be guided by it. There is silence in the streets. The indifferent are left in peace. There is nothing to disturb them, now, but the detonations of saboteurs, and the hideous outbursts of secret society savagery.

Censored, Banned, Gagged

(1963)[1]

Repression in South Africa in the early 1960s was not confined to the political domain; culturally, too, the government began to limit the scope for any kind of opposition to its policies. For one thing, censorship was now organised more systematically than it ever had been before, under the Publications and Entertainments Act of 1963. Linked to the political legislation of the period, as Gordimer shows in this essay, for the first time writers now became specific political targets. Here Gordimer initiated her long-standing campaign against censorship, a campaign which continues to the present day.

Peter Abrahams, Harry Bloom, Hans Hofmeyer, Daphne Rooke, Ezekiel Mphahlele, and I myself are some of the South African writers who share the experience of having had books banned in our own country. Why were our books banned? If one were to judge by the monotonous insistence with which the necessity to protect pure young minds from 'cheap filth', etc., was invoked as justification for the new censorship bill in recent parliamentary debates in South Africa, one would conclude that these books must be pornographic. In fact, of the six writers I have mentioned, none deals sensationally or with more than passing frankness with sex, and two (in those books of theirs which were banned) do not, by reason of their subjects, touch upon sexual relations at all. Although the Minister of the Interior and the Nationalist Members of Parliament never mention political reasons for censorship, these books, and almost without exception *all* those books by South African writers which have been banned, have been banned for a political reason: non-conformity with the picture of South African life as prescribed and proscribed by apartheid.

I think I am the only one who has ever been favoured with

an explanation for a book banning. I was informed that the official attitude to my second novel — banned in the Penguin edition in which it would have reached its widest public in my country — was that the book 'undermines the traditional race policy of the Republic'.*

That was the truth, for once, the truth behind pious concern for young minds: it's not four-letter words that menace them, but the danger that they may begin to think, and, under the stimulus of certain books, come up with some doubts about the way their lives are ordered. The minds of people who can afford five shillings for a paper-cover edition of a book are apparently considered more tender (or more susceptible?) than those of people who pay eighteen-and-six for a hard-cover edition, since some books are banned in the paper-cover edition only. This is not as illogical as it seems; it assumes that more affluent people (affluent = white) are likely to be living too easy to want to see any change in the 'traditional race policy of the Republic' whereas poorer people (poorer = black) are likely to be encouraged by any suggestion that it is possible to 'undermine' it.

The machinery of censorship which has served to ban all these books has now been superseded by a more stringent, sin-mongering, and all-devouring system under the new censor-ship laws, promulgated in the Publications and Enter-tainments Act of 1963. Among the defects of the old machinery — from the point of view of a state evidently bent on introdu-cing thought-control — was that it did not provide for internal censorship (that is, of publications produced within the Republic itself) other than in respect of pornography. This is not quite such a gap as it sounds; English-language publishers in South Africa are few, and they stick mainly to graceful, gift-book Africana and adventure yarns; the thriving Afrikaans publishing houses draw both authors and readers from that section of the community which loyally supports the govern-

* My latest novel, *Occasion for Loving* (London: Gollancz; New York: Viking; 1963), was held under embargo for a while, but has now been released; its fate, once it is published in a cheaper edition, probably will be the same as that of the earlier novel. [In fact *Occasion for Loving* was not ultimately banned; possibly because, amongst other things, it dealt with the failure of an inter-racial love affair.]

ment and, so far,* has been unlikely to produce anything that undermines any government policy.² At any rate, whatever is published within the country will now be subject to censorship along with whatever is imported, and the decisions as to what should be banned and what may be read will be made by a Publications Control Board, presently to be set up by the Minister of the Interior.

The Board will consist of nine members, all appointed by the Minister, of whom not fewer than six shall be 'persons having special knowledge of arts, language, and literature, *or* {my italics} the administration of justice.' The chairman (Minister-designated, again) must be one of the 'special knowledge' members, but a quorum is constituted by only four members and, in the absence of the chairman and vice-chairman, an ordinary member may preside. Special committees can be set up to deal with the work of the Board – which will be prodigious, to say the least, since it covers films, plays, 'objects', magazines, etc., as well as books. A committee is to consist of one member of the Board (not specified that this should be one with 'special knowledge') and at least two other persons appointed as members from a panel designated by the Minister. So that, in fact, whether South Africans will be permitted or not to read any particular piece of literature can and frequently will be decided by three persons, all appointed by the Minister, not one of whom need have even the dubious qualification, where literary judgment is required, of 'special knowledge' of the 'administration of justice'.

There will be no representation whatsoever on the Board or committees outside the Minister's personal choice; but any person may, at any time, upon payment of a nominal fee, submit for the consideration of the Board a publication which *he* personally thinks ought to be banned. Under the old system there was a board of censors which examined books referred to it by Customs, Post Office, or other officials under various relevant Acts, including the Suppression of Communism Act; but the old Board was not a Grundy ombudsman to whom, as

* Some of the younger Afrikaans writers are beginning to feel stifled by a literary tradition that ignores the glaring realities of our country's life. If they are moved to write books that do not conform to the tradition of Afrikaans writing, who is to publish them? Afrikaans is not spoken outside South Africa, the Protectorates, and the Rhodesias.

well, cranks, crack-pots, and political informers could take their grudges, confident, on the incredibly wide grounds on which there is provision for them to claim offence, of a hearing.

A publication is deemed 'undesirable' if it, or any part of it, is

> indecent or obscene or is offensive or harmful to public morals; is blasphemous or offensive to the religious convictions or feelings of any section of the inhabitants of the Republic; *brings any section of the inhabitants into ridicule or contempt; is harmful to the relations between any sections of the inhabitants*; is prejudicial to the safety of the State, the general welfare, or the peace and good order.

The definition of what may be considered indecent, obscene, offensive or harmful to public morals includes the portrayal of:

> murder, suicide, death, horror, cruelty, fighting, brawling, ill-treatment, lawlessness, gangsterism, robbery, crime, the technique of crimes and criminals, tippling, drunkenness, trafficking in or addiction to drugs, smuggling, sexual intercourse, prostitution, promiscuity, white-slaving, licentiousness, lust, passionate love scenes, sexual assault, rape, sodomy, masochism, sadism, sexual bestiality, abortion, change of sex, night life, physical poses, nudity, scant or inadequate dress, divorce, marital infidelity, adultery, illegitimacy, *human or social deviation or degeneracy*, or any other similar or related phenomenon.

My italics are there as a reminder that the racial laws of the country, and its traditional race policies, are such that social as well as sexual intercourse between white and coloured people could be interpreted as 'human or social deviation or degeneracy'; and that, in the practical and ideological pursuit of apartheid, *any* mixing between the races is considered 'harmful', and criticism of or satire on this curious belief could easily be construed, by those who uphold it, as 'ridicule and contempt'.

In determining whether a book should be censored or not, 'no regard shall be had to the purpose' of the author; which means that no distinction can be drawn between *Ulysses* and *What the Butler Saw in the Boudoir*, or between a revolutionary pamphlet advocating the bloody overthrow of the white man and a serious study of such aspirations. There is a provision that the Board may exempt, at its pleasure to recall the exemption at any time, a publication of a 'technical, scientific, or professional nature *bona fide* intended for the advancement of or for use in any particular profession or branch of arts, literature, or science'. But how the Board will go about deciding what is *bona fide* and what is not, is not stated.

Much has been made of the concession of the right of appeal to the courts, not included in the Act in its earlier forms (there have been three), but now granted. An author now has the right of appeal to the Supreme Court after his book has been banned by the Board, but he must lodge notice of the appeal within thirty days of the Board's decision. As a book may be banned, at the instigation of anyone, at any time (maybe months or years after publication) and the notice of its banning is not communicated to the author but merely published in the *Government Gazette*, it could easily happen that the thirty days might elapse before the author became aware of the ban. And a Supreme Court action is an extremely costly privilege by means of which one is allowed, at last, to defend a work which has already been condemned without trial.

The censorship system applies to magazines and periodicals as well as books, of course, and also to exhibitions, films, plays, and entertainment of any kind. (The long list of special restrictions on films includes any scene that 'depicts in an offensive manner intermingling of white and non-white persons'.) The daily and weekly press, both opposition and government, is exempt because the Newspaper Press (Proprietors) Union of South Africa accepted a 'code' – self-censorship responsible to their own organisation – as the lesser evil, when confronted with the alternative of government censorship. The radical left-wing and liberal publications – weeklies, fortnightlies, and monthlies – have been successfully decimated (the last may have disappeared by the time this is in print) without the help of the new Act, by the simple means of making them staffless – first under the Suppression of Communism Act, by prohibiting all people banned under the Act, or who were even only members of an organisation suppressed by it, from association with any organisation which 'in any manner prepares, compiles, prints, publishes, or disseminates' a newspaper, magazine, pamphlet, handbill, or poster; second, under the General Law Amendment Act, 1962 (commonly called the Sabotage Act),[3] by prohibiting five journalists from in any way carrying on their profession.

The special provisions governing paperbacks are making booksellers wish they had become bakers instead. For example, the importation of paperbacks that cost the bookseller less than 2s. 6d. each is forbidden. This piece of legislation was no doubt genuinely intended to keep out trash; but it failed to take into account that thousands of reputable books, including classics, reference, and hand-books prescribed for schools and universities, are imported in paperback editions. If the bookseller wants to import any particular book or series, he may apply, on payment of a fee, to have the Board examine it, decide whether it is 'undesirable' and, if not, grant him permission to import it. Similarly, exemptions may be granted in the case of books published by a specified publisher; or a specified class of publication from such a publisher; or if they deal with any specified subject. Of course, these blanket releases work t'other way about, too: blanket bans may be invoked for specified books; series; editions; and publishers. As for magazines, presumably if one number were to be pronounced undesirable, either that particular number could be banned, or a blanket ban could descend on the magazine.

All the dreary legalese through which I have followed the writer's situation thus far belongs to the hot war of censorship. But there is also a cold war going on all the time, outside the statute books, and as it is likely to get colder and colder with the new Act, I should like to explain it. One hears a lot (quite rightly) about the effect the new internal censorship will have on South African (virtually, Afrikaans) publishers: how they will hesitate to publish if they feel there is any risk of banning, so prejudicing the chances of existing or aspirant writers who publish in the Republic. But this censorship cold war began long ago for writers with a wider public, that is abroad as well as in their own country, whose books are published in England

and imported to South Africa as part of the literature of the English-speaking world.

South African booksellers are wary of books by serious South African writers who deal with the contemporary scene. Whatever the interest of the book, whatever the selling power of the author's name, the booksellers risk only very small orders, perhaps a third of what they know they could sell, because they fear to find themselves burdened with hundreds of copies of a book that may be banned either on arrival in the country, or later. (Some publishers ship copies on the understanding of return in the case of banning; others do not.) Publishers are afraid to risk advance publicity for the book in the Republic; the general idea is that it is better to have the book slip in quietly and sell modestly than to be unable to sell it at all. If the book is subsequently banned, the author has the satisfaction of knowing that at least it has had some chance to be read, if not widely. If it is not banned, its potential distribution and readership have been limited by the intimidation of censorship to an extent that, especially in the case of lesser-known writers, cannot easily be made up by subsequent sales. By the time the bookseller feels 'safe' to re-order (remember, anyone can submit the book to the Board at any time), interest in the book may well have died down.

Back to the hot war, now. As I have already indicated, not only censorship afflicts writing and writers in my country. So far as I know, only one author has been affected as yet by what one might call the Mutilation Act, one of the gagging provisions of the Sabotage Act. Tom Hopkinson – South African by adoption for a number of years – was obliged to remove from his autobiographical record of experience in Africa a statement by Chief Luthuli, who, like all banned persons, may not be quoted. Not a matter of much importance in this particular book, maybe; not enough to distort it seriously: but quite enough to establish the principle of mutilation of books through censorship. Enough to show the authors of non-fiction – the sociological, historical, and political studies, the analyses, reminiscences, and biographies – that they are no longer free to present as full a picture of South African life and thought as their subjects and talents can command. The balance has gone from the picture; and the truth, in direct proportion to what must be left out.

The links between this and the Sabotage Act are clear. Under the Sabotage Act it may be considered a crime 'to further or encourage the achievement of any political aim, *including the bringing about of any social or economic change in the Republic*'. (As usual, my italics.) The gagging clauses of the Act make the incredible provisions whereby more than 102 people have been forbidden to make any communication whatsoever with the public, either in speech or in the written or quoted word. Among these people are twelve journalists and two or three creative writers – the number does not matter; so long as there were to be even one, this Act would provide an example of suppression of writers that far exceeds any restrictions suffered by any other profession. The gagged journalist and writers are prohibited from publishing *any writing whatever*, however remote from politics it might be. This means that Dennis Brutus,[4] writing poetry, Alex La Guma,[5] writing a novel while under twenty-four-hour house-arrest, cannot publish either.

Censored, banned, gagged – the writers of my country may be said to be well on the way to becoming a victimised group. They have resisted variously. So far as censorship is concerned, English-speaking writers began to oppose its growth several years ago, with vigour in the case of individuals, rather ponderously and timidly in the case of our only English-speaking writers' organisation, PEN. Nevertheless, PEN did submit to the Select Committee on the Publications and Entertainments Bill an excellent memorandum that probably had a mitigating effect on the form in which the Bill finally became an Act. With the exception of a few splendidly outspoken people, such as the poet Uys Krige, the Afrikaans writers seemed to feel that censorship was none of their business until the new Publications and Entertainments Act, with its provision for internal censorship, right here at home where their books are published, changed their minds for them. Once this happened, they began the familiar round of collecting signatures for protest, etc., with which the English-speaking writers were already so familiar, and which, alas, while in the combined effort may have softened the Act a little between its first draft and final form, did not, could not hope to succeed in getting it scrapped.

The attitude towards gagged writers and journalists is more complicated, because organisations and individuals in general are inclined to be frightened off by the fact that these are leftist* writers and journalists, some of them named Communists. The sad old paradox arises of those who will fight for the freedom to write what *they* want to write, but are not sure it really ought to be extended to other people who may want to write something different. Perhaps, like the Afrikaans writers, who thought censorship wouldn't touch them, people who keep silent on the subject of gagged writers will wake up, too late, to find that freedom is indivisible and that when professional freedom was withheld from one or two little known leftist writers, it was lost to them, too. Individual writers and PEN have issued protests on behalf of gagged persons. The South African Society of Journalists is putting up a strong fight on behalf of the gagged journalists.

Within the small group of intellectuals in South Africa, writers represent an even smaller group; and for that reason perhaps the people of the country might be content to ignore what is happening to them.

But what of the readers? What of the millions, from university professors to children spelling out their first primers, for whom the free choice of books means the right to participate in the heritage of human thought, knowledge, and imagination?

Yes, they still have a great many uncensored books to read, Shakespeare, Plato, Tolstoy, and many modern writers in world literature – though even the classics have been shown not to be immune from South African censorship (much of Zola; *Moll Flanders*; some of Maupassant as well as Marx); serious writers of all times and origins have been axed. But surely the people realise that no one can be well-read or well-informed or fitted to contribute fully to the culture and development of his own society in the democratic sense while

---

* An imprecise definition in South Africa, at the best of times. Randolph Vigne and Peter Hjul are members of the Liberal Party who were running a liberal fortnightly, as was its founder, Patrick Duncan, at the time he was put under ban – subsequently he went into exile in Basutoland, left the Liberal Party and aligned himself with the anti-Communist, militantly black nationalist Pan-Africanist Congress.

he does not have absolutely free access to the ideas of his time as well as to the accumulated thought of the past, nor while, in particular, there are areas of experience in the life of his own society and country which, through censorship, are left out of his reading? It is interesting to note, in this context, that while the South African government is anxious to convince the world of its eagerness to raise to 'civilisation' the African people, it has at the same time largely suppressed the first proofs that some Africans have indeed already achieved complete emergence into the intellectual standards of the civilised world. Most of the writings of black South Africans who have recorded the contemporary experience of their people – including Peter Abrahams's autobiography, the literary essays of Ezekiel Mphahlele, the autobiographies of Alfred Hutchinson and Todd Matshikiza, and an anthology of African writing which included stories and poems of a number of black writers from South Africa – are banned.[6] These books were written in English and they provide the major part of the only record, set down by talented and self-analytical people, of what black South Africans, who have no voice in parliament nor any say in the ordering of their life, think and feel about their lives and those of their fellow white South Africans. Can South Africa afford to do without these books?

And can South Africans in general boast of a 'literature' while, by decree, in their own country, it consists of *some* of the books written by its black and white, Afrikaans- and English-speaking writers?

Why Did Bram Fischer
Choose Jail?

(1966)[1]

By the mid-1960s Gordimer's political consciousness was fully roused in her fiction: her fourth novel, The Late Bourgeois World,[2] *was based on the sabotage campaigns of the immediately preceding years, even though it focused on an organisation of the period called the African Resistance Movement, rather than any of the mainstream political bodies. Beyond her fiction at that stage, however, was a more particular interest. One of the major figures involved when the movements opposed to the government went underground after the early 1960s was Abram ('Bram') Fischer, a white member of the South African Communist Party. His story evidently fascinated Gordimer. Thus, when he was brought to trial at this time, she attended the proceedings and published two accounts, of which this essay is one.[3] It was a fascination which endured, ultimately entering her fiction in her seventh novel,* Burger's Daughter *(1979).[4]*

In South Africa on May 9 1966, Abram Fischer, Queen's Counsel, a proud Afrikaner and self-affirmed Communist, was sentenced to imprisonment for life. The main counts against him (conspiring to commit sabotage and being a member of, and furthering the aims of, the Communist Party) were framed under the Suppression of Communism Act,[5] but anti-Communists could take no comfort from that: this Act is the much-extended one under which all extra-parliamentary opposition to apartheid, whether inspired by socialism, capitalism, religious principles, a sense of justice or just plain human feeling, is at least under suspicion in South Africa. In his address to the court a few days before, Fischer himself had pointed out, 'The laws under which I am being prosecuted were enacted by a wholly unrepresentative body ... in which three-quarters of the people of this country have no voice whatever.' He went on to say, 'These laws were enacted not to prevent the spread of communism, but for the purpose of silencing the opposition of a large majority of our citizens to a Government intent upon depriving them, solely on account of their colour, of the most elementary human rights.'

All through his trial, Fischer listened and took notes – even when some erstwhile friends turned state witnesses stood a few feet away, testifying against him – with the same composed alertness that had been his demeanour when appearing as counsel in this same Palace of Justice at Pretoria. The smile, beginning in the brilliant, flecked blue eyes, was his familiar one, as he turned from the dock to face the public gallery, and sought the faces of family or friends. The panoply of the court, the shouts drifting up from the cells below, the press tiptoeing restlessly in and out, his colleagues in their robes, Mr Justice Wessel Boshoff on the bench – all this was the everyday scene of his professional working life as an advocate. But he stood in the prisoner's dock. Hemmed in by the intimidating presence of plain-clothes security men and scrutinised by uniformed policemen, the spectators in the gallery stared into the well of the court as into Fischer's private nightmare, where all appeared normal except for this one glaring displacement.

Yet it was clear that Abram Fischer recognised the reality of his position, and knew it to be the climax of the collision course upon which he and his countrymen were set, nearly thirty years ago, the day he rejected his student belief in segregation. He told the court:

All the conduct with which I have been charged has been directed towards maintaining contact and understanding between the races of this country. If one day it may help to establish a bridge across which white leaders and the real leaders of the non-whites can meet to settle the destinies of all of us by negotiation and not by force of arms, I shall be able to bear with fortitude any sentence which this court may impose on me. It will be a fortitude strengthened by this knowledge at least, that for twenty-five years I have taken no part, not even by passive acceptance, in that hideous system of discrimination which we have erected

in this country and which has become a byword in the
civilised world today.

Not even those Afrikaners who regard Abram Fischer as the
arch-traitor to Afrikanerdom would deny that if he had been
able to stomach white overlordship and the colour bar there
would have been no limit to the honours and high office he
might today have attained in the republic his forebears won
from British imperialism. He comes from the right stock, with
not only the brains but also the intellectual *savoir-faire* coveted
by a people who sometimes feel, even at the peak of their
political power, some veld-bred disadvantage in their dealings
with the sophistications of the outside world.

He was born in 1908 in the Orange River Colony – formerly
the old Boer republic of the Orange Free State – grandson of
its only Prime Minister before Union in 1910. His father
became Judge-President of the Orange Free State – after
Union a province of South Africa. The Boer War defeat at the
hands of the British remained a bitter taste in the mouth of the
grandfather; as a school cadet, it is said that the grandson
refused to be seen in the British conqueror's military uniform.

He was a brilliant scholar, and when he had taken his law
degree at Bloemfontein, won a Rhodes scholarship to New
College, Oxford. At twenty-nine he married the daughter of
another distinguished Afrikaner family, Susannah (Molly)
Krige, and began a thirty-year career at the bar in Johannesburg. He reached the top of his profession and was regarded as
an expert on mining law. His services were engaged by the
insurance companies, the newspaper consortiums and the big
mining houses.

His success coincided with the growth of Afrikaner political
power, but his recognition of the subjection of the black man on
which this power was built precluded him from taking any part
in it. While he saw his people as the first in Africa to win
liberation from colonial domination and therefore well able to
understand and fitted to encourage African aspirations, they
were busy codifying the traditional race prejudice of white
South Africans, whether of Boer, British or any other descent,
as an ideology and the 'South African way of life'.

It was within this situation that Fischer, as a young man, had become a Communist. The rise of Fascism in the world at that time was turning many of his contemporaries in other countries to the left. In England, for example, his counterpart would have gone off to fight with the International Brigade in the Spanish Civil War. But Fischer's battle was to be fought at home. His instigation was not youthful idealism, but the injustice and indifference to injustice that he saw around him every day, and that, indeed, as the first Nationalist prime minister of a student parliament, and a segregationist, he had been party to. It was Hitler's sinister theory of race superiority, combined with a 'strange revulsion' that Fischer experienced when, as a formality at a philanthropic meeting he had to take a black man's hand, that had opened his eyes. Since the days when, as a child, he had made clay oxen with black children on his family's farm, he had been conditioned to develop an antagonism for which he could find no reason. He came to understand colour prejudice as a wholly irrational phenomenon.

At his trial in Pretoria, he told the court why he had been attracted to the Communist Party. There was this

> glaring injustice which exists and has existed for a long time in South African society ... This is not even a question of the degree of humiliation or poverty or misery imposed by discrimination ... It is simply and plainly that discrimination should be imposed as a matter of deliberate policy, solely because of the colour which a man's skin happens to be, irrespective of his merits as a man.

Three decades ago there was certainly not much choice for a young man looking for participation in political activity unequivocally aimed to change all this. The Communist Party was then, and for many years, the only political party that observed no colour bar and advocated universal franchise. (Today, more than thirty years later, there is only one other white political party advocating universal franchise – the Liberal Party, founded in 1953.) At his trial Fischer explained:

My attraction to the Communist Party was a matter of personal observation. By that time the Communist Party had already for two decades stood avowedly and unconditionally for political rights for non-whites, and its white members were, save for a handful of courageous individuals, the only whites who showed complete disregard for the hatred which this attitude attracted from their fellow white South Africans. These members ... were whites who could have taken full advantage of all the privileges open to them because of their colour ... They were not prepared to flourish on the deprivations suffered by others.

But apart from the example of white members, it was always the Communists of all races who were prepared to give of their time and their energy and such means as they had, to help ... with night schools and feeding schemes, who assisted trade unions fighting desperately to preserve standards of living ... It was African Communists who constantly risked arrest ... in order to gain or retain some rights ... This fearless adherence to principle must always exercise a strong appeal to those who wish to take part in politics, not for personal advantage, but in the hope of making some positive contribution.

Fischer's contemporaries among the angry young men in the Western world of the thirties have lived to see a peaceful social revolution in England and the vigorous pursuit of civil-rights legislation against segregation in the United States. Within the same span, in South Africa, Fischer has seen the deeply felt grievances of the non-white population of his country increasingly ignored, their non-violent campaigns against discriminatory laws in the fifties ruthlessly put down, in the sixties their Congresses banned, responsible leaders jailed and house-arrested, along with white people of many political beliefs who have supported them, and a year-by-year piling up of legislation – Bantustans,[6] job reservation,[7] ghetto acts[8] – increasing restriction by colour in every aspect of human activity.

Those contemporaries who shared what now seems to them a hot-headed youth may sit back in good conscience and ask why Fischer did not leave behind leftist beliefs, as they did, in the disillusion of the Stalinist era. One can only state the facts. Though Fischer never proselytised, he was and remains a doctrinaire Marxist; South Africa, in her political development in relation to the colour problem, has never offered him an acceptable alternative to his socialist beliefs.

At his trial he affirmed in orthodox Marxist terms the theory that political change occurs inevitably when a political form ceases to serve the needs of people who are living under new circumstances created by the development of new economic forces and relations. He obviously sees the colour problem in South Africa as basically an economic one: the white man's fear of losing his job to the overwhelming numbers of Africans, the black man so insecure economically that the numbers of unemployed Africans are never even recorded accurately. Fischer said, 'South Africa today is a clear example of a society in which the political forms do not serve the needs of most of the people,' and pointed out that ownership of factories, mines and land used for productive purposes is becoming more and more concentrated – in the hands of whites, of course.

Outside the banned Communist Party, there is no group or party open to whites that, however it proposes to go about removing colour discrimination, also visualises radical change in the ownership of the means of production which underpins the present system of white supremacy. Fischer openly told the court: 'I believe that socialism in the long term has an answer to the problem of race relations. But by negotiation, other immediate solutions can be found ... Immediate dangers {a civil war which he visualised as dwarfing the horrors of Algeria} can be avoided by bringing our state at this stage into line with the needs of today by abolishing discrimination, extending political rights, and then allowing our people to settle their own future.'

In prison or out, Abram Fischer maintains a dramatic position in South African life. For some years, circumstances surrounding him have been extraordinary. If Afrikaner Nationalist propagandists present him as the anti-Christ, then, curiously moved to lay aside his socialist rationalism, he has taken upon himself some of their sins in an almost Christlike way. In addressing the court he returned again and again to statements like

> What is not appreciated by my fellow Afrikaner, because he has cut himself off from all contact with non-whites, is that ... he is now blamed as an Afrikaner for all the evils and humiliations of apartheid. Hence today the police-man is known as a 'Dutch'[9] ... When I give an African a lift during a bus boycott, he refuses to believe that I am an Afrikaner ... All this has bred a deep-rooted hatred for Afrikaners among non-whites ... It demands that Afri-kaners themselves should protest openly and clearly against discrimination. Surely there was an additional duty cast on me, that at least one Afrikaner should make this protest actively ...

Those people, including Afrikaner Nationalists, who know Fischer personally have a special affection and respect for him, no matter how anti-Communist they may be. He himself has always shown respect for the right of anyone to work for social reform in his own way, just so long as the obligation is not smugly ignored. No other figure is at once so controversial and so well-liked. Even people who have never been able to under-stand his adherence to, let alone accept, his socialist views will add: 'But he is a wonderful *person*.' This is due to nothing so superficial as charm – though Fischer has plenty of that; there has been, about Abram Fischer and his wife and children, the particular magnetism of deeply honest lives. Paradoxically, the pull is strong in a country where so many compromises with conscience are made by so many decent citizens.

In his profession, as well, Fischer has borne something of a charmed life. From the fifties, when political trials got under way in South Africa, he would refuse conventionally important briefs in order to take time to defend rank-and-file Africans, Indians and whites on political charges. Such was his pro-fessional prestige that the financial Establishment continued to seek his services as before. From 1958 to 1961 he devoted himself to the defence of Nelson Mandela, the African National Congress leader, and twenty-nine other accused in the first mass political trial that, because it represented so many shades

– both skin and ideological – of political thought, became known as 'the Opposition on trial'.[10] In 1964 Fischer was leading defence counsel at the trial of the 'High Command' of combined liberation movements, which had been based at Rivonia, north of Johannesburg.[11] Later that year, his invisible armour was pierced for the first time; he was imprisoned, briefly, under the ninety-day-detention law. And then, in September of 1964 he was arrested, with thirteen others, on five charges including those of being a member and furthering the objects of the Communist Party.

Because of the esteem in which Fischer was held, his request for bail was supported by many of his legal colleagues and granted by the court, although he had been named chief accused. During the course of the trial, he was even given a temporary passport to enable him to go to London to represent an internationally known pharmaceutical company at the Privy Council. He could expect as much as a five-year sentence at his own trial: would he come back? He had given his word, and he did. Having won the case, he returned discussing the new plays he had seen in the West End, just as if he had come home to face nothing more than the letdown after a holiday.

He had been in South Africa a month or so when, on January 25, 1965, he disappeared overnight, leaving a letter to the court saying that he was aware that his eventual punishment would be increased by his action, but that he believed it was his duty both to remain in South Africa and to continue to oppose apartheid by carrying on with his political work as long as he was physically able. He referred to his career at the Bar, in relation to the injustice of apartheid upheld by the law: 'I can no longer serve justice in the way I have attempted to do during the past 30 years. I can do it only in the way I have now chosen.'

For ten months he eluded a police hunt that poked into every backyard and farmhouse in the country, and brought into detention anyone suspected of being able to blurt out, under persuasion of solitary confinement, Fischer's whereabouts. On November 11 last year, he was arrested in Johannesburg, thin, bearded, his hair dyed. Except for the eyes, he was unrecognisable as the short but well-set, handsome man with curly white hair that he had been – and was to be again, by the time he appeared in court on January 26 of this year to face fifteen instead of the original five charges against him.

Why did Abram Fischer abscond? What did he achieve by it? So far as is known, he does not seem to have managed to initiate any significant new political activity while in hiding.

His fellow white South Africans, the majority of whom are indifferent to the quality of life on the other side of the colour bar, living their comfortable lives in the segregated suburbs where, once, he too had a house with a swimming pool, and among whom, last year, he lived as a fugitive, express strong opinions about what he had done with his life. His colleagues at the Bar, taking the position that absconding from his original trial was conduct unseemly to the dignity of the profession, hurriedly applied within days of his disappearance to have him disbarred. Some people assure themselves that he acted in blind obedience to 'orders from Moscow' – the purpose of which they cannot suggest. Well-meaning people who cannot conceive that anyone would sacrifice profession, home, family, and ultimately personal liberty for a gesture affirming what he believed to be right, say that the tragic death of his wife, Molly, in a motor accident in 1964, must have disorientated him. Others, who have themselves suffered bans and lost passports as a result of courageous opposition to apartheid, feel that Fischer's final defiance of the law was a gratuitous act, ending in senseless tragedy: 'Why has Bram thrown himself away?'

While Fischer was 'at large' for those ten months, some people were saying, 'Now he is our Mandela.' (The reference was to the period when Nelson Mandela escaped a police net for more than a year, travelled abroad, and worked among his people from 'underground'.)[12] In the jails last year (where there were more than three thousand political prisoners), when African politicals were allowed to see anybody, their first question was commonly not about their families but whether 'Bram' was still 'all right'. And a few days before sentence was to be passed on him, an African couple begged his daughter to let them borrow one of his suits, so that a witchdoctor might use it in a spell to influence the judge to give a deferred sentence.

For the Fischer family, 1964–5 was a year to turn distraught any but the most tough and selfless minds. It has since become clear that, as defence counsel at the Rivonia Trial, Fischer had to muster the nerve and daring to handle evidence that might at any moment involve himself. Directly after the trial, he and his wife were driving to Cape Town to celebrate the twenty-first birthday of their daughter Ilse, a student at the University of Cape Town, and to enable Fischer to visit Mandela and the other convicted trial defendants imprisoned off the coast on Robben Island, when his car plunged into a deep pool by the side of the road and Molly Fischer was drowned.

The Fischers have always been an exceptionally devoted family, sharing as well as family love a working conviction that daily life must realise in warm, human action any theoretical condemnation of race discrimination. In Molly Fischer the very real tradition of Afrikaner hospitality triumphantly burst the barriers it has imposed on itself; her big house was open to people of all races, and, unmindful of what the neighbours would say, she and her husband brought up along with their own daughters and son an orphaned African child.

Molly Fischer taught Indian children, worked with women's non-racial movements and spent five months in prison, detained without trial, during the 1960 State of Emergency. At her huge funeral people of all races mourned together, as if apartheid did not exist. No one who saw him at that time can forget the terrible courage with which Fischer turned loss into concern for the living; neither could they confuse this with the workings of an unhinged mind. Almost at once, he set out again for Cape Town to visit the men on Robben Island.

If one wants to speculate why he disappeared in the middle of his trial and yet stayed in South Africa, fully aware that when, inevitably, he was caught he would incur greatly increased punishment, one must surely also ask oneself why, when he was allowed to go abroad while on bail, he ever came back. Some friends half hoped he wouldn't; a government supporter nervously remarked that there was nothing to stop Fischer turning up at The Hague, where, at the time, the World Court was hearing the question of South Africa's right to impose apartheid on the mandated territory of South West

Africa [Namibia]. There would have been no extradition, but a hero's role for him there.

People of different backgrounds who know Fischer best seem to agree that what brought him back from Europe and what made him turn fugitive were one and the same thing, the touchstone of his personality: absolute faith in human integrity. It seems reasonable to conclude that he came back because he believed that this integrity was mutual and indivisible – he believed he would never be betrayed by the people with whom he was working in opposition to apartheid, and, in turn, he owed them the guarantee of his presence.

As for the 'gesture' of the ten months he spent in hiding, he has given, in court, his own answer to those fellow citizens – legal colleagues, firms, enemies, the white people of South Africa – who seek to judge him:

> It was to keep faith with all those dispossessed by apartheid that I broke my undertaking to the court, separated myself from my family, pretended I was someone else, and accepted the life of a fugitive. I owed it to the political prisoners, to the banished, to the silenced and to those under house arrest not to remain a spectator, but to act. I knew what they expected of me, and I did it. I felt responsible, not to those who are indifferent to the sufferings of others, but to those who are concerned. I knew that by valuing, above all, their judgment, I would be condemned by people who are content to see themselves as respectable and loyal citizens. I cannot regret any such condemnation that may follow me.

The judge sentenced him to prison 'for life' and, while others wept, Fischer himself received the pronouncement with fortitude. No one can guess what goes on in a man's mind when he hears such words; but perhaps Abram Fischer, sitting it out in prison, now, may ask himself, taking courage, 'Whose life? Theirs – the government's – or mine?'[13]

One Man Living Through It

(1966)[1]

*The 1950s were not only a period of political revival — the kind
which Gordimer recorded in her biographical essay on Albert
Luthuli. It was also a period of extraordinary cultural and literary
renaissance. At this time a generation of black writers arose, based
for the most part in Sophiatown, and writing for the mass
circulation newspapers and periodicals such as* Drum *magazine.
Gordimer became friendly with most of them, and many of their
names recur in these and other essays: Ezekiel Mphahlele, Lewis
Nkosi, Can Themba, Bloke Modisane and Todd Matshikiza. One
of this generation was Nat Nakasa, to whom Gordimer became
close. In a way he embodied a wider history. Largely self-taught
and working his way up from hardship, he became one of the best
known writers and journalists in South Africa. But this the
apartheid government could not tolerate. When Nakasa was
awarded a Nieman Fellowship to Harvard University, he was
allowed to leave the country on an exit permit only, which meant he
could never return. Some time after in America, Nakasa — who had
been part of the joyous and anguished, vibrant life of Sophiatown —
committed suicide. By the time this occurred most of his colleagues
had also gone into exile, some — such as Can Themba — also to
suffer untimely deaths.[2] Hearing the news of Nakasa's death,
Nadine Gordimer remembered him . . .*

My memory for the sequence of events in getting to know
people is bad — the preliminaries tend to run together into the
colour and quality of the relationship that develops. But I do
remember clearly the first time I met Nat Nakasa. It was
perhaps seven years ago and I was expecting Lewis Nkosi. He
brought with him that day a round-faced boy who, faced with
the prospect of being left alone to amuse himself while Lewis

and I went off for a private talk, said, just as if there were not plenty of books and papers in the room – 'Haven't you got any records I can play?' He was not ill-at-ease, but carried the youthful confidence in his own interests that marks the city-bred. Here was someone who would skid through the conventions of white houses as nippily as, a few years earlier, he would weave a bicycle in and out of the stream of Durban's big cars.

I knew he must mean jazz records, and felt he would find mine meagre and 'commercial', but I gave them to him. And when Lewis and I came back to the room he was stretched full-length in a chair, attentive to the music and inoffensively indifferent to both our absence and return.

That was Nat, newly arrived in Johannesburg. That was Nat at the beginning of the period he describes in the essay 'Johannesburg, Johannesburg'.[3] That was the period of no fixed abode. And yet he was going somewhere; by the very nature of the way he was living, he was set upon the only course that was valid for him: the course of independent self-realisation. Although I barely recognise that boy sitting in the chair stirring his toes inside his shoes to the beat, just as I barely recognise the man who ended his own life early one summer morning in New York, both were part of the young man who became my close friend. So do the limits of human relationships constantly fling us back; so do one's hands fall, helpless, before the quintessential loneliness of each human being. It is keeping this in mind that I write of him, respecting the ultimate despair that took him beyond the understanding of friends, aware that what each of us knows of him was only part of what he was, and lived, and suffered, and that even when we have put it all together there will always be something – perhaps the unbearable sum of the total in itself? – that he kept to himself and died of.

I saw quite a lot of Nat at parties or when friends simply gravitated together to talk, but it was when he launched out into the founding of the *Classic*, and I became a member of the small committee formed to help him run it, that he was drawn into the working life of our house. He heard squabbles and learnt private jokes. He lost his fear of the bulldog and endured its smelly presence at his feet; he was asked to pick up a schoolboy from the bus-stop or to buy a pint of milk while on the way from town. The process is known as becoming one of the family and it implies chores as well as privileges. He and I found that one of the times that suited both of us best, if we had *Classic* matters to work on, was about two o'clock in the afternoon. Very often he would rush in then, carrying his bulging attaché case, and we would eat bread and cheese on the verandah in the sun, laughing a lot (he was a brilliant mimic) and getting on with the work at the same time. His social instincts were sure, and even in easy friendship he never lost his precise judgment of exactly the time to get up and go. He always seemed to sense when you had work or some other preoccupation that you must get back to. This leads me, only now, while writing, to realise that I never ever remember him being a bore. He didn't even have those moments of recurring tediousness on pet subjects that most of us have. Sensitivity is a term whose mention may itself cause a suppressed yawn, but the fact is that he was too sensitive to be a bore. Too conscious, in the best and most open way, of the feelings of other people. And this reminds one how, on the last evening of his life, when in all his final anguish of mind he talked until late with his friend Jack Thomson and his wife, he had still some instinct that made him shrink from burdening them with the mention of his impulse to suicide.

Nat's approach to the *Classic* was serious and yet light-handed, gay; candid and unflustered. He was a clever young newspaperman but had no literary background or experience – yes. There was not enough money for the venture and there were endless practical difficulties – yes. But he felt that day-to-day journalism floated, like oil indicating the presence of a submarine, on the surface of African life, and he wanted to make soundings of his own. He asked for help, and what's more, he did so aware that help more often than not must take the form of criticism, and in the self-knowledge that he could take *that*, too. As for money, he managed as best he could with what there was; and as for the other difficulties, he dealt with them with what I am prepared to say is a particularly African resilience, vigorously born of harsh necessity, early on.

One of the practical difficulties was that it was hard to get white printers (our first one, certainly) to accept that this black man was the editor and not a white editor's office boy. Nat's manner with the man was amusing and highly successful – he treated him kindly but firmly as someone who has had a nasty shock, but really not *so* bad, after all, and wasn't he getting used to it, wasn't he feeling better already? Nat did not do as well with the wife, an ink-haired, flour-faced lady sitting up among her invoices on a high stool, like a grim *madame* in a late nineteenth-century French painting, but he had the husband confiding his business troubles to him, and *almost* calling him 'Mr Nakasa' . . .

He would bring to me a manuscript that he liked particularly, to share the pleasure of it, and he brought me those whose interest or quality he felt uncertain about. If he was strongly in favour of something, he would publish it anyway, no matter what anyone thought of it. He had read no poetry outside a school primer and I often told him that some poems he considered publishing in the magazine were rubbish. He would say, 'Oh. Well, why?' And would force me to state the grounds of my attack, line by line. Sometimes he would come back days later – scratching down through the nest of dog-eared manuscripts in the attaché case – and dig out one of the same poems over again. 'What about this line here? – you said it was meaningless but I think what he's getting at here – ' And so he sometimes caught me out.

Once he planked down a poem – 'Now that's really got something!' I read it over; 'Yes, but what it's got is not its own,' and I fetched down the Lorca and showed him the poem from which the other had borrowed the form and imagery that distinguished it. He was not at all touchy about gaps in his knowledge and experience; he had none of the limitations of false pride. He sat down to Lorca with the pleasure of discovery. One of the reasons why he hoped to go to Harvard was because he wanted time to read the great poets and imaginative writers; he felt strongly that he needed a wider intellectual context than the day-to-day, politically-orientated, African-centred one in which he had become a thinking person, and on which, so far, even his artistic judgments must be empirically based. I wonder if he ever found that time to read; somehow, I don't think he did. Too many well-meant invitations to speak here and there about Africa, too many well-meant requests to appear on television programmes about

Africa, too many requests to write articles about how an African looks at American this and that. Nat remained trapped in the preoccupations of his time — the time measured by those multiple clocks on airports, showing simultaneously what hour it is at Karachi, Vladivostok, Nairobi and New York, and not the dimension in which one can sit down and read. There seems to be no fellowship that provides for that.

Nat was a good talker and had the unusual ability to tell an anecdote in such a way that he himself was presented as the 'feed', and the bright lights illuminated the character of someone else. The oblique picture that emerged of him was one of wit and calm, sometimes in bizarre situations. He was given to analysis — of himself and others — rather than accusations and self-pity, and so did not react with self-dramatisation to the daily encounters with white laws and prejudices. White people used to say of him that he, unlike others, was not 'bitter'; I don't know quite what they meant by this — because he was as bitterly hurt by the colour bar as the next man — unless they mistook for resignation the fact that he managed to keep his self-respect intact.

In the years I knew him fragments and segments of his life came out in talk, without chronology, as these things do between friends; he was telling me, one Sunday, how as a small boy he used to be up at four in the morning to be first on the streets with the newspapers. He was not telling me about his hardships as a poor black child, but of how mysterious and exciting Durban was at that hour, for a little boy — the deserted city coming up with the sun out of the mist from the sea. Then, last year while I was in London, I met his younger brother, who was about to go up to Oxford. When I told Nat — who had helped to pay for the boy's schooling — how impressed I had been by his brother's keen mind, he told me how he had been in the room when the boy was born, and how, since the mother became ill soon after and was never again able to look after her children, he had simply 'taken the baby around with me until he could walk'. Again, it was the quality of the experience he was conveying, not a hard-luck story presenting himself as a victim. Of course, he *was* a victim of this country; but never accepted the character of the victimised in himself.

I always hoped that one day he would write about these

things — the child in Durban, the life he and Lewis Nkosi shared, homeless and yet, curiously, more at home in Johannesburg than those behind their suburban front doors. I think that the writing in his weekly column in the Johannesburg *Rand Daily Mail* was a beginning, and is the best writing he did. It was journalism, yes, but journalism of a highly personal kind; all the news came from inside Nat. He dredged into his mind and feelings as he had never done before, he wrote only of what was real to him, throwing away all the labels conveniently provided by both protest writing and government handouts, accepting without embarrassment all the apparent contradictions in the complexity of his reactions to his situation — and ours, black and white. (He didn't even balk at coming out with the pronouncement that he felt sorry for young Afrikaners!) 'Bitterness'; 'resentment'; 'prejudice'; these terms are as easy to use as the airmail stickers free for the taking in post offices. Nat presented the reality, in daily life and thought, from which these abstractions are run off. He showed us what it was all about, for one man living through it.

This writing — reflecting the gaiety of a serious person — came from his central personality and, in giving himself the fullest expression he had yet known, during the year that he was writing his column and concurrently running *Classic* he developed amazingly. It was a strange time, that last year in South Africa. On the one hand, he was making a name for himself in a small but special way that no African had done before; his opinions and ideas were being considered seriously by white newspaper-readers whose dialogue across the colour line had never exceeded the command, do-this-or-that, and the response, yes-*baas*. On the other hand, he had been awarded a fellowship to Harvard and was involved in the process of trying to get a passport — for an African, a year-long game in which the sporting element seems to be that the applicant is never told what you have to do to win, or what it was he did that made him lose. Knowing the nature of the game, Nat had to consider from the start how the refusal of a passport would affect his life. He had to decide whether the place he had made for himself, astride the colour bar, merited electing to stay, should the passport be refused; or whether he should, like others, accept exile as the price of a breath of the open world. It was not a decision to be dictated only by personal ambition; part of his development was that he had come to the stage, now, when he had to weigh up the possible usefulness to his people of the position he had gained. It was not, of course, a political position, and its value was not something that could easily be measured; there is no scale for the intangibles of the human spirit.

Quite suddenly, he made the decision to go, although he had been refused a passport. He took what every other young man of outstanding ability — but of a different colour — takes for granted, and gets without the necessity of an agonising decision to exile himself from home, country, friends and family — a chance to travel and seek education. I saw him off at the airport — twice. The first time he missed the plane (no, it was not what white people call African time; it was a hitch over the issue of traveller's cheques) and the crowd of friends who had come to say goodbye dispersed rather flatly. Not all could come back again next day; but this time it went without a hitch, weigh-in, customs, finally passport control and the exit permit open on the counter. I looked at it; it was valid for one exit only, and the undersigned, Nathaniel Nakasa, was debarred from 'entering the Republic of South Africa or South West Africa' again. There was the printed admonition: 'This is a valuable document. Keep it in a safe place.'

Nat was gone. He never came back. But he was the beginning, not the end of something. In so many ways he was starting where others left off. I have heard that shortly before his death he made an impassioned anti-white speech before a Washington audience; but the report comes third-hand and I do not know whether this interpretation of his address is a true one. Similarly, if in direct contradiction, I have heard it said that through his association with white friends he had become a 'white' black man. The truth is that he was a new kind of man in South Africa — he accepted without question and with easy dignity and natural pride his Africanness, and he took equally for granted that his identity as a man among men, a human among fellow humans, could not be legislated out of existence even by all the apartheid laws in the statute book, or all the racial prejudice in this country. He did not calculate the population as thirteen million or three million, but as sixteen. He belonged not between two worlds, but to both. And in him one could see the hope of one world. He has left that hope behind; there will be others to take it up.

Speak Out:
The Necessity for Protest

(1971)[1]

A student for only a short time in her own life, one of the responsibilities which Nadine Gordimer has taken seriously is the need to keep in touch with the universities in South Africa, especially to respond to the various and separate calls by students on any number of matters. Talks on literature, censorship and writing; graduation addresses; contributions to protest meetings: all these have been part of her sustained activity over the years. Latterly she has been closely associated with the National Union of South African Students (NUSAS) — a national student body which has been renowned for its enduring opposition to and protest against the policies of apartheid for many years.

The address reproduced here was given as an Academic Freedom Lecture — an institution perhaps peculiar to South Africa in its specific form, which may need some explaining. In 1959 the National Party government passed the Extension of University Education Act, which set up various tribal or ethnic colleges, but also — as Gordimer remarked in 'Great Problems in the Street' — restricted the universities by segregating them. As far as the 'white' universities were concerned, there was now a prohibition on the attendance of almost all black students. Ever since that time it has been a tradition at the English-language universities to reaffirm their commitment to the renewal of academic freedom in an annual Academic Freedom Lecture.

When Gordimer gave this particular lecture at the University of Natal in 1971, there were two main topics on her mind. One was the continued assault on white liberal institutions by the state — a process which she records in some detail here. The second was an attack on white liberalism from a very different quarter — by the black students themselves. For these years saw the rise of what became known as the Black Consciousness movement. Its two main organisations were the South African Students' Organisation

87

(SASO) and the Black Peoples' Convention (BPC), and its central theme (much like Africanism before it) was that black liberation could be achieved only by blacks themselves. It focused on the psychological liberation of blacks, and it attacked white liberals for having undermined this. For — ran the Black Consciousness argument — white liberals were intrinsically part of white supremacy: even when ostensibly opposed to it they had acted on behalf of blacks instead of letting blacks act for themselves. It was in accordance with this position that soon after its formation SASO withdrew from any contacts with NUSAS. These then were the issues underlying Gordimer's approach in this address.

I've come to talk to you about protest, and you wish and I wish I might have been able to choose some other subject. After all, I am a writer of novels and stories, you are studying a dozen different branches of knowledge — there are so many subjects that would interest us, that we'd like to be able to pursue in peace: subjects where we shine, and where, perhaps, we have the best of ourselves to offer. But instead I turn where we are all amateurs, driven to response by an historical situation — not of your making — in which we share the common lot of our humanity, undifferentiated by any special interests.

Protest was the subject of last year's Academic Freedom Lecture, and no doubt that of the previous year. Like those laws hastily promulgated as emergency measures and then never repealed, the issue, properly associated with crisis, is now always with us. Turn away from it though we may, it asserts itself in the gorge that rises daily with the opening of a newspaper. The tragic, mean and shabby happenings we read of are the concrete expressions of the state, in our country, of those high-sounding unmentionables, freedom, justice and civilisation. That sick taste at the base of the throat is protest, the protest of an organism at what it knows it shouldn't, can't stomach without harm. The state of emergency for freedoms — I use the plural because we have been shown that, indeed, freedom is almost infinitely divisible in our country — has been with us for a long time. It is the way we live now; there is no escaping, not even for those who, feeling their own morsel to be secure, don't care.

So I make no apology for taking up where someone else left off last year or the year before, or for believing that I may have something to add. And I want to say now what I didn't in the polite preamble expected of the Academic Freedom lecturer, the preamble I skipped because I wanted to say outside the context of polite and grateful platitudes: I am honoured to have been invited to address you because many of you have shown you *do* care. Students all over South Africa have made that clear.

The fact is that it is the students of the English-language universities who have kept alive the spirit of protest among whites in South Africa over the last five years or more. To their shame, and with the exception of a few isolated groups, notably the Black Sash[2] and the Christian Institute,[3] and a few individuals, white South Africans of my generation have abdicated their responsibility to speak out. Swopping the true horror stories of the callousness and hypocrisy that are never in short supply in public life in our country, they deplore in the privacy of their own dining-rooms what they listlessly condone in public. Deploring, in the same breath, the scruffy irresponsibility of the younger generation, they have allowed themselves to be frightened and silenced, while their 'effeminate' long-haired sons and 'unladylike' daughters voice thoughts that are safer left unspoken, ask aloud the awkward questions, and endure the unquestionably adult experience of being watched by the Security Police.

It was not always so. Protest arises as an ancillary to political opposition in situations where the political machinery is defective in allowing opposition its due voice and corrective influence. Ours is and always has been such a situation, since the vast majority of our population never has had the vote or direct representation in the places of power where our laws are made and the structure of our society determined. Therefore the tradition of protest in South Africa is old and honourable, and as a social phenomenon it could not always conveniently be attributed — as it so often is by spokesmen of our present government — to parental over-permissiveness and the natural exhibitionism of the young. There are times when you may find it heartening to remind yourselves that the tradition of protest, far from being a kind of nursery tantrum, nor yet alien to the

South African way of life, has been entrenched in that way of life since the days of early settlement. In terms of age, it is almost as venerable as the colour bar itself. But let's be content to confine ourselves to the contemporary tradition, which flowered and, not unaccountably, withered within the lifetime of your parents' generation. I say not unaccountably because we all know what happened to the political and para-political movements that in the 1950s and '60s represented the perfectly legal, if sometimes radical opposition that even our peculiar whites-only, élitist minority-democracy had to tolerate if it were to be allowed its dubious claim to be a democracy. These movements were all banned or so persistently beheaded of leadership, by government decree or imprisonment, that they died. The most important of the black mass-movements – the African National Congress, the Pan-Africanist Congress and the South African Indian Congress – had existed outside that self-styled democracy anyway, because they had no access to parliamentary processes for change. The fringe movements, for the most part pressure groups where white and black found contact quite naturally in their opposition to a colour bar that denied them a common humanity, had precariously straddled the wall separating that democracy and the black majority.

Now the focus of protest through the burning glass of political movements is hooded. No one knows if, or when, by what methods or by whose hand the hood will be lifted. And few share the ultimate convictions, or could summon the courage on behalf of convictions of their own, to follow those brave ones, like Bram Fischer and Nelson Mandela, who are in Pretoria prison or on Robben Island for what they believe. But the tradition of protest was always much wider than this. It was flung centrifugally from, rather than concentrated centri-petally on, a core of political movements. In the fifties and early sixties, hundreds of ordinary men and women who were neither communists nor revolutionaries took part in demon-strations, marches and street meetings, not out of political conviction but out of a basic sense of right and wrong. It was as simple as that. When they saw one discriminatory law after another being passed, while the rest of the world was beginning to dismantle the social machinery of race and colour prejudice, when they saw even the separate freedom of white privilege being pared down by restriction after restriction on freedom of speech and association, they reacted out of human decency and self-respect. When the gorge rose they didn't swallow it. Yes, they were naïve enough to feel outraged. The great passive resistance campaigns were waged by the power of controlled outrage. They were non-violent; and they were based on profound respect for law and order: respect for the basic human laws, the unwritten charter that exists inside you and me just as surely as the mechanism that keeps us balanced on our two feet. The unwritten charter that makes us *know*, out of the deepest source of collective knowledge and experience, that I have no right that you should not have. This concept of protest recognised that the law of the land in any country does not always conform to that unwritten charter. In Gandhi's own words, 'The convenience of the powers that be is the law in the final analysis.'⁴ Perhaps the best definition of progress would be the continuing efforts of men and women to narrow the gap between the convenience of the powers that be and the unwritten charter.

The concept of protest has changed in South Africa in the last decade. This has been brought about by a double process. On the one hand, the token defiance, on principle, of what might be called non-criminal laws now carries the penalty that one is regarded as a potential violent enemy of the state, although one has neither plotted, nor connived, nor harmed a hair on anyone's head. On the other hand, the idea that one may have a moral right and necessity to *judge* laws to be unjust, and to oppose them in speech and spirit, has been buried as laws enforcing more and more conformity of thought have been passed. And as so often happens, strictured already, there comes to people the twilight need to stricture themselves still further, to try to anticipate, in order to be left in peace, what the authorities may ask of them next. There is much to be afraid of, in the way of the state's retribution for non-conformity to the official ideology, in our country; but South Africans have become afraid even when there is nothing to fear. Hold a perfectly legal meeting, circulate a perfectly legal petition – people will tell you they think preventive detention an abomination, but they would prefer not to be associated with your meeting; they will tell you they think it dreadful that censorship should be extended, but they dare not risk putting their names to a petition. The margin of safety white South Africans feel they must claim for themselves extends yearly. Their 'respect' for the law grows proportionately. That respect is a sham. In a democracy — even if it is a so-called democracy like our white-élitist one — the greatest veneration one can show the rule of law is to keep a watch on it, and to reserve the right to judge unjust laws and the subversion of the function of the law by the power of the state. That vigilance is the most important proof of respect for the law.

No doubt in your generation there are very many men and women as cowed and intimidated as their parents, happily strumming *We Shall Overcome* on their guitars even while remarking that, after all, the Prime Minister may know something we don't know when he says there are people in the universities 'who are making it their business to cause another Sharpeville'. I don't believe the Prime Minister knows anything about the activities and aims of NUSAS or the Federation of Catholic Students that we don't know; I don't think there is anything *to* know except what is plain for everyone to see, and that, indeed, is what the Prime Minister himself has seen: there are enough young people among the students at the English-language universities to dig up, alive and kicking, the concept of protest that was buried under the weight of the Suppression of Communism Act and its satellite laws and overgrown — an unmarked grave from which people prefer to avert their eyes — by a dusty ivy of intimidation. I don't believe that anyone, given the list of issues that students have taken up in the last five years, issues which, without exception, show them to be concerned with preventing or abolishing the pain, physical and mental, caused by a certain government legislation, could think that these same students could have the desire ever to see repeated in our country that day when the police shot sixty-nine and wounded one hundred and eighty people.

George Steiner, a great contemporary scholar who has given some time to the meaning and nature of protest, has said: '*Men are accomplices to that which leaves them indifferent.*'[5] The students have refused to become accomplices to those features of present-day South African life, interrogatory detention, house arrest, the arbitrary banning and restriction of individuals, the practice of endorsing out and resettling people. They have declared themselves unequivocally against all forms of racial discrimination. They have marched, sat-in, picketed, held forums and seminars, spoken and written on many issues, from the Mafeje affair,[6] the detention of the 22[7] and the expulsion of student leaders such as Rex Heinke,[8] to the house arrest of Father Cosmas Desmond.[9]

We come now to a question you may be asking yourselves. I have been asked it quite often lately, when I have talked with students in Johannesburg. What has student protest achieved? More broadly, what use is non-violent, legal protest? Is there any sense in gathering together in a hall, talking, going off home again to the same old life under the same old conditions? Is protest *action*? Is there any truth, despite its suspiciously complacent ring, in the perennial suggestion that protest does more harm than good? And are critics perhaps not so wrong when they sneer that brave words on the platform send everyone home in a self-righteous, sterile euphoria?

Protest is not a revolutionary means but a reforming one. The only treason it serves is one of those 'necessary treasons' Steiner remarks on with reference to Socrates, when he says there are 'necessary treasons to make the city freer and more open to man'.[10] Protest is the need to speak out in a silenced society; it seeks, usually on specific issues, to expose injustices, set wrongs right, ameliorate hardship. The very term 'protest' implies acceptance of an ear of authority and power to·hear and take heed; therefore protest is not anarchic, either. When we look for results from various forms of protest, the measure is whether any change for the better has been brought about by them. Well, let's take a look at protest in its more obvious form: the demonstration. Father Trevor Huddleston,[11] that lean flame of a man who warmed all Sophiatown with love and trust in place of contact and dialogue, first suggested the fact that colour-bar cricket wasn't 'cricket' might make granite white South Africa vulnerable to change in at least one area of national life. That was a long time ago; the possibility seemed remote; the white Springboks[12] were travelling the inter-national circuit yearly, and South Africa was still taking part in the Olympics. But we have lived to see concessions towards the idea of the non-racial team made by both sporting bodies and the government – not yet the complete abolition of the colour bar in sport, but a backing-down from white exclusiveness that would have crumbled the walls of the country clubs, a few years back. This has come about solely as a result of demonstrations against South African white sportsmen abroad, even while the sportsmen themselves and the white public back home have warned that demonstrations repel the delicate antennae of willingness for change put out in South Africa, and one South African government spokesman went so far as to remark bravely, in Australia, that demonstrations worry our government about as much as a buzzing fly. Some fly, that; some bite. Stung into action by it, a group of South African sportsmen have even taken over the tactics of demonstration themselves, and walked off a home field in protest at segregated teams.

Turning to student mass protest, would the 22 have been brought to trial – twice over, as it turned out, and with an acquittal both times – without the determined and persistent protest of the students of the University of the Witwatersrand? Or would those twenty-two people still have been confined in interrogatory detention for who knows how many more months, without ever having faced charges? Of course, I do not suggest, nor would any person in his right mind wish, that the processes of the courts could or should be influenced by the public. But this was a matter of protesting that, indeed, the due process of the law, by which a man is entitled to meet charges and defend himself, was *not* being made available to people. So I think there are grounds for accepting that the arousal of public conscience over this group of people brought results. And it was student protest that woke the sleepers, including, it seems, important and influential spokesmen of the legal profession itself.

The effectiveness or otherwise of student protest on other issues cannot be measured in quite such a clear-cut fashion. The Mafeje affair – truly an issue of Academic Freedom, specifically – didn't end with the reappointment of Mr Mafeje, and in fact produced the salutary sidelight of Mr Mafeje's remark that he thought the issue of one black lecturer in a white university unimportant in comparison with a generations-long segregation in schools. The demonstrations in protest against the banning of student leaders, against censorship, and against the house arrest of various individuals and the arbitrary removals of black communities have not – have not yet – brought about any changes one can weigh up as events.

But the public has been made aware.

With the combinations of the provisions of the Riotous Assemblies Act, the Suppression of Communism Act, etc., and the nervousness of the city fathers, places of public assembly in our cities are really only open to flower shows and pop groups these days. When there's a request to hold a public meeting, it's a case of the Town Clerk asks the Chief of Police, and the Chief of Police asks the Magistrate – and in the end the answer is 'no'. City halls are not places where city people may speak their minds. It is a strange situation. The campuses are almost the only places left, now, where mass meetings on contentious issues may be held. When students collect in halls and sometimes on the open campus, the word that goes forth from that forum is often the only public debate, outside parliament, on these issues. And some, indeed, are not debated in parliament, either. Because the students meet and invite speakers, because the students march, because they stand in the street with posters, and because SRC leaders give statements to the press, people outside the universities are made to notice happenings that might otherwise pass, unremarked, as an inch of newsprint somewhere.

I don't think one can overestimate the importance of this aspect of protest. To speak, to pamphleteer, to march is frustrating. To pass resolutions at meetings seems futile. To be perpetually in the position – as one is from a stand of protest – of saying 'no', of refusal instead of acceptance, brings a feeling of sterility. To find oneself joined by the lunatic fringe, out for exhibitionism and little else, is distasteful. To suspect oneself of self-righteousness is nauseating. To see little concrete action as a result of enduring all these unheroic things may seem to be the final disillusion. But protest does not have your well-being as its object. That object is to bring awareness to those people, among yourselves, and in the world outside the campus gates, whose responses are blunted by unquestioning conformity. If student protest were to achieve nothing but this, the shock of recognition of things as they really are, affecting the daily lives of real, flesh-and-blood people, instead of rows of statistics or incomprehensible clauses in a statute book, or strange abstractions like 'Other Coloured' or 'Surplus people' — if protest were to achieve nothing else, it still would be performing an absolutely vital function in our society.

Other forms of protest have risen out of awareness: the spirit of enquiry and testimony, for example. And this form of protest has not been without results. Harold Strachan's personal account of prison life, and the Gandar and Pogrund accounts, collated from various sources, on the same subject, brought these men to court.[13] But Mrs Helen Suzman, the Progressive Party[14] MP, has placed on record that after these court cases there was a significant improvement in prison conditions.

Father Cosmas Desmond recorded the conditions he found in black resettlement areas, published them in his book, *The Discarded People*, and assisted in the making of a television film on some resettlement areas. Father Desmond is now under house arrest and his book is banned, but Mrs Helen Suzman confirms that the conditions under which African communities are uprooted and removed have been improved, at least in some places, and the most basic of needs provided for. So you can see that there is something to be said for my fellow novelist, the German writer Günter Grass's choice of a crowing cock as the symbol of what's needed in a society burdened with the legacy of a shameful past — as his and ours is — and (in our case) a not less shameful present. The more of us who are not afraid to speak out, the less there will be to fear. We could take courage from the example of Helen Joseph,[15] whose first public act after nine years of enforced silence under house arrest was to address a mass meeting of protest against the house arrest of Cosmas Desmond.

The view that South African student protest is a youthful aberration and as such will pass as this generation moves up the seven-age scale and becomes 'responsible', is one that brings comfort to many people. What worries me most, on the contrary, is that this will indeed happen: you will graduate, marry, grow fat around your nerves of social response and moss over your sense of outrage. You will become responsible only to a life of material privilege paid for by other people's deprivation and the demeaning of your own spirit. You will settle down: at worst, to what Günter Grass calls that 'mistaken sense of loyalty {that} heaps late blessings on yesterday's crime',[16] in your country; at best, to that private dissent and public assent which seems to represent the flower of white civilisation here, at present. If I might have one wish for the students in our universities, it is that they might never 'settle down' and forget the sort of responsibility they were once prepared to take up, the responsibility for being culpable and aware in their society.

But for the time being, you are still here; still with us. And as men and women who see themselves in this light of culpability and responsibility, you now have a particular problem. I have said earlier that so far as the need for protest is concerned, we live in a chronic state of emergency. Recent events have shown, however, that for the students a new internal crisis has arisen. I think it the most crucial your leaders and you have ever had to deal with, not forgetting that the very existence of NUSAS has been threatened from time to time in the past few years. To have been outlawed by government decree would have been a disaster; but to have brought in question the entire basis from which the greater part of your activities has sprung can be tragic, in the ancient Greek sense in which tragedy is the fate that one brings down upon oneself, as the result of a fatal flaw in one's own being. I'm referring of course to the principle and practice of black disinvolvement which is affecting student affairs, now. To put it bluntly: NUSAS is the only mass organisation in the country that has persistently and doggedly attempted to implement its non-racial charter, even within the near-impossible confines of the segregated universities. Under NUSAS or individual SRC leadership, the issues taken up by student protest all have been, almost without exception, concerned with opposition to racial legislation, the colour bar in practice, and the restriction of freedom of movement, speech and conscience arising out of the maintenance of a white supremacy. More important, the students have attempted, over years, a direct co-operation and consultation with black students which was constantly frustrated and blocked by authorities carrying out a policy of isolation of black students that did not stop short of intimidation. Yet now, while the Rosetta stone of 'contact' is frantically being sought by way of Malawi, Madagascar, the Ivory Coast and Ghana,[17] white students find that their long-established if minimal contact seems likely to disappear altogether. While the Holiday Inn at Jan Smuts airport provides, indeed, a holiday from apartheid, a neutral Never-never land with just about everything a good mixed party needs, with blacks and whites, local as well as imported ones, Nationalist Party dignitaries as well as liberals, conferring and quarrelling there, white students find their association with black ones barred, not only by apartheid laws but also by the edict of the South African Students Organisation, the black students themselves. They have stated quite firmly that they see no point in working with white students whose needs — and presumably, by extension, whose aims — are different.

Outside the world of student activity, this view finds its context in the Bantustan leaders' pragmatic acceptance of the homelands policy and apparent determination to make of the government's self-justifying ethnic separation something the government didn't bargain for.[18] Beyond both the Bantustans and the ethnic colleges, the movement is taken up by urban leaders such as Mr David Thebehali of Soweto, with the call for Africans to 'buy black' and put their spending power into their own communities rather than into the white man's pocket. On the ideological side, none of these things springs from a political base, a political philosophy in the Western sense, in the way that the creed, methods and actions of the mass organisations of the fifties and sixties sprang from European political ideology. On the contrary, this movement is purely African. The white South African government perhaps unwittingly foreshadowed it in their phrase, 'developing along your own lines'; some people borrow for it the American term, Black Power; what it really is closest to, at its present stage, is good old-fashioned négritude, conceived just after the Second World War by the West Indian negro poet Aimé Césaire and the Senegalese poet-president Léopold Senghor, and defined most simply as black cultural nationalism.

Négritude is rather old hat, now, in West Africa, where it was developed originally, and in the other parts of independent black Africa, where it was adopted in one form or another and served its purpose towards the end of the colonial era. Those countries have no need of it any more. They have finally broken the shell of the white man's projected image and reinhabited their identity with the assumption of political power; they are now preoccupied like nations the world over with the problems of that power. But one can well see why the blacks of South Africa are rediscovering négritude, if somewhat late; why they need to discover négritude.

Their mass political movements were based not upon the cohesion of shared blackness so much as that of shared deprivation, their dispossession by white power. In the case of the African National Congress, the declared aim was not a black country but a non-racial one. If they were shut out of parliament, both the African National Congress and the Pan-Africanist Congress had great leaders among their own people and well-disciplined, legal political movements to give expression to their identity as human beings and citizens. Many of their political tactics were learned from a black political movement that predated them – the South African Indian Congress – and had been devised by one of the great men of our century, who also happened to be a black man: Mahatma Gandhi.[19] But the banning of their political organisations made statutory criminals of their leaders, and the shame of their mass submission, however little choice they have had in the matter, has eaten into their self-respect. Without the cohesion of a political identity and leadership, simply doing what one's told, moving when one's bid, working where the law says one's restricted to – all these conditions are imposed because of the colour of one's face; in the end, one must come to look askance at that face when one meets it in the glass of a passing shop window. It is to blame for all one endures. In the end, the shameful situation of blacks creates a shame of being black. Not to be white is to be taken over by the Hegelian condition of 'existing for others'. One can say of Africans, Indians and Coloureds as Jean-Paul Sartre did of the victims of anti-semitism, that they feel they have allowed themselves to become poisoned by other people's opinion of them.[20]

Concurrent with the disappearance of a black political identity came the dispersion and ultimate failure of the liberal ideal in South Africa. That centuries-long creation of a tiny minority of whites is today reviled by Africans in harsher terms than they use for Nationalists. White liberals abroad join the attack, disowning their 'colonial' kin as mealy-mouthed do-gooders who justify their presence in South Africa by being kind to their servants. It's not uncommon, now, to see quoted as 'liberal' white utterances the sort of white-leadership-with-justice statements that any South African recognises immediately as coming from people who are not and never have been liberals, but are good United Party members. To advocate the pat on the head instead of the sjambok on the back is not to be liberal.

Nevertheless, the genuine liberals, many of whom would prefer to be called radical in view of the sort of context into which the term 'liberal' has fallen – the real liberals honestly did want to abolish white supremacy; some of their number formed the Liberal Party, the only white-inspired political group, outside the banned Communist Party, that stood for one-man one-vote; they had no colour feeling and they did struggle to work *with* Africans and other coloured people rather than lead them.

The sin for which retribution is now falling on their heads from all sides was the sin of failure. The upholders of white supremacy, whether they called it *baasskap* ['boss-ship'] or white-leadership-with-justice, never really offered the black man anything more than a handout. The radical liberals offered everything, and were powerless to give anything. Even the worth of personal friendships that were formed between black and white, out of affinity, not patronage, became soured by this circumstance. Against the cold measure of the needs of our historical situation, the liberals with small or large 'L' failed twice over; first, to gain a following where political power existed, among whites; second, by inevitably falling into the role of acting proxy for black aspirations. Nosipho Majeke defined it the way the blacks have come to see it, rather differently, as 'the role of the liberal as the conciliator between oppressor and oppressed'.[21]

And so we have the black people of South Africa, in danger

of losing self-respect through living in the 'shameful' situation of being black, and reinforced in their feeling of impotence by having to delegate expression of their deepest grievances to whites who, paradoxically, claim no privilege, but still are obliged to exercise it on behalf of blacks — one can see how négritude, the prideful assertion of blackness as a positive value, is the only antidote to this spiritual sickness. Moreover, given the peg of separate development, it has some sort of chance to hitch itself to official recognition and countenance.

It is hard to accept a rebuff, even in terms of other people's needs. But I think the ironic refusal of black students to co-operate with white students who have fought many battles on their behalf, and on behalf of Africans generally, must be seen in the light of a healing négritude. Student protest has been white and has always belonged within the spectrum of radical-liberal thinking in South Africa. The activity of students has fallen with the same inevitability into the necessity to speak *for*, demand on *behalf* of, people whose colour sets them aside, along with half-wits and children, as not considered capable of speaking for themselves or deciding their own destiny. Nearly a century ago, Matthew Arnold wrote:

> if experience has established any one thing in this world, it has established this: that it is well for any great class and description of men in society to be able to say for itself what it wants, and not to have other classes, the so-called educated and intelligent classes, acting for it as its proctors, and supposed to understand its wants and to provide for them ... A class of men may often itself not either fully understand its wants, or adequately express them; but it has a nearer interest and a more sure diligence in the matter than any of its proctors, and therefore a better chance of success.[22]

Whether we like it or not, whether we support or oppose apartheid, we whites belong by virtue of our faces to white power. If those of us who are outraged by and prepared to take responsibility for the injustices of our society must relinquish the role of proctor, what is left to us?

I don't believe the question is as simple as that, and I know that the answer certainly isn't simple at all. As of now, the power structure remains the same: the whites make the law and the blacks must direct their lives in accordance. Our fundamental social problem remains daubed crudely black-and-white. But what is needed to approach it honestly now is a change of emphasis. We shall need to see our efforts not so much as attempts to right wrongs on behalf of the blacks, as to set our society free of the lies upon which it is built. The role of proctor, honourable though it may have seemed, and great courage though it undoubtedly showed in certain individuals at certain times, is one of those lies. If you students are to go on speaking out, it will be on behalf of yourselves, and that part of yourselves which exists tangled inextricably in human inter-dependence with the lives of those you live among, whether or not on the surface of the skin it's their turn to reject you. You will affirm your right and desperate need to protest against the hurt and injustice done in your midst, not because you are white but because you are human. Of course, there always has been some recognition that the privileged whites are not quite so privileged as they like to think, that while the Dorian Gray reflected in the swimming-pool remains eternally bronzed and fit, fear, guilt, shame or that coarsening and blunting of the spirit that is the price of indifference, presents a different picture when he is alone with himself. Many psychological studies have pointed out that segregation is harmful both to those who impose it and those who submit to it. Yet we who live here see around us that any white man, whatever the state of his soul, lives the *dolce vita* in comparison with the black man bulldozed out of his home by resettlement, or the Indian banished from his livelihood by the Group Areas Act. Speaking out beyond humbug and in full cognisance of that particular reality, you still have the right to demand to be fully human, and to reject the plush white reserve along with the black dumping grounds, as a denial of the meaning of a society of men.

I do not know whether the time will come when young black South Africans will want to work with young white South Africans. I think that, whatever one's feelings of regret that things have perfectly predictably fallen out like this, the turning of their backs on the white man's back door is necessary for the younger generation of blacks. This does not mean that any of you, black or white, need forget the reflection of another thinker, Frantz Fanon, black but not African, who has had much influence on African thought in general. Most of his writings are banned in our country, but this quotation comes from one of his books that I have seen freely on sale. In it he wrote: 'Every time a man has contributed to the victory of the dignity of the spirit, every time a man has said no to an attempt to subjugate his fellows, I have felt solidarity with his act.'[23]

A Writer's Freedom

(1975)[1]

*As suggested in the general introduction, along with a growing
political awareness for the writer in South Africa comes a related set
of issues based on the principal one: how does one respond as a
writer to apartheid? What obligations are cast on one by the
imperatives of freedom in one's country? What freedoms must the
writer insist upon in relation to his or her own vocation in order best
to further that wider struggle? These issues, describing a basic
duality in the approach of the writer to politics, have continued to
preoccupy Nadine Gordimer; as we see in later essays she returns to
them again and again. In this address, given in 1975, she began to
fashion a position which would become strengthened in the 1980s,
though a few of her emphases here may be surprising to those
expecting any simple definitions. At the same time Gordimer
revealed some of the primary influences on her literary and political
commitments.*

What is a writer's freedom?

To me it is his right to maintain and publish to the world a
deep, intense, private view of the situation in which he finds his
society. If he is to work as well as he can, he must take, and be
granted, freedom from the public conformity of political interpretation, morals and tastes.

Living when we do, where we do, as we do, 'Freedom' leaps
to mind as a political concept exclusively — and when people
think of freedom for writers they visualise at once the great
mound of burnt, banned and proscribed books our civilisation
has piled up; a pyre to which our own country has added and is
adding its contribution. The right to be left alone to write what
one pleases is not an academic issue to those of us who live and
work in South Africa. The private view always has been and

always will be a source of fear and anger to proponents of a way of life, such as the white man's in South Africa, that does not bear looking at except in the light of a special self-justificatory doctrine.

All that the writer can do, as a writer, is to go on writing *the truth as he sees it*. That is what I mean by his 'private view' of events, whether they be the great public ones of wars and revolutions, or the individual and intimate ones of daily, personal life.

As to the fate of his books — there comes a time in the history of certain countries when the feelings of their writers are best expressed in this poem, written within the lifetime of many of us, by Bertolt Brecht:

When the Regime ordered that books with dangerous
    teachings
Should be publicly burnt and everywhere
Oxen were forced to draw carts full of books
To the funeral pyre, an exiled poet,
One of the best, discovered with fury, when he studied the
    list
Of the burned, that his books
Had been forgotten. He rushed to his writing table
On wings of anger and wrote a letter to those in power.
Burn me, he wrote with hurrying pen, burn me!
Do not treat me in this fashion. Don't leave me out. Have I
    not
Always spoken the truth in my books? And now
You treat me like a liar! I order you:
Burn me![2]

We South African writers can understand the desperate sentiments expressed while still putting up the fight to have our books read rather than burnt.

Bannings and banishments are terrible known hazards a writer must face, and many have faced, if the writer belongs where freedom of expression, among other freedoms, is withheld, but sometimes creativity is frozen rather than destroyed. A Thomas Mann survives exile to write a *Doctor Faustus*; a Pasternak smuggles *Doctor Zhivago* out of a ten-year silence; a

Solzhenitsyn emerges with his terrible world intact in the map of *The Gulag Archipelago*; nearer our home continent, a Chinua Achebe, writing from America, does not trim his prose to please a Nigerian regime under which he cannot live;[3] a Dennis Brutus grows in reputation abroad while his poetry remains forbidden at home; and a Breyten Breytenbach, after accepting the special dispensation from racialist law which allowed him to visit his home country with a wife who is not white, no doubt accepts the equally curious circumstance that the book he was to write about the visit was to be banned, in due course.[4]

Through all these vicissitudes, real writers go on writing the truth as they see it. And they do not agree to censor themselves ... You can burn the books, but the integrity of creative artists is not incarnate on paper any more than on canvas – it survives so long as the artist himself cannot be persuaded, cajoled or frightened into betraying it.

All this, hard though it is to live, is the part of the writer's fight for freedom the *world* finds easiest to understand.

There is another threat to that freedom, in any country where political freedom is withheld. It is a more insidious one, and one of which fewer people will be aware. It's a threat which comes from the very strength of the writer's opposition to repression of political freedom. That other, paradoxically wider, composite freedom – the freedom of his private view of life – may be threatened by the very awareness of *what is expected of him*. And often what is expected of him is conformity to an orthodoxy of opposition.

There will be those who regard him as their mouth-piece; people whose ideals, as a human being, he shares, and whose cause, as a human being, is his own. They may be those whose suffering is his own. His identification with, admiration for, and loyalty to these set up a state of conflict within him. His integrity as a human being demands the sacrifice of everything to the struggle put up on the side of free men. His integrity as a writer goes the moment he begins to write what he is told he ought to write.

This is – whether all admit it or not – and will continue to be a particular problem for black writers in South Africa. For them, it extends even to an orthodoxy of vocabulary: the jargon of struggle, derived internationally, is right and adequate for the public platform, the newsletter, the statement from the dock; it is not adequate, it is not deep enough, wide enough, flexible enough, cutting enough, fresh enough for the vocabulary of the poet, the short story writer or the novelist.

Neither is it, as the claim will be made, 'a language of the people' in a situation where certainly it is very important that imaginative writing must not reach an élite only. The jargon of struggle lacks both the inventive pragmatism and the poetry of common speech – those qualities the writer faces the challenge to capture and explore imaginatively, expressing as they do the soul and identity of a people as no thousandth-hand 'noble evocation' of clichés ever could.

The black writer needs his freedom to assert that the idiom of Chatsworth, Dimbaza, Soweto is no less a vehicle for the expression of pride, self-respect, suffering, anger – or anything else in the spectrum of thought and emotion – than the language of Watts or Harlem.

The fact is, even on the side of the angels, a writer has to reserve the right to tell the truth as he sees it, in his own words, without being accused of letting the side down. For as Philip Toynbee has written, 'the writer's gift to the reader is not social zest or moral improvement or love of country, but an enlargement of the reader's apprehension.'

This is the writer's unique contribution to social change. He needs to be left alone, by brothers as well as enemies, to make this gift. And he must make it even against his own inclination.

I need hardly add this does not mean he retreats to an ivory tower. The gift cannot be made from any such place. The other day, Jean-Paul Sartre gave the following definition of the writer's responsibility to his society as an intellectual, after himself having occupied such a position in France for the best part of seventy years: 'He is someone who is faithful to a political and social body but never stops contesting it. Of course, a contradiction may arise between his fidelity and his *contestation*, but that's a fruitful contradiction. If there's fidelity without *contestation*, that's no good: one is no longer a free man.'

When a writer claims these kinds of freedom for himself he begins to understand the real magnitude of his struggle. It is not a new problem and of all the writers who have had to face it, I don't think anyone has seen it as clearly or dealt with it with such uncompromising honesty as the great nineteenth-century Russian, Ivan Turgenev. Turgenev had an immense reputation as a progressive writer. He was closely connected with the progressive movement in Czarist Russia and particularly with its more revolutionary wing headed by the critic Belinsky and afterwards by the poet Nekrasov. With his sketches and stories, people said that Turgenev was continuing the work Gogol had begun of awakening the conscience of the educated classes in Russia to the evils of a political regime based on serfdom.

But his friends, admirers and fellow progressives stopped short, in their understanding of his genius, of the very thing that made him one – his scrupulous reserve of the writer's freedom to reproduce truth and the reality of life even if this truth does not coincide with his own sympathies.

When his greatest novel, *Fathers and Sons*, was published in 1862, he was attacked not only by the right for pandering to the revolutionary nihilists, but far more bitterly by the left, the younger generation themselves, of whom his chief character in the novel, Bazarov, was both prototype and apotheosis. The radicals and liberals, among whom Turgenev himself belonged, lambasted him as a traitor because Bazarov was presented with all the faults and contradictions that Turgenev saw in his own type, in himself, so to speak, and whom he created as he did because – in his own words – 'in the given case, life happened to be like that'.

The attacks were renewed after the publication of another novel, *Smoke*, and Turgenev decided to write a series of autobiographical reminiscences which would allow him to reply to his critics by explaining his views on the art of writing, the place of the writer in society, and what the writer's attitude to the controversial problems of his day should be. The result was a series of unpretentious essays that make up a remarkable testament to a writer's creed. Dealing particularly with Bazarov and *Fathers and Sons*, he writes of his critics:

generally speaking {they} have not got quite the right idea of what is taking place in the mind of an author or what exactly his joys and sorrows, his aims, successes and failures are. They do not, for instance, even suspect the pleasure which Gogol mentions and which consists of castigating oneself and one's faults in the imaginary characters one depicts; they are quite sure that all a writer does is to 'develop his ideas' ... Let me illustrate my meaning by a small example. I am an inveterate and incorrigible Westerner. I have never concealed it and I am not concealing it now. And yet in spite of that it has given me great pleasure to show up in the person of Panshin (in *A House of Gentlefolk*) all the common and vulgar sides of the Westerners: I made the Slavophil Lavretsky 'crush him utterly'. Why did I do it, I who consider the Slavophil doctrine false and futile? Because, *in the given case, life, according to my ideas, happened to be like that*, and what I wanted above all was to be sincere and truthful. In depicting Bazarov's personality, I excluded everything artistic from the range of his sympathies, I made him express himself in harsh and unceremonious tones, not out of an absurd desire to insult the younger generation ... but simply as a result of my observations ... My personal predilections had nothing to do with it. But I expect many of my readers will be surprised if I tell them that with the exception of Bazarov's views on art, I share almost all his convictions.[5]

And in another essay, Turgenev sums up regarding what he calls 'the man of real talent': 'The life that surrounds him provides him with the contents of his works; he is its *concentrated reflection*; but he is as incapable of writing a panegyric as a lampoon ... When all is said and done — that is beneath him. Only those who can do no better submit to a given theme or carry out a programme.'[6]

These conditions about which I have been talking are the special, though common ones of writers beleaguered in the time of the bomb and the colour-bar, as they were in the time of the jack-boot and rubber truncheon, and, no doubt, back through the ages whose shameful symbols keep tally of oppression in the skeleton cupboard of our civilisations.

Other conditions, more transient, less violent, affect the freedom of a writer's mind.

What about literary fashion, for example? What about the

cycle of the innovator, the imitators, the debasers, and then the bringing forth of an innovator again? A writer must not be made too conscious of literary fashion, any more than he must allow himself to be inhibited by the mandarins if he is to get on with work that is his own. I say 'made conscious' because literary fashion is a part of his working conditions; he can make the choice of rejecting it, but he cannot choose whether it is urged upon him or not by publishers and readers, who do not let him forget he has to eat.

That rare marvel, an innovator, should be received with shock and excitement. And his impact may set off people in new directions of their own. But the next innovator rarely, I would almost say never, comes from his imitators, those who create a fashion in his image. Not all worthwhile writing is an innovation, but I believe it always comes from an individual vision, privately pursued. The pursuit may stem from a tradition, but a tradition implies a choice of influence, whereas a fashion makes the influence of the moment the only one for all who are contemporary with it.

A writer needs all these kinds of freedom, built on the basic one of freedom from censorship. He does not ask for shelter from living, but for exposure to it without possibility of evasion. He is fiercely engaged with life on his own terms, and ought to be left to it, if anything is to come of the struggle. Any government, any society — any vision of a future society — that has respect for its writers must set them as free as possible to write in their own various ways in their own choices of form and language, and according to their own discovery of truth.

Again, Turgenev expresses this best: 'without freedom in the widest sense of the word — in relation to oneself . . . indeed, to one's people and one's history — a true artist is unthinkable; without that air it is impossible to breathe.'[7]

And I add my last word: In that air alone, commitment and creative freedom become one.

Selecting My Stories

(1975)[1]

*Though Gordimer has frequently discussed the work of other writers
and the tasks and obligations of writing in South Africa, she has
seldom given explicit attention to the ways and means of her own
fiction, its inner and outer logic, the way it actually* works. *In this
essay, originally the introduction to her* Selected Stories, *she does
exactly that. Retrospectively considering her stories over a period of
some thirty years, she gives thought to the deep internalities and
paradoxes of her craft, as well as the way in which these
unexpectedly correspond to an outer history.*

'After I had selected and arranged these stories, their present
publisher asked me to provide some kind of introduction to
them. If they were now making their first appearance I might
have recoiled from this invitation, but they have all been
printed and some reprinted, and have therefore been through a
period of probation. Whatever I may say about them now
cannot alter what has been said by others, and can hardly
increase or lessen the likelihood of their being read – that must
depend on the stories themselves.'[2]

The words are William Plomer's, but the attitude comes so
close to my own that I do not hesitate to fly his declaration at
the masthead of a selection of my own stories. William Plomer
not only wrote some stories that have become classic, he also
had a special interest in and fascination with the short story as
a form used in widely diverse ways by others. His code holds
good for me; for all of us. I take it further; if the story itself does
not succeed in conveying all the writer meant it should, no
matter when he wrote it, neither explication nor afterthought
can change this. Conversely, if the story has been *achieved*, the
patronising backward glance its writer might cast upon it, as

something he could now do with one hand tied behind his back but no longer would care to do at all, will not detract from it.

I wrote these stories over thirty years. I have attempted now to influence any reader's judgment of or pleasure in them only to the extent implied by the fact that I have chosen some and excluded others. In this sense, I suppose, I have 'rewritten': imposed a certain form, shaped by retrospect, upon the collection as an entity. For everything one writes is part of the whole story, so far as any individual writer attempts to build the pattern of his own perception out of chaos. To make sense of life: that story, in which everything, novels, stories, the false starts, the half-completed, the abandoned, has its meaningful place, will be complete with the last sentence written before one dies or imagination atrophies. As for retrospect as a valid critique, I realise it has no fixed existence but represents my own constantly changing effort to teach myself how to make out of words a total form for whatever content I seize upon. This I understood only too clearly when I was obliged to read through my five existing collections of stories and saw how there are some stories I have gone on writing, again and again, all my life, not so much because the themes are obsessional but because I found other ways to take hold of them; because I hoped to make the revelation of new perceptions through the different techniques these demanded. I felt for the touch that would release the spring that shuts off appearance from reality. If I were to make a choice of my stories in five years' time, I might choose a different selection, in the light of what I might have learnt about these things by then. My 'retrospect' would be based upon which stories approached most nearly what I happened to have most recently taught myself. That is inevitable.

Why write short stories?

The question implies the larger one: what makes one write? Both have brought answers from experts who study writers as a psychological and social phenomenon. It is easier and more comforting to be explained than to try and explain oneself. Both have also brought answers of a kind from many writers, devious answers; as mine may be. (If one found out exactly how one walks the tightrope, one would fall immediately?) Some have lived — or died — to contradict their own theories.

Ernest Hemingway said we write out our sicknesses in books and shot himself. Of course I find I agree with those writers whose theories coincide at least in part with mine. What is experienced as solitude (and too quickly dubbed alienation) is pretty generally agreed to be a common condition conducive to becoming a writer. Octavio Paz speaks of the 'double solitude', as an intellectual and a woman, of the famous early Spanish American writer, Sor Juana Inés de la Cruz.[3] Growing up in a goldmining town in South Africa as a member of a white minority, to begin with, my particular solitude as an intellectual-by-inclination was so complete I did not even know I was one: the concept 'intellectual', gathered from reading, belonged as categorically to the Northern Hemisphere as a snowy Christmas. Certainly there must have been other people who were intellectuals, but they no doubt accepted their isolation too philosophically to give a signal they scarcely hoped would be answered, let alone attract an acolyte. As for the specific solitude of the woman-as-intellectual, I must say truthfully that my femininity has never constituted any special kind of solitude, for me. Indeed, in that small town, walled up among the mine dumps, born exiled from the European world of ideas, ignorant that such a world existed among Africans, my only genuine and innocent connection with the social life of the town (in the sense that I was not pretending to be what I was not, for ever hiding the activities of mind and imagination which must be suspect, must be concealed) was through my femaleness. As an adolescent, at least I felt and followed sexual attraction in common with others; that was a form of communion I could share. Rapunzel's hair is the right metaphor for this feminity: by means of it, I was able to let myself out and live in the body, with others, as well as — alone — in the mind. To be young and in the sun; my experience of this was similar to that of Camus, although I did not enter into it as fully as he did, I did not play football . . .

In any case, I question the existence of the specific solitude of woman-as-intellectual when that woman is a writer, because when it comes to their essential faculty as writers, all writers are androgynous beings.

The difference between alienation and solitude should be clear enough. Writers' needs in this respect are less clear, and certainly less well and honestly understood, even by themselves. Some form of solitude (there are writers who are said to find it in a crowded café, or less romantically among the cockroaches in a night-time family kitchen, others who must have a cabin in the woods) is the condition of creation. The less serious — shall we say professional? — form of alienation follows inevitably. It is very different from the kind of serious psychic rupture between the writer and his society that has occurred in the Soviet Union and in South Africa, for example, and that I shall not discuss here, since it requires a study in itself.

I believe — I *know* (there are not many things I should care to dogmatise about, on the subject of writing) that writers need solitude, and seek alienation of a kind every day of their working lives. (And remember, they are not even aware when and when not they are working ...) Powers of observation heightened beyond the normal imply extraordinary disinvolvement; or rather the double process, excessive preoccupation and identification with the lives of others, and at the same time a monstrous detachment. For identification brings the superficial loyalties (that is, to the self) of concealment and privacy, while detachment brings the harsher fidelities (to the truth about the self) of revealment and exposure. The tension between standing apart and being fully involved; that is what makes a writer. That is where we begin. The validity of this dialectic is the synthesis of revelation; our achievement of, or even attempt at this is the moral, the human justification for what we do.

Here I am referring to an accusation that every writer meets, that we 'use' people, or rather other people's lives. Of course we do. As unconscious eternal eavesdroppers and observers, snoopers, nothing that is human is alien to the imagination and the particular intuition to which it is a trance-like state of entry. I have written *from the starting-point* of other people's 'real' lives; what I have written represents alternatives to the development of a life as it was formed before I encountered it and as it will continue, out of my sight. A writer sees in your life what you do not. That is why people who think they recognise themselves as 'models' for this character or that in a story will protest triumphantly, 'It wasn't that way at all'. They think they know better; but perhaps it is the novelist or short story writer who does? Fiction is a way of exploring possibilities present but undreamt of in the living of a single life.

There is also the assumption, sometimes prurient or deliciously scandalised, that writers write only about themselves. I know that I have used my own life much the same way as I have that of others: events (emotions are events, too, of the spirit) mark exits and entrances in a warren where many burrows lead off into the same darkness but this one might debouch far distant from that. What emerges most often is an alternative fate, the predisposition to which exists in what 'actually' happened.

How can the eavesdropper, observer, snooper ever be the prototype? The stories in this book were written between the ages of twenty and fifty. Where am I, in them? I search for myself. At most, reading them over for the first time in many years, I see my own shadow dancing on a wall behind and over certain stories. I can make a guess at remembering what significatory event it was that casts it there. The story's 'truth' or lack of it is not attached to or dependent upon that lost event.

But part of these stories' 'truth' does depend upon faithfulness to another series of lost events — the shifts in social attitudes as evidenced in the characters and situations. I had wanted to arrange the selection in sequence from the earliest story collection to the latest simply because when reading story collections I myself enjoy following the development of a writer. Then I found this order had another logic to which my first was complementary. The chronological order turns out to be an historical one. The change in social attitudes unconsciously reflected in the stories represents both that of the people in my society — that is to say, history — and my apprehension of it; in the writing, I am acting upon my society, and in the manner of my apprehension, all the time history is acting upon me.

The white girl in 'Is There Nowhere Else Where We Can Meet?'[4] whose first *conscious* encounter with a black is that between victim and attacker — primary relationship indeed — is several years and a book away from the girl in 'The Smell of Death and Flowers', experiencing her generation's equivalent of religious ecstasy in the comradeship of passive resistance action in the company of blacks. Both white girls are twenty-five years and several books away from the whites in 'Open House' and 'Africa Emergent', experiencing the collapse of white liberalism. The humble black servant bemoaning fatalistically in 'Ah, Woe Is Me' (a very early story) could never have occurred in my writing by the time, again several books later, the young black political refugee is awaiting military training in exile and the 'Some Monday For Sure' when he will return to a South Africa ruled by a black majority. Even the language changes from book to book: 'native' becomes first 'African' then 'Black', because these usages* have been adopted, over three decades, by South Africans of various opinions, often at different stages. For example, the old Afrikaner in 'Abroad' (a recent story) still speaks quite naturally of 'natives', whereas for English-speaking whites the use of the term 'African' is now general, no longer even indicating, as it would have ten years ago, that the speaker was showing his political colours as liberal if not leftist. The use of the blunt term 'Black' is now the reverse of pejorative or insulting: indeed it is the only one, of all generic words used to denote them, that has not been imposed upon but has been chosen by blacks themselves. (Though not all, in particular older and more conservative people, feel happy with it.) Its adoption by whites has a somewhat left-of-liberal tone, but much more significant is the fact that here whites are following black, not white usage.

What I am saying is that I see that many of these stories *could not have been written* later or earlier than they were. If I could have juggled them around in the contents list of this collection without that being evident, they would have been false in some way important to me as a writer.

What I am also saying, then, is that in a certain sense a writer is 'selected' by his subject — his subject being *the consciousness* of his own era. How he deals with this is, to me, the fundament of commitment, although 'commitment' is usually

---

* There is a fourth, roughly concurrent with 'African', but I don't think it occurs in any of these stories: 'Bantu'. The word means 'people', and so, used in conjunction with the English word, as it often is – 'Bantu people' – it produces the idiotic term 'People people'. The use of 'Bantu' is official government *politesse*, adopted to replace the more offensive appellations with a term almost as negative – and revealing, so far as the user is concerned – as 'non-white'.

understood as the reverse process: a writer's selection of a subject in conformity with the rationalisation of his own ideological and/or political beliefs.

My time and place have been twentieth-century Africa. Emerging from it, immersed in it, the first form in which I wrote was the short story. I write fewer and fewer stories, now, and more novels, but I don't think I shall ever stop writing stories. What makes a writer turn from one to the other? How do they differ?

Nobody has ever succeeded in defining a short story in a manner to satisfy all who write or read them, and I shall not, here. I sometimes wonder if one shouldn't simply state flatly: a short story is a piece of fiction short enough to be read at one sitting? No, that will satisfy no one, least myself. But for me certainly there is a clue, there, to the choice of the short story by writers, as a form: whether or not it has a narrative in the external or internal sense, whether it sprawls or neatly bites its own tail, a short story is a concept that the writer can 'hold', fully realised, in his imagination, at one time. A novel is, by comparison, staked out, and must be taken possession of stage by stage; it is impossible to contain, all at once, the proliferation of concepts it ultimately may use. For this reason I cannot understand how people can suppose one makes a conscious choice, *after* knowing what one wants to write about between writing a novel or a short story. A short story *occurs*, in the imaginative sense. To write one is to express from a situation in the exterior or interior world the life-giving drop – sweat, tear, semen, saliva – that will spread an intensity on the page; burn a hole in it.

Letter from Johannesburg 1976[1]

On 16 June 1976 Johannesburg's black township of Soweto exploded in revolt. Ostensibly the cause was the enforced use of Afrikaans — 'the language of the oppressors', as the black students were calling it — as the medium of instruction in certain subjects in the schools; but a whole range of issues accreted around this one. What was new was that this was primarily a revolt of school-children. Drawing its impetus from Black Consciousness ideology, the revolt started in the schools in Soweto and spread countrywide to others, though it reached the universities and the wider communities as well. It was more than a year before the state managed to quell the uprising as a whole. The cost, however, was tremendous: official (and probably underestimated) figures put the toll at 575 dead — most of them schoolchildren shot by the police — and 2,389 wounded.[2] The Soweto Revolt, as it became known, was a concerted challenge to the state, and it set the tone for the decade to come. At the same time, however, it was also a challenge to white sympa-thisers. The Black Consciousness movement had categorised white liberals and radicals as being integrally caught up in the structures of white supremacy. Now the revolt of the children appeared to marginalise any white role entirely; white opposition to the government seemed to have been bypassed by history. The revolt itself — and the reaction by the state — had a profound effect on Nadine Gordimer, as this essay shows very clearly. With a deeper gravity now she attempted to come to terms with a new brutality exercised in defence of apartheid, her own marginality in opposition to it, and the bravery of the children.

I flew out of Johannesburg on a visit abroad two and a half months after the first black schoolchild was killed by a police bullet in Soweto. Since June 16, when the issue of protest against the use of the Afrikaans language as a teaching medium in black schools, long ignored by the white authorities, finally received from them this brutal answer, concern had been the prevailing emotion in South Africa.

Concern is an over-all bundle of like feelings in unlike people: horror, distress, anguish, anger – at its slackest manifestation, pity.

There was no white so condemnatory of black aspirations, so sure of a communist plot as their sole source, that he or (more likely) she didn't feel 'sorry' children had died in the streets. Black children traditionally have been the object of white sentimentality; it is only after the girls grow breasts and the boys have to carry the passbook that chocolate suddenly turns black.

There was no black so militant, or so weary of waiting to seize the day, that he or she did not feel anguish or regret at the sacrifice of children to the cause. Not even a mighty rage at the loathed police could block that out.

I was away for the month of September. Henry Kissinger came to South Africa to discuss the Rhodesia settlement with Mr Vorster;[3] six children were killed while demonstrating against his presence. A day or two after I arrived home in October, a girl of fifteen was shot by police at the Cape. The six were already merely a unit of the (disputed) official figures of the dead (now 358), some adult but in the main overwhelmingly the young, in unrest that has spread from blacks to those of mixed blood, and all over the country by means of arson, homemade bomb attacks, boycotts, and strikes. The fifteen-year-old girl was added to the list of fatalities; no one, I found, was shocked afresh at the specific nature of this casualty; the killing of a child by a police bullet.

Like the passing of a season, there was something no longer in the air. People had become accustomed, along with so much else unthinkable, to the death of children in revolt.

I try to recognise and set out the reasons for this acclimatisation before daily life here, however bizarre, makes me part of it.

When striking children met the police that Wednesday morning in June in the dirt streets of Soweto and threw stones that promptly drew bullets in return, who would have believed that the terrible lesson of white power would not be learned? The lesson for these children wasn't free, any more than their schoolbooks are (white children get theirs for nothing); they paid with the short lives of some of their number. No one could conceive they would ever present themselves again, adolescent girls bobbing in gym frocks, youths in jeans, little barefoot boys with shirts hanging out as in a wild game of cops and robbers — to police who had shown they would shoot real bullets. But the children did. Again and again. They had taken an entirely different lesson: they had learned fearlessness.

Of course, white attitudes towards them began to change, even then. It was immediately assumed by the government and the majority of white people that since the issue of the Afrikaans language had been quickly conceded, and the children now demanded the abolition of the entire separate educational system for blacks, and then bluntly 'everything whites get', such intransigence must be the work of agitators. Among black people — among the outlawed liberation organisations inside and outside the country, and those perforce confined to balancing cultural liberation on a hair's breadth of legality within it — all began to claim credit for the first popular uprising since the early sixties. No one will know, for years perhaps, how to apportion the influence of the banned African National Congress and Pan-Africanist Congress — their leadership in prison and exile — in the development of schoolchildren's defiance into the classic manifestations of a general uprising.

Neither can one measure how much of the children's determined strategy was planned by older students of the black university-based South African Students' Organisation. There surely were — there are — agitators; if agitators are individuals able and articulate enough to transform the sufferings and grievances of their people into tactics for their liberation. There surely was — there is, has never ceased to be — the spirit of the banned political movements in the conceptual political attitudes and sense of self, passing unnamed and without attribution to their children from the tens of thousands who once belonged to the mass movements.

What neither the accusations of the white government nor

the claims of black adult leadership will ever explain is how those children learned, in a morning, to free themselves of the fear of death.

Revolutionaries of all times, who know this is the freedom that brings with it the possibility of attaining all others, have despaired of finding a way of teaching it to more than a handful among their trained cadres. To ordinary people it is a state beyond understanding. We knew how to feel outrage or pity when we saw newspaper photographs of the first corpses of children caught by the horrible surprise of a death nobody believed, even in South Africa, would be meted out by the police. Blacks still burn with an anger whose depth has not yet been fathomed − it continues to show itself as it did at the Soweto funeral of Dumisani Mbatha, sixteen, who died in detention. Seven hundred mourners swelled to a crowd of 10,000 youths that burned R100,000 worth of the Johannesburg municipality's vehicles and buildings. Yet − not without bewilderment, not without shame − black people have accepted that the weakest among them are the strongest, and thus by grim extension also accept the inconceivable: the death of children and adolescents has become a part of the struggle.

We whites do not know how to deal with the fact of this death when children, in full knowledge of what can happen to them, continue to go out to meet it at the hands of the law, for which we are solely responsible, whether we support white supremacy or, opposing, have failed to unseat it.

When you make men slaves you deprive them of half their virtue, you set them in your own conduct an example of fraud, rapine, and cruelty, and compel them to live with you in a state of war . . .

Olaudah Equiano
18th-century black writer[4]

White people have turned away from concern to a matter-of-fact preoccupation with self-protection. A Johannesburg parents' committee has a meeting to discuss whether or not teachers at a suburban school should be armed, as they might once have planned a school fête. I bump into a friend who tells me, as if he were mentioning arrangements for a cattle show, that he and fellow farmers from a district on the outskirts of

Johannesburg are gathering next day to set up an early warning system among themselves – one of them uses a two-way radio for cattle control, the gadget may come in handy. Now it is not only the pistol-club matrons of Pretoria who regard guns as necessary domestic appliances. At the house of a liberal white couple an ancient rifle was produced the other evening, the gentle wife in dismay and confusion at having got her husband to buy it. Gunsmiths have long waiting lists for revolvers; 50 per cent of small arms come illegally from Iron Curtain countries who call for a total arms embargo against South Africa at the UN. Certainly, in that house a gun was an astonishing sight. Pamphlets appear with threats to whites and their children; although the black movements repudiate such threats, this woman feels she cannot allow her anti-apartheid conviction to license failure to protect her children from physical harm. She needn't have felt so ashamed. We are all afraid. How will the rest of us end up? Hers is the conflict of whites who hate apartheid and have worked in 'constitutional' ways to get rid of it. The quotes are there because there's not much law-abiding virtue in sticking to a constitution like the South African one, in which only the rights of a white minority are guaranteed. Gandhi had our country in mind when he wrote, 'The convenience of the powers that be is the law in the final analysis.'[5]

My friend Professor John Dugard, Dean of the Faculty of Law at the University of the Witwatersrand, says that if whites do not show solidarity with blacks against apartheid, their choice is to 'join the white *laager* or emigrate'. Few, belonging to a country that is neither in the Commonwealth nor the Common Market, have the chance to emigrate. Of the *laager* – traditionally, a defensive circle of ox-wagons – my friend David Goldblatt, the photographer, says to me: 'How can we live in the position where, because we are white, there's no place for us but thrust among whites whose racism we have rejected with disgust all our lives?'

There is not much sign that whites who want to commit themselves to solidarity with blacks will be received by the young anonymous blacks who daily prove the hand that holds the stone is the whip hand. They refuse to meet members of the Progressive-Reform Party, who, while assuming any new society will be a capitalist one, go further than any other white constitutional group in genuine willingness to share power with blacks – at the same time insisting on 'guarantees' for the protection of the white minority. These young blacks will not even talk to white persons who accept one-man one-vote and the rule by a black majority government without qualification as the aim of any solidarity, and understand, as John Dugard puts it, that 'the free enterprise system is not the only system' to be discussed.

The black moderate, Chief Gatsha Buthelezi,[6] whose position as a Bantustan leader fiercely attacking the government that appointed him has made him exactly the figure to whom whites have talked and through whom they hope to reach blacks, lately is reported to have made a remark about 'white ultra-liberals who behave as though they are making friends with the crocodile so they will be the last to be eaten'. He also said, 'Nobody will begrudge the Afrikaner his heritage if it is no threat to the heritage and freedom of other people.' It seems old white adversaries might be accepted but white liberals will never be forgiven their inability to come to power and free blacks.

Nevertheless, I don't think the whites he referred to would be those with the outstanding fighting record of Helen Suzman, let alone radical activists like Beyers Naudé[7] of the Christian Institute, and others, of the earlier generation of Bram Fischer, who have endured imprisonment and exile alongside blacks in the struggle.

If fear has taken over from concern among whites, it has rushed in to fill a vacuum. In nearly six months, nothing has been done to meet the desperate need of blacks that seems finally to have overcome every threat of punishment and repression: the need, once and for all and no less, to take their lives out of the hands of whites. The first week of the riots, Gatsha Buthelezi called for a national convention and the release of black leaders in prison to attend it. As the weeks go by in the smell of burning, the call for a national convention has been taken up by other Bantustan leaders, black urban spokesmen, the press, the white political opposition. After five months, the Prime Minister, Mr Vorster, answered: 'There will be no national convention so far as this government is concerned.' Most of the time he leaves comment to his Minister of Justice, Police and Prisons, Mr Jimmy Kruger. The only attempt to deal with a national crisis is punitive. It is Mr Kruger's affair. He continues to project an equation that is no more than a turn of phrase: 'South Africa will fight violence with violence.'

Three hundred and sixty people have died, of whom two were white. The police, who carry guns and still do not wear riot-protective clothing but army camouflage dress and floppy little-boy hats that could be penetrated by a slingshot, have not lost a single man.

Neither the Prime Minister nor his minister in charge of black lives, M. C. Botha (Bantu Administration, Development and Education), has yet talked to urban black leaders more representative than members of the collapsed Urban Bantu Councils.[8] (They do not have normal municipal powers.) On their own doleful admittance, these are dubbed 'Useless Boys' Clubs' by the youths who run the black townships now.

Of the black leaders whom the vast majority of urban blacks would give a mandate to speak for them, Nelson Mandela and his lieutenants Walter Sisulu and Govan Mbeki, of the banned African National Congress, are still imprisoned for life on Robben Island. Robert Sobukwe of the Pan-Africanist Congress is banished to and silenced in a country town.[9]

Black intellectuals who might stand in for these have been detained one by one, even while whites of unlikely political shades continue to affirm a fervent desire to talk to blacks, just *talk* to them — as if three hundred years of oppression were a family misunderstanding that could be explained away, and as if everyone did not know, in the small dark room where he meets himself, exactly what is wrong with South African 'race relations'.

The government leaders refuse to meet the Black People's Convention, perhaps in the belief that by not recognising Black Consciousness organisations the power of blacks to disrupt their own despised conditions of life and (at the very least) the economy that sustains the white one will cease to exist. Fanonist theory of the black man as an image projected upon him by the white man[10] takes a new twist; the white man goes to the door of his shop in central Johannesburg one September

morning this year and fails to recognise the black man marching down the street shouting, in his own image, 'This is our
country.'

The government won't speak to the Black Parents' Association, formed originally to finance the burial of Soweto children in June. In this ghastly bond, the association moved on
under the leadership of Nelson Mandela's wife and Dr Manas
Buthelezi, an important Black Consciousness leader about to
be consecrated Lutheran Bishop of Johannesburg. It became a
united front combining youthful Black Consciousness inspiration with the convictions of older people who followed the
African National Congress and Pan-Africanist Congress.

Finally, the government does not consider speaking to the
militant students themselves who are still effectively in leadership, sometimes preventing their parents from going to work
(two successful strikes in Johannesburg). Daily and deter-
minedly, they pour into the gutters the shebeen liquor they
consider their elders have long allowed themselves to be
unmanned by.

Meanwhile, since June, 926 black schoolchildren have
received punishments ranging from fines or suspended sentences to jail (five years for a seventeen-year-old boy) and
caning (five cuts with a light cane for an eleven-year-old who
gave the black power salute, shouted at the police, and stoned a
bus). They are some of the 4,200 people charged with offences
arising out of the riots, including incitement, arson, public
violence, and sabotage. Many students are also among the 697
people, including Mrs Winnie Mandela, detained in jail for
'security reasons'; the other week one hanged himself by his
shirt in the Johannesburg prison, an old fort two kilometres
from the white suburban house where I write this.* Several
students, not twenty years old, have just begun that reliable
apprenticeship for African presidents, exile and education in

* The South African Institute of Race Relations in Johannesburg released on
November 8 the following analysis gleaned from cases reported in the national press
between June 16 and October 31: 1,200 people have already stood trial. Three
thousand are facing trials not yet completed. Of the 926 juveniles tried and
convicted, 528 have been given corporal punishment, 397 have received suspended
sentences or fines, and one has been jailed.

  The Minister of Justice's figure of 697 people detained for 'security reasons' is
broken down thus: 123 held under the Internal Security Act without charges
pending against them; 217 held under the Terrorism Act who will either be brought
to trial or released; 34 detained as witnesses; 323 held in cases 'relating to security'.

Britain. When, in September, Mr Vorster met blacks with
whom he *will* talk – his appointed Bantustan leaders – he
would not discuss urban unrest or agree to a national conference of blacks and whites to decide what ought to be done
about it.

There is a one-man commission of inquiry into the riots,
sitting now. Mr Justice Cillie, the white judge who constitutes
it, complains that few people actually present at these events
have volunteered evidence. In fact, the schoolchildren and
students themselves boycott it, and for the rest, South Africans'
faith in the efficacy of commissions to lead to positive action
has long gone into the trash basket along with the recommen-
dations the government steadily rejects. The Cillie Commission keeps extending the period in which it will sit, as the riots
continue to be part of the present and not a matter of calm
recollection. January 27 next year is the latest limit announced.
Historical analogies are easily ominous. But a commission of
inquiry was Czar Nicholas II's way of dealing with the
implications of the 'unrest' of Bloody Sunday, the beginning of
the 1905 revolution.

A chain-store owner whose business has been disrupted by
strikes and the gutting of a store has burst out of the conventions of his annual report to shareholders to say, 'Decades of
selfishness and smugness by South African whites is the
principal reason for widespread unrest among blacks.'

Yet most changes suggested by whites do not approach a call
for a national convention, with its implication of a new
constitution and the end of white supremacy. Black certainty
that *nothing* will bring equality without power is dismantled by
whites into component injustices they can admit and could
redress without touching the power structure. The Federated
Chamber of Industries calls for job 'reservation' discriminat-
ing against blacks in industry to be ended, and has the support
of the most powerful trade union group and the opposition
parties. The National Development and Management Foundation goes further and calls for the ending of business and
residential apartheid as well. Afrikaner big business, government supporters all, in their *Afrikaanse Handelsinstituut* [Afri-
kaans Institute of Commerce] ask for blacks to be given

'greater' rights in their own urban areas and training to increase their skills. Although the Progressive-Reform Party has demanded a national convention and the release of all people from detention, it was still necessary, before its 1976 congress agreed to change its education policy to enforced desegregation, for Helen Suzman to remind rank-and-file members that the separate-but-equal dictum for education had been 'thrown out by the United States twenty years ago'.

With unprecedentedly strong criticism of the government coming from its own newspapers and prominent Afrikaners as well as the opposition, it is baffling to read that at the same time 60 per cent of whites – an increase of 5 per cent over the majority gained by the government in the 1974 election – support Mr Vorster's National Party. The reliability of this particular poll is in some doubt; but perhaps the contradiction is not so unlikely after all. It is possible to see a dire necessity for change and fear it so greatly that one runs to give oneself to the father figure who will forbid one to act.

For months the white political opposition parties – Progressive-Reform, United Party, and Democratic Party – have been trying to agree to some sort of realignment. If a liberal front comes about, it will trample the old sand-castle fort of the United Party, the conservative official parliamentary opposition, already eroded by the departure of most of its politically vigorous members to the Progressive-Reform Party.

The numerical strength of such a front cannot be measured until it is known whether a major part of the United Party, which still polled 31·49 per cent in the 1974 elections, will enter it alongside the Progressive-Reform Party, in the last few years grown from a pressure group to a real presence in parliament, with twelve seats and 6·25 per cent of the vote. (The crankish Democratic Party has a minute following.) Only when the extent of United Party commitment is revealed will it be possible to estimate roughly what percentage of the 40 per cent who voted against the government in the last election are liberals. There are rumours that some disaffected *verligte* ('enlightened') National Party MPs may defect to the front too.

The declared aim of the front is to protect the rights of whites while giving Blacks, Coloureds, and Indians a direct say in government — which careful phrasing suggests its policy will be to the right of the present Progressive-Reform Party. The spectral raison d'être of such a realignment is surely not the chance of ousting Vorster's government but of getting ready a white 'negotiating party' to treat with blacks on a shared power basis when he finds he can no longer govern. The viewpoint of enlightened white politics now includes urgently the wide angle of acceptability to blacks, although they have no vote to be wooed. When Mr Vorster can no longer govern, it is not likely any other white government will be able to.

No one knows whether the Bantustan leaders are, in their different circumstances, preparing themselves for a particular role on that day. They meet at a Holiday Inn at Johannesburg's airport, exactly like Holiday Inns all over the world, down to its orgy-sized beds and cosy smell of French fried potatoes piped along with muzak, but deriving its peculiar status as neutral country outside apartheid from the time when it was the first hotel here to be declared 'international': not segregated — for foreign blacks, anyway.

From there the Bantustan leaders demand 'full human rights for blacks and not concessions'. With the exception of the Transkei and Bophuthatswana — the former having celebrated the homeland brand of independence on October 26,[11] the latter soon to do so — they reject ethnic partitions of South Africa. Which means they walk out on the many-mansions theory of apartheid, abandoning the white government which set them up inside; and they identify themselves as part of the liberation movement for an undivided South Africa. They present themselves to the black population in general as *black* leaders, not tribal leaders. Is this a bid for power? If Nelson Mandela were to come back from the prison island, would they step aside for him? Has the most imposing of them, Gatsha Buthelezi, a following cutting across his Zulu tribal lines?

Whites believe so. He attracts large audiences when he speaks in cosmopolitan black townships. Many blacks say no; and the African National Congress in exile continues to deride the Bantustan leaders as collaborators, making no exceptions. Other blacks imply that the best of the Bantustan men are keeping warm the seats of leaders in prison. Among politically articulate blacks, this year's is their (Southern hemisphere) hot summer of brotherhood. Tsietsi Mashinini, the student leader who fled the police to exile in Britain, suggests that the tremendous force his movement shows itself to represent is loyal to Mandela. It does not seem to matter to blacks whether it is a Gatsha Buthelezi or anyone else who is the one to say to whites, as he has, 'The future is a Black future and we Blacks want our future now.'[12]

From the Market Theatre, newly opened in what was the Covent Garden of Johannesburg, comes a strange echo – Cucurucu, Kokol, Polpoch, and Rossignol, asylum clowns in Peter Weiss's *Marat/Sade*, singing '*Give us our rights ... and we don't care how – We want – our re-vol-u-tion – NOW*.' The author granted performances on condition everyone could see the work and has donated his royalties to a Soweto riot victims fund. His play has never been performed before in a city atmosphere such as ours, it has never been heard as we hear it.

During the 'quiet' years of successful police repression, before the young emptied the Dutch courage of shebeens down the drain and sent through people's veins the firewater of a new spirit, there have been political trials in progress continually in South Africa. Not only those of blacks who have left the country for military training and re-entered illegally, but also those reflecting aspects of the struggle against apartheid carried on by an intellectual élite.

While the riots have been taking place, two young white university lecturers in Cape Town have given the black power clenched fist salute and, avowing 'no regrets', have accepted long sentences under the Terrorism and Internal Security Acts; their uncompromising personal suffering serves as proof of solidarity with blacks that must be granted even by those whites who abhor the white far left. In Johannesburg I have been to hear the trial of four white university students and a lecturer accused of trying 'to change South Africa' by organising black workers, who have no recognised trade unions. The five were charged under the Suppression of Communism Act, and the state's principal evidence consisted of papers read at a seminar.

The backs of these young men in blue jean outfits suggested

a pop group; but when they turned in the witness stand it was not to greet fans but to smile at the wife of one of them, whose hands, while she followed the proceedings, were working at a complicated length of knitting – the danger of active dissent does make risk of imprisonment part of the daily life of courageous people. Yet I felt events had overtaken them. The segregated public gallery was almost empty of white and black spectators. The struggle was a few miles away in the streets of Soweto.

But it is another trial, which has gone on almost two years, that seems to have the opposite relation to present events. Four years ago, the nine black members of the South African Students' Organisation accused under the Terrorism Act seemed to the ordinary public, black and white, to represent a radical fringe movement on the far side of the generation gap. The state's evidence against them was literary and clumsily esoteric – it consisted of black plays in the idiom of New York black theatre of seven years ago, mimeographed Black Consciousness doggerel that couldn't compete with comic books, poetry readings that surely could appeal only to the educated young.

The paper flowers of literary rhetoric have come alive in the atmosphere of tragic exaltation and discipline that can't be explained.

In the city streets of Johannesburg black people go about their white-town working lives as they always did: the neat clerks, waiters in their baggy parody of mess dress, dashing messengers in bright helmets on motor scooters, shop-cleaners, smart girls who make tea in offices or shampoo the clients' hair in white hairdressing salons. Polished shoes, clean clothes; and most of the time, when the youngsters don't stop them from boarding township trains, people get to work every day.

How do they do it? Daily life in Soweto is in hellish disruption. One-third of the country's school-leavers may not be able to write the final exams of the school year that ends in December; not all schools in the Johannesburg area have reopened. Those that have function irregularly, either because militant pupils stop classes, or teachers suspected of sympathetic alignment with them are detained. Buses and trains don't run when stoning and burning start; commuters crush into the big old American cars that serve as taxis or walk to stations outside the area. No one knows when his neighbour's house may cave in, set alight because he is a policeman. If he himself owns a precious car, it too may burn, should he be suspected of being, or even be mistaken for, some less obvious form of collaborator.

While we white people picnic, Sundays are the most dreadful days of all in Soweto: funerals, the only category of public gathering not banned, have become huge mass meetings where the obsequies of the riot victim being buried are marked by new deaths and fresh wounds as the police attack mourners singing freedom songs and shaking black power salutes. A black intellectual whose commitment to liberation no one would question, although he risks the violent disapproval of blacks by still having contact with whites, tells me, 'When I go home tonight, I don't know which to be more afraid of – the police getting me when they shoot at anything that moves, or my own people getting me when I walk across the yard to the lavatory.'

White Johannesburg appears as it always was. Across the veld to the south-west Soweto has been severed from the city, to drift in its fury and misery. Refuse, carted away in municipal vehicles that are vulnerable symbols of white rule, is collected when it can be. The Johannesburg medical officer of health has warned of possible outbreaks of measles and diphtheria in Soweto, and the reappearance of poliomyelitis; the white doctors and nurses who staffed most clinics have had to be withdrawn. It is no longer safe for any white to enter there. Only the white police go in; stand guard, their chrome whiplash aerials giving away the presence of riot squad cars and men in leaf-spattered jumpsuits at the crossroads where Soweto leads to Johannesburg. And the black workers come out every morning and go back every night, presenting faces that won't distress the white city.

What may the clean, ironed clothes and calm faces carry concealed, of disease and violence, to a city that has cut such things loose from itself?

Postscript

A Johannesburg newspaper asks if I will accept nomination for the 'Woman of the Year'. I decline. Someone else will have that honour, perhaps even a woman from the small black professional élite. But this year the only candidates are surely Winnie Mandela, who came out of house arrest to stand between the police and the schoolchildren and be imprisoned, or any one of the black township women who have walked beside their marching children, carrying water to wash the tear-gas from their eyes.

Relevance and Commitment

(1979)[1]

If Nadine Gordimer felt the Black Consciousness movement and the Soweto Revolt as a direct challenge to the role of the white writer in South Africa, then it is clear she was not prepared to accept this as a stopping point. Indeed, one salutary effect of these challenges was to galvanise South African literary culture into a much deeper and stronger thinking on its situation. Thus, in 1979 Gordimer attended a conference on 'The State of Art in South Africa' at the University of Cape Town, where she gave the following address. Again, the impact of Black Consciousness is appreciable in the entire framework and tenor of the speech, the very terms in which it is conceived. Gordimer explores now not only the different social and political conditions which apply to white and black writers, but also the seemingly ineradicable gap of existential and psychological distance which lies between them. At the same time there are signs of a new synthesis emerging: having accepted some of the undeniable insights of Black Consciousness, there is a determination here to see further, to find ways of working beyond separatism to a renewed vision of a culture unfragmented by apartheid. But how to achieve this was still the question; and other issues broached earlier in 'A Writer's Freedom' remained. How far could this new synthesis be achieved by black and white writers responding to external, political demands? How far did it depend on their internal and private dedication to their writing? Radicalised now by the Soweto Revolt, and confronting the extraordinary range of conflicts she saw in South African society, Gordimer attempted to answer these questions through the terms of 'relevance' and 'commitment'.

There is a question that bursts with the tenacity of a mole from below the surface of our assumptions at this conference: Do men and can men make a common culture if their material interests conflict?

Don't let us ignore the mole; though blind it knows instinctively where the daylight is.

The nature of art in South Africa today is primarily determined by the conflict of material interests in South African society. We gather, rent by that conflict, in this auditorium. On the very ground of one of South Africa's institutions, this 150-year-old university, we gather within a philosophy of spiritual liberation that requires, among other fundamentals, a frank appraisal of the institutions and policies of the white communities that affect the arts in South Africa. We are all paradox. We have all the questions and few answers. Yet there is left to us no less embattled ledge from which to speak honestly and meaningfully about the arts. We must face the fact that the Apollonian brotherhood is no safer from fratricide than any other, where divided loyalties are demanded by immediate survival. We are here to challenge ourselves, without cant. That seems to me what this conference is about – and, for myself, that is why I have agreed to speak on this platform.

For I take it we acknowledge that as racial problems, both material and spiritual, can hope to be solved only in circumstances of economic equality, so the creative potential of our country cannot be discussed without realisation and full acceptance that fulfilment of that potential can be aimed for only on the premise of the same circumstances.

Equal economic opportunity, along with civil and parliamentary rights for all 26 million South Africans, is rightly and inevitably the basis for any consideration of the future of the arts. Man has no control over the measure in which talent is given to this one and withheld from that; but man, through the state, controls the circumstances in which the artist develops. Innate creativity can be falsified, trivialised, deflected, conditioned, stifled, deformed and even destroyed by the state, and the state of society it decrees.

'Courage in one's life and talent in one's work' is the artist's text, according to one of the greatest of them, Albert Camus.*

---

* *Carnets 1942–51*, translated with an introduction and notes by Philip Thody (London: Hamish Hamilton, 1966), p. 92.

Every artist, in any society, has to struggle through what the poet Pablo Neruda calls the 'labyrinths' of his chosen medium of expression;* that is a condition of his being. As to his place in the outer world, I doubt if any artist ever finds himself in the ideal condition of Hegel's 'individual consciousness in wholly harmonious' relationship to the external power of society'.†
But there can have been few if any examples in human history of the degree, variety and intensity of conflicts that exist between the South African artist and the external power of society. That external power is at its most obvious in the censorship laws, running amuck through literature and lunging out at the other arts. But it is at the widest level of the formation of our society itself, and not at any specific professional level, that the external power of society enters the breast and brain of the artist and determines the nature and state of art. It is from the daily life of South Africa that there have come the conditions of profound alienation which prevail among South African artists. The sum of various states of alienation *is* the nature of art in South Africa at present.

I am not invoking the concept of alienation in the Marxist sense, as the consequence of man's relation to the means of production, although that undoubtedly has its appositeness in the industrialisation of blacks under apartheid and therefore our society as a whole. There are many ways in which man becomes divided from others and distanced from himself. Alienation as such is a condition of rejecting and/or being rejected. The black artist lives in a society that rejected his culture for hundreds of years. He has turned his alienation in the face of those who rejected him and made of his false consciousness the inevitable point of departure towards his true selfhood. The white artist belongs to the white culture that rejected black culture, and is now itself rejected by black culture. He is the *non-European* whose society nevertheless refused to acknowledge and take root with an indigenous culture. He is the *non-Black* whom blacks see as set apart from

* Pablo Neruda, *Memoirs*, translated by H. St Martin, (London: Souvenir Press; New York: Farrar, Straus & Giroux; 1977).
† G. F. W. Hegel [as quoted by Lionel Trilling, *Sincerity and Authenticity* (London: Oxford University Press, 1972), p. 35, in his discussion of Hegel's *Phenomenology of Mind* in the translation by J. B. Baillie (London: Allen & Unwin, 1949; New York: Harper & Row, 1967)].

indigenous culture. He does not know as yet whether this is a dead-end or can be made a new beginning.

Any homogeneity in the nature of the work produced by these artists is brought about by what shackles them together rather than what they share. South African artists belong to the Dionysiac 'disintegrated consciousness' that Hegel defines by its antagonism to the external power of society* — if by nothing else, they are united in the wish to be free of imposed social circumstances, although they would define these in accordance with a widely differing experience of circumstantial reality. From a disintegrated consciousness, all seek wholeness in themselves and a reconnection with the voltage of social dynamism. Opposition to an existing society implies a hunger to create and identify with another and better one. The abjuration of a set of values implies an intention to create and relate to another set. For the artist, these implications become part of the transformations of reality which are his work.

'Relevance' and 'commitment' are conceptualisations of this movement. They become the text claimed by artists who, individually, understand different things by them; they also become the demands made upon the artist by his people. Relevance and commitment pulse back and forth between the artist and society. In a time and place like this one, they have become, in the words of Lionel Trilling, 'the criteria of art and the qualities of the personal life that may be enhanced or diminished by art'.†

How close are these terms that question the existence of the painter, sculptor, writer, composer, photographer, architect in South Africa today? In fact, they are juxtaposed as much as cognate. And in this, again, they are a signification of the tension between the artist and his society in which his creativity is generated. For relevance has to do with outside events; and commitment comes from within.

For the black artist at this stage in his development relevance is the supreme criterion. It is that by which his work will be judged *by his own people*, and *they* are the supreme authority

---

* Hegel [from Trilling, *Sincerity and Authenticity*, p. 114].
† Paraphrased from *Sincerity and Authenticity*, p. 134. Trilling is discussing here authenticity as such a criterion.

since it is only through them that he can break his alienation. The poet Mafika Pascal Gwala states that the black artist must be ready to phase himself out of the role of being carrier to what he calls white official 'swimming pool and caravan culture'.* The external reality to which relevance paces out the measure of his work is not a step away from him: Gwala says 'blacks are operating' from within 'a crushing intellectual and educational environment'.† Sartre's philosophical dictum sums up: 'The exploited experience exploitation *as their reality*'‡ – the artist has only to do what every artist must in order to become one: face his own reality, and he will have interiorised the standard of relevance set up outside. Then, theoretically, he has solved the aesthetic and social problem, put himself in meaningful relationship to his society.

But relevance, in the context of the absolutes placed upon the black artist by the new society to which he is dedicated, has another demand. Struggle is the state of the black collective consciousness and art is its weapon. He accepts this as the imperative of his time. Weapons are inevitably expected to be used within an orthodoxy prescribed for the handling of such things. There is a kit of reliable emotive phrases for writers, a ready-made aesthetic for painters and sculptors, an unwritten index of subjects for playwrights and list of approved images for photographers. Agitprop binds the artist with the means by which it aims to free the minds of the people. It licenses a phony sub-art. Yet the black artist is aware that he is committed, not only as a voluntary act, but in the survival of his own being and personality, to black liberation. It is at this point that, as an artist, commitment takes over, from within, from relevance, and the black artist has to assert the right to search out his own demotic artistic vocabulary with which to breathe new life and courage into his people. His commitment is the point at which inner and outer worlds fuse; his purpose to master his art and his purpose to change the nature of art, create new norms and forms out of and for a people re-creating themselves, become one aim.

* See Mafika Pascal Gwala, 'Towards the Practical Manifestations of Black Consciousness', in *Black Renaissance*, (ed.) T. Thoahlane (Johannesburg: Ravan Press, 1975), pp. 31, 32.
† Ibid., p. 26.
‡ Jean-Paul Sartre (from my notebooks, precise work not recorded).

For the black artist, the tendentiousness of the nature of art goes without question. He cannot choose the terms of his relevance or his commitment because in no other community but the predicated one which blacks have set up inside themselves are his values the norm. Anywhere else he is not in possession of selfhood. The white artist is not quite in the reverse position; that would be too neat for the complexity of the state of art, here. He can, if he wishes, find his work's referent in an aesthetic or ontological movement within the value-system traditional to whites. White South African culture will not repudiate him if he does. Even if he were to decide to be relevant to and find commitment only to himself, he could still find some kind of artistic validity so long as he were to be content to stay within the kind of freedom offered by that closed value-system. Yet the generally tendentious nature of art in South Africa – overwhelming in writing, if less consciously so in painting and the plastic arts – shows that few white artists take up these options. One could reverse the proposition and say they don't 'opt out' – if it were not for the fact that the rejection of whites-only values by no means implies a concomitant opting in: to black culture. The white artist, who sees or feels instinctively that exclusively white-based values are in an unrecognised state of alienation, knows that he will not be accepted, cannot be accepted by black culture seeking to define itself without the reference to those values that his very presence among blacks represents. Yet for a long time – a generation at least – the white artist has not seen his referent as confined within white values. For a long time he assumed the objective reality by which his relevance was to be measured was somewhere out there between and encompassing black and white. Now he finds that no such relevance exists; the black has withdrawn from a position where art, as he saw it, assumed the liberal role Nosipho Majeke defined as that of the 'conciliator between oppressor and oppressed'.*

If the white artist is to break out of his double alienation, he too has to recognise a false consciousness within himself, he too has to discard a white-based value-system which it is fashion-

* [Dora Taylor, pseud. Majeke], *The Role of the Missionaries in Conquest* [Johannesburg: Society of Young Africa, 1952], p. 26.

able to say 'no longer' corresponds to the real entities of South African life but which in fact never did. But unlike the black, he does not have a direct, natural, congenital attachment to these entities. We are not speaking of artistic modes and forms, here, but of the substance of living from which the artist draws his vision. Exploitation, which the blacks *experience as their reality*, is something the white artist repudiates, refuses to be the agent of. It is outside himself; he experiences it through a moral attitude or a rational empathy. The black creation of new selfhood is based on a reality he, as a white, cannot claim and that could not serve him if he did since it is not of his order of experience. If he is to find his true consciousness, express in his work the realities of his place and time, if he is to reach the stage where commitment rises within him to a new set of values based on those realities, he has to admit openly the order of his experience as a white as differing completely from the order of black experience. He has to see the concomitant necessity to find a different way, from that open to the black artist, to reconnect his art through his life to the total reality of the disintegrating present, and to attempt, by rethinking his own attitudes and conceptions, the same position the black artist aims for: to be seen as relevant by and become committed to commonly-understood, commonly-created cultural entities corresponding to a common reality — an indigenous culture.

I suppose I shall be accused of using the schema of a Black Consciousness philosophy. It is an indication of the rethinking, remaking needed in South African cultural contexts that for years no one, not even blacks, ever questioned the exclusive use of white cultural analyses. In my view, this conference should not be afraid of having kick-me political labels pinned on its back; it should assert the urgent need and right to use whatever ideas, from whatever source, that may reflect the facts of life here and penetrate the cataract of preconceptions grown over our vision. This is consistent with an abandonment of the old positions, the deserted gun-emplacements of white and black in culture, and the scrapping — for white as well as black — of the assumption that white-based culture is the mean. I want to emphasise that. A purely white-based culture is as meaningless for white as black, in the future of South Africa.

What I have outlined so far is a brief analysis of the

imperatives laid upon South African artists by their society. Of course it is all not so clear-cut as that. When we turn to the nature of the work the artist produces, we become aware of the terrible problems in which the artist is enmeshed while following those imperatives, even if, as in the case of black artists, he feels sure he knows his way. The nature of contemporary art here, in the aspect of subject-matter, is didactic, apocalyptic, self-pitying, self-accusatory as much as indicting. Apartheid in all its manifestations, the petty jigger that niggles under the skin, the bullet that reaches the heart, informs the ethos of what is produced even by a non-objective painter or an architect seeking an aesthetic for cheap housing to replace a demolished squatters' camp. As Pieyre de Mandiargues says in one of his novels, 'When you have been given a disaster which seems to exceed all measure, must it not be recited, spoken?'[2]

But when we posit a post-apartheid art – and we must, right *now*, out of the necessity implied by the facts examined so far – we switch off the awful dynamism of disintegration and disaster. The black artist is aware of a great force ready to charge *him*, the Yeatsian drive to 'express a life that has never found expression',[*] his part in the re-creation of his people in their own image. For him, the new orientation may be already psychologically established; but it is by no means fully formulated. The important cultural debate that was taking place, in the early and mid-seventies in publications like the yearly *Black Review* and the publications of the Black Community programmes, has been cut off by the banning of organisations and individuals concerned. Black art has not really visualised itself beyond protest. It has not even dealt with aspects of present-day art that do a disservice to the very purpose relevance imposes upon them – for example, the commodity-maker of 'black image' sculpture and painting, the production of artifacts of protest that the white man hangs on his wall as he keeps a carved walking-stick in his hall. These aspects may have grave effects on the future of art, carry over a distortion of the moment of identification between the artist and the subject that Proust defines as style.[†] In the dragon's breath heat of the

---

[*] W. B. Yeats, letter to J. M. Synge.
[†] Marcel Proust, as quoted by George D. Painter in his *Marcel Proust: A Biography* (London: Chatto & Windus; New York: Random House; 1965), vol. 2.

present, this neglect is more than understandable. But understanding does not shift aside problems that will confront the new black culture. Black thinkers are aware of them. Ezekiel Mphahlele and Lewis Nkosi began an inquiry twenty years ago, and their essays were banned. In this decade, it is a continuingly shameful and criminally stupid action on the part of the South African government to have reduced the black cultural debate to conferences of exiles and exiles' publications and at home to a clandestine affair showing itself here and there in white and/or literary journals.

Black artists are primarily concerned with a resuscitation of the pre-colonial culture as a basis, concreted over by the interruption of a purely white-based culture, for an indigenous modern African culture. They break through the concrete with the drums and folk epics that celebrate the past and effectively place the heroes of the present liberation struggle — Mandela, Sobukwe, Biko,[3] Hector Petersen[4] — in a parthenon of inspirational culture-heroes along with the pioneers of black literature itself, Plaatje[5] and Mofolo.[6] But to embody the objective reality of modern blacks, writers and artists must synthesise with all this the aspirations of people who still want TV and jeans — what George Steiner calls 'the dream-life and vulgate'* of contemporary, individual lives. It is comparatively easy to create a people's art — that is to say an aesthetic expression of fundamentally-shared experience — during a period when the central experience of all, intellectuals, workers and peasants alike, is oppression: the pass laws are a grim cultural unifier. It is quite another matter when the impact of experience breaks up into differing categories of class-experience.

The avowed black aim is a culture springing from and belonging to the people, not an élite. This new orientation involves turning away from Europe but at the same time setting up an essential relationship between the past and the technological present recognised as something distinct from the inherent threat of all-white culture. For the technological age is something that cannot be denied and is with blacks in Africa for ever. Similarly, the tools of white culture — most importantly, written literature with all its forms, from blank

* 'To Civilise Our Gentlemen', *Language and Silence* (Harmondsworth: Penguin, 1969), p. 82.

verse to secular drama and the novel — that have been appropriated by blacks, and rightfully, since the evolution of means of expression belongs to all who have the will to use them, should be recognised as independent of that threat. Post-apartheid, beyond liberation in the political sense, and moving on within the total context of liberation in which black culture sees its future — unless black artists can achieve a strong, organic synthesis on these lines their art will be nostalgic, there will be an hiatus between modern life and art, for them. They will be in danger of passing into a new phase of alienation. The questions of relevance and commitment will come up again. This may not seem much of a concern in the fierce urgency of present dangers, but it is one of the many that make the black artist's struggle towards true consciousness a continuing one, and the future of art in South Africa uncertain.

If the white artist is to move on to express a life that has never found expression, this presupposes, on the one hand, that white culture will remake itself, and on the other that black culture will accept him as one who has struck down into liens with an indigenous culture. That remaking could inform his vision, it could replace the daemonic forces of disintegration which both drove him into alienation and were his subject. But unless this happens he will know less and less and see less and less, with the deep comprehension and the inner eye necessary to creation, of the objective realities he came to recognise when he rejected the false consciousness constituted in traditional white-based culture. In the post-apartheid era, the white's position will depend much more on external forces than will that of the black artist. Having changed his life, the white artist may perhaps stake his place in a real indigenous culture of the future by claiming that place in the implicit nature of the artist as an agent of change, always moving towards truth, true consciousness, because art itself is fixed on the attainment of that essence of things. It is *in his nature* to want to transform the world, as it is a *political decision* for those who are not artists to want to transform the world. The revolutionary sense, in artistic terms, is the sense of totality, the conception of a 'whole' world, where theory and action meet in the imagination. Whether this 'whole' world is the place where black and white culture might become something other, wanted by both black and white, is a question we at this conference cannot answer; only pursue.

Throughout this address, when I have used the pronoun 'we' I have been referring specifically to this assembly. Although I am white and fully aware that my consciousness inevitably has the same tint as my face, when I have spoken of white attitudes and opinions I have not taken it upon myself to speak for whites, but have quoted attitudes and opinions expressed by whites themselves, or manifest (in my opinion) in their work. When I have spoken of black attitudes and opinions, I have not taken it upon myself to speak for blacks, but have quoted attitudes and opinions expressed by blacks themselves or (in my opinion) manifest in their work.

It's difficult to end on the customary high note; the state of culture in South Africa does not encourage it. Yet when I go so far as to use 'we' to speak for this assembly, the pronoun in itself expresses some kind of obstinate collective intention to assume that there is at least the possibility of a single, common, indigenous nature for art in South Africa. Any optimism is realistic only if we, black and white, can justify our presence, talking here, by regarding ourselves as what Mannoni, in his study of the effects of colonialism, terms 'apprentice{s} to freedom'.* Only in that capacity may we perhaps look out for, coming over the Hex River Mountains or the Drakensberg, that '*guest from the future*',† the artist as prophet of the resolution of divided cultures.

---

* O. Mannoni, *Prospero and Caliban: The Psychology of Colonisation*, translated by Pamela Powesland (London: Methuen, 1956), p. 65.
† From Anna Akhmatova, 'Poem Without a Hero', in *Requiem and Poem Without a Hero*, translated by D. M. Thomas (London: Elek, 1976), p. 43.

A Writer in Africa

Nadine Gordimer's travels in Africa began when she visited Egypt in 1954. Though stimulated to write about her journeys from early on, it was not until later in the decade that her accounts began to be published. Where editors were interested or invited her, Gordimer was sent on commission; at the same time she used these trips as opportunities to travel, to deepen her knowledge of and feel for her continent. The discipline of work meant a heightened attention to detail; and besides the benefit to the essays themselves, some of this was later transmuted indirectly into fiction. Always there was a dual perspective as Gordimer sought the link between place and people. These essays are, consequently, environmental, social and political.

This selection gives a record of her journeys. In 1958 Gordimer returned to Egypt and wrote 'Egypt Revisited'. In 1960, as the Belgian Congo (now Zaire) was about to gain its independence, she undertook a remarkable trip up the Congo (Zaire) River, over the Ruwenzori Mountains and into East Africa. Geographically absorbed, and poised between past and future, 'The Congo River' is surely one of her finest pieces. In 1969 she visited Madagascar; in 1970 the Botswana desert. In 1971 she went to that symbol of failed promise and enduring hope in post-independence Africa, Ghana, as well as its more pragmatic and conservative neighbour, the Ivory Coast — and compared them. For her last essay included here, in 1977 she visited a different kind of 'country' — the Transkei, South Africa's showpiece 'homeland', in the wake of its 'independence'. North to South, East to West, these are the records of a writer in Africa.

Egypt Revisited

(1958)¹

The friend who had come to meet me at the airport said with satisfaction, 'It's worse than ever here, it's lovely.' He was a foreigner, expressing in seven words a viewpoint doubly foreign: no citizen of the United Arab Republic² would admit that graft is thriving in Egypt more rankly than ever, and no other member of the remnant of the foreign community whom I met would agree that life there is lovely. Yet the eccentric viewpoint given by my friend, who has spent the whole middle thirty years of his life in Egypt, is less than half a joke. Perhaps you have to come, as I do, from Africa and not from Europe, to pick the truth from the laugh. All over the Afro-Asian world there must be isolated Europeans who secretly rejoice in the bitterness of their own banishment, because they love the life and temperament of the country of their adoption so much and so tolerantly that they luxuriate even in the intensification of national failings that so often seems to follow on independence of foreign domination.

I was last in Cairo nearly five years ago, in March 1954, during the week when Nasser deposed Neguib.³ There were machine guns snouting at you through the dusty leaves of the shrubs in the Ezbekieh Gardens, then, and military trucks delivered their loads of soldiers at the street corners every morning, where they sipped coffee on the alert, all day. Now the impromptu, trigger-happy atmosphere has gone. Suez⁴ hangs in the air, a confidence that inflates even the meanest street-urchin chest. Nasser has had the good sense and the imagination to do one or two things that show: a beautiful corniche has swept away the jumble of little villas that used to obscure the town bank of the Nile, there are new bridges, and new wide roads, and white blocks of newly-built workers' flats that, spaced on their cleared ground, look as much like institutions as all workers' flats seem to everywhere in the world. One of the new roads, which leads up to the Mokattam hills, cuts a wide tarred swathe through the Dead City, and in another part of the city the great dunes of rubble that are ancient Cairo, crumbled to dust, are being bitten into and smoothed to a new level for the dwelling places of the latest wave of civilisation. (Watching the cranes and bulldozers, you can see an archaeological discovery of the future in the actual making.) All this, along with the colossus that has been raised from the sands of Memphis and put up outside the main railway station, and the boyishly-grinning pictures of Nasser that cover the faded squares where once Farouk's picture hung on the walls of shops, is the maquillage on an old face that has known so many. But it's an impressive job, and one which encourages one to believe that there's been some bone-surgery too, some improvement of the structure beneath the paint.

I soon discovered that there are two almost completely different versions of the range and effect of this surgery, and that while I should have full opportunity to hear one, I should have to gather the other, and most important, one chiefly by sharpening my own eyes and ears and the shiver of receptivity on my skin. As a European visitor without any Arabic, I naturally found myself socially stranded among the remnants of the European 'foreign' community; I could not expect to cross the very few old and personal bridges between European society and Egyptian society that have survived, successfully, the Palestine War, the Officers' Revolution and Suez, and I could not expect, without a word of their language, to reach a confession of the hopes, fears and prides of the people of the streets. While I was in Cairo I did not let myself forget that the voice in my ear — a measured, intelligent and mostly unembittered voice — was not the voice of the people; that coarse and muffled note I should have to pick up for myself.

Cairo as seen by the few members of the old community who still manage to live there is a depressing place; an intimate whose sight is going and from whose mind the mobility of memory is fading. This is not entirely blimpish nostalgia for good old days. The ancient city that only a few years ago was one of the elegant centres of the modern world has forgotten its sophistication. Lack of foreign currency has emptied the

Kasr-el-Nil shops of nearly everything imported; they are filled with decent cloth of uninspired design made in Egyptian textile mills, and unbeautiful shoes fairly well made by Egyptian factories. Even Groppi's famous delicatessen exposition has shrunk; there *are* one or two delicacies you cannot buy there, now. In those smart restaurants which are still open, the head chef has gone (banished to that 'home' in France from which he came perhaps two generations ago?) and the second-in-command is following the recipes, but not the flair. The great artists and musicians of the world no longer come to Egypt, and there are few who come to hear them if they do. The only evidence I saw of the cultural life of the year in Cairo was the peeling remains of tremendous posters advertising a Soviet ballet and theatre company (a third-rate one, I was told) that had come and gone. The *luxe* of Europe has been banished, but what is left, of course, is the pandemic inania of Hollywood. The entertainment life of Cairo has become that of a complex of villages, each with its ten-foot-high paper face of Marilyn Monroe.

In the eloquent silence of a departed presence that Europe has left behind in Cairo − a silence that you are aware of beneath the unchanged racket and tinkle of the street − a sound forms. The hoarse scraping of the palms of deserted gardens in Maadi is the nervous clearing of the throat; the faint stir of air in the peacock's tail of fallen leaves before the door of the British Embassy is the taking of a preparatory breath − and there, it is out. 'Sequestrated'.[5] Sibilant and fateful, this is the last word on the destiny of nearly every European you meet and every second shop or bank you pass. It is the excuse, the explanation and the apotheosis of city life.

With the immediate past of the city under sequestration, the present seems to be passing into the hands of the army officers and their wives. They are the new élite; the officers' wives are the women who spend hours and money at the beauty parlours, now, and (it is said with a touch of malice) picnic on the Gezirah Club golf course because they haven't yet got so far as learning the game itself. There is a splendid new officers' club, too, where the officers take the ease of top men. No doubt these are the people for whom the new suburb, dubbed Mokattam City, is intended. The development has the authentic, sad, *nouveau riche* stamp; bold, cocky, unsure in taste but sure of *right* – in this case the right to plan ugly villas on the moon-landscape of the Mokattam hills. This certainly is one of the most beautiful places in the world to live, if you feel you could stand the unearthliness of it. Withdrawn from the softening presence of the Nile, these austere heights have no geological memory of green or root or growth; as some mountains are above the tree belt, so these are, so to speak, above the life belt. They drop sheerly from level to level, the higher ones carved into deep escarpments of rock and sand, and the lower ones pitted and cragged by the quarrying that has built Cairo for years. From the foot you see a landslide of hardened Demerara sugar, sliced here, scooped out there, gouged and layered. From the top, with the strange, coarse crumbs of a substance that does not seem to be the surface of the earth, underfoot, you look, far below, on the peace of the Dead City, a place from which at this height only the sound-track seems missing; and beyond it to the whole marvellous city, from the medieval minarets and domes to the cubist shapes of light and shade made by modern blocks; and, at last, to the desert itself. I went into a Fatimid tomb that has stood alone, up there, through the centuries; and I had lunch at the new casino, a vast grand-piano of a building whose 'free lines' have begun to peel before it is quite completed.

On another day I drove past deserted Mena House – open, I believe, but listless – and went to eat *tahina* and *kebab* at another new restaurant, this time at the foot, or rather under the nose, of the Sphinx. This one is called 'Sahara City' and it is run by a Sudanese who looks like Uncle Tom and as a small boy was a page at the court of Franz Joseph of Austria. Both the casino restaurant and 'Sahara City' were empty; 'Nobody goes anywhere,' said my friends. But that night, at a restaurant I had remembered from my last visit, the tables were full and people stood ten deep around the bar – avaricious-looking women, men who watched everyone who came in. 'Then who are these?' I asked. 'The local representatives of international crooks,' said my companion boredly.

The cosmopolitan city of Cairo is dead as the Dead City itself. But does it matter? Does it really count? When I sat in the train, waiting to leave for Upper Egypt, I had a sense of release from involvement with a prevalent emotional atmosphere that had little or nothing to do with me; my emphatic identification with the dispossessed foreign community left me, and I very properly took up my own role again, which was that of a stranger in a strange land. The train took a long time to get started; a boy with rings of sesame-studded bread braceleting his arms from armpit to wrist ran up and down the platform; trolleys full of fowls in cane cages were wheeled past; the crowd, predominantly male, as usual, took an elaborate farewell of the passengers. I had plenty of time to think, and look. The scene on the platform was just as it would have been, five years ago. The streets of Cairo, too, with the exception of the 'foreign' streets, were just as before. At sunset that afternoon, I had stood on the balcony of the flat where I was staying, and had watched the people below, never ant-like as in big cities of the West, but leisured, in full cry, pushing carts, selling peanuts and roasted maize cobs, balancing coffee cups, zigzag-ging the hazard across hooting cars and the little red petrol tanks (from which householders buy the spirit for their stoves) drawn by jingling, brass-cluttered donkeys. As I had come out of the building to make for the station, I had passed the caretaker, sitting resting his back against the blast-wall that was put on during the War and has never been taken down; he was eating his bean soup supper preparatory to his night's work, which consists of climbing into the bed that is pushed into the foyer every evening, and falling asleep under his yellow coverlet.

Here, among the real population, the people themselves, not enough seemed to have changed. Nasser's infant industrial plans are not yet sufficiently under way to thin out the ranks of the thousands who exist on half-jobs, waiting for a share of a half-job, or simply waiting for the opportunity to turn some absurd and unwelcome service into a job — the urban manifes-tation of an over-populated country that is increasing its count of souls by the disastrous number of a million every two years. And while the military caste is raising its standard of living hand over fist along with its social position, the civil servants are struggling to keep up decent appearances on salary scales that would have been adequate before the last war. Many people told me that these totally unrealistic salaries were largely responsible for corruption; families could not hope to make ends meet without the 'little extra' brought in by bribes.

Yet though these facts were disappointing – they were at least negative – by and large, they had not been brought about by the new regime; the new regime had failed, as yet, to change them.

One of the things I had liked about Cairo, five years after the revolution, I decided, was what I cautiously call national confidence – something that I don't believe has anything to do with the braggart 'Voice of Cairo' or Pan-Arabism, or, indeed, anything more ambitious or aggressive than an inner assurance that each man is a man measured against his own people, and not a cipher found wanting against the standards of those who are born of other countries and to other opportunities. All of a piece with this was my satisfaction when I saw what good care the new government is taking to preserve many of those great hunks of the past which jut out here and there, all over Cairo – walls and city gates as well as more obvious and spectacular monuments. When I went to the Cairo Museum, that very morning of my last day in Cairo, I was not surprised to see that although the tourists were reduced to myself, two whispering Indian girls and an American couple sitting exhaustedly in a window embrasure, the museum was full of parties of Egyptian schoolboys and girls; it seemed to me natural that a young and poor nation should be eager to teach its children that it is not so young or so poor, after all.

But what *was* a horrifying surprise was the state of the museum. It was dusty and dingy as a second-hand dealer's; many exhibits had lost their labels, and those of others were almost indecipherable. Vaguely military-looking attendants lounged about, their sticky tea-glasses stowed away in dark corners. Even in the Tutankhamen rooms the jewellery is falling to pieces and the gold is flaking off the incomparable splendour of the shrine. Such neglect of the exquisite work of human hands that has survived time almost long enough to have achieved immortality gives you a feeling of real distress; I had hastened back into town to find someone who could explain to me why this was being allowed to happen. And then I heard about another side of national pride, a foolish, childish side, that will see its wonderful artistic heritage rot rather than let the foreigner – any foreigner – bring the expert help and knowledge that is needed to preserve it.

The train finally did go, and I woke up next morning in an Egypt that is not Cairo. For the next few days I followed the life of the Nile. Where in the world do you get a statement of the human condition as simple and complete as this? Look out of the train or car window and the entire context of the people's lives is there – the river, the mud, the green of crop and palm it nurtures, the desert. There is no existence outside the beneficence of the river, the scope of the mud, the discipline of the desert. This pure statement comes like peace, after the complexity and fragmentariness of life as we know it.

The land looks as it has always looked – 'always' is an impudent five years, for me, out of many thousands. Although the big estates have been broken up under a fairly vigorous and, most people agree, fairly successful agrarian reform, they are worked by the same people in the same way. I was struck again by the unfair picture of these people that soldiers who had been in Egypt during the War gave to their Western countries. I know that South Africans built up for me a caricature of a squinting, cringing, night-shirted Egypt – 'those old Gyppos'. The fact is that many of the peasants, who went on with their work in dogged dignity, as we walked past, are good-looking, while the youths, especially the Nubians round Aswan, are as beautiful as the lovely faces in tomb carvings. This is extraordinary when you remind yourself that these people have been underfed and debilitated by bilharzia and malaria for many generations, and that ever since year-round irrigation was achieved, they have been over-worked as well.

Strung along the Nile, their villages appear as single units – no straggler houses, and a shelter of palms drawn in around them, fortressed against the sun. In the distance they seem to be those very oases that appear in the deserts of fairy tales. The beauty of this poverty has to be shaken off. Then you see that these people are breath-takingly poor, even by the standards of African poverty that I know in South Africa. How, you ask yourself, mentally groping down to confine comparisons only to those things which seem reasonably essential to life – how can they live, so possessionless, so stripped? Apart from a more equitable distribution of land – no one is allowed to own more than 300 feddans (315 acres) and fifty feddans for each of his first two children, and the vast absentee-owned estates have been distributed among the landless – the regime has brought one obvious enrichment to village life. Nearly every village now has a fine modern school, just outside its confines, and it was good, in the mornings, to see the children running out of the dark, close mud walls across to the spanking new white buildings with big windows. Oddly enough, contemporary architecture does not look out of place beside mud brick and tea-cup domes; I wondered about this until I remembered the model of an ancient Egyptian villa that I had seen in a dusty case in the Cairo Museum – it made use of the same juxtaposition of simple rectangles as one sees in contemporary buildings.

At last, I stood at the Aswan on the barrage and felt the power of the Nile water thudding up through the concrete under my hands as it forced through the sluices. 'Aswan' has become a place-name of immense overtones to anyone who reads a newspaper; since 1956 its pronouncement has stirred feelings – loyalties, resentments, fears, satisfactions, guilts – rather than conjured up the imaginative picture of a town.[6] It was quite a surprise – it was as if I had forgotten – to find that Aswan was a place where people lived; a lively Arab town, a view of the Nile flowing in great hanks of calm water round islands of granite behind which the feluccas appeared and disappeared in scythes of white. A few miles from the town, standing on the barrage itself, it is difficult not to indulge in the dramatic feeling that you have all the life of Egypt piled up there behind you in the great dam, and in the still greater dam whose plan lies, bandied about in the abstractions of inter-national politics and finance, but marked out clearly on the landscape, not many miles behind it. I walked along the barrage to the hydro-electric power station which is under construction, cutting into the west shore. The clumsy steel giants of Europe were busy there; great turbines and cables and cranes from Switzerland, Germany and Austria. A workman waved me back; and laughed like a boy with a firecracker when I jumped at the hollow boom of an explosion. We leaned together over the steel rail and watched the granite dust settle, far down in the immense rock basin that has been blasted out.

I am not a watcher at the peep-holes so considerately provided by builders when they are at work; the sight of men swarming about their jobs on some project that will swallow the work in their hands anonymously in its immensity is more likely to depress than thrill me. But I found myself watching the Egyptian workmen labouring below on their power station, and I felt I could go on watching for a long time. There was something hopeful and even exciting about the sight of these men with their energies caught up by the demands of a huge imaginative task — not the labour of the cotton and the bean field whose fruits are used up, each day by the day's existence, and nothing more to show for it. When the power station is completed, it will be theirs to use; it does not merely feed them now, but will change their lives. Surely these people need so badly not merely to be fed better and to live better, but also, after so many centuries of humbleness, to achieve, as other people do? I hope that Nasser will not forget them in dreams of world power, as all their rulers in the past have forgotten them or sold them out, for one reason or another. People who 'know Egypt' and deplore the Nasser regime tell me that 'kings and governments come and go, but it makes no difference to the fellah.' How tragic is the smug comfort of this remark if, this time again, it should prove to be true.

The Congo River

(1960–1)[1]

... a place of darkness. But there was in it one river especially, a mighty big river, that you could see on the map, resembling an immense snake uncoiled, with its head in the sea, its body at rest curving afar over a vast country, and its tail lost in the depths of the land.

Joseph Conrad
Heart of Darkness

Begin with a stain in the ocean. Three hundred miles out to sea, off the west coast of Africa, the mark of a presence the immensity of seas has not been able to swallow. Mariners saw it in the age of exploration, when each voyage held the fear that a ship might sail off the edge of the world. They knew it was the stain of land; mountains had coloured it, the rotting verdure of forests, perhaps, the grass of plains. A massive land, a continent, giving rise to and feeding a river great enough to make a dent in the sea.

The continent parts; the river opens a way in. Many journeys have beginnings flat and unworthy, but not this one.

I stayed a day or two at a beach on the west coast of Africa at the river's mouth. Though the water was salt to my tongue and the tides rose and withdrew, it was not the sea that lay below the ochre cliff. It was the Congo River. All the Atlantic Ocean, as far as I could see, was the Congo River. In the bright sun, the water glittered like a seal's coat; under the heavy skies of the rainy season, it was quite black. When I swam in it, even in the evening, it was warmer than the warm air. I had read that the Congo, measured by its year-by-year flow, is the second greatest river in the world; now the conception of the dry fact flowed around me, a vast environment.

Strange creatures live in the Congo River. From a small boat following the water maze of mangroves, with their cages of whitish roots set over a footing of black ooze, I saw the climbing fish *periophthalmus*. Pop-eyed, startled little creatures, they ran nimbly up the roots, but hobbled and flopped on the ooze. They are the colour of mud, they live in mud that is neither land nor water, and their lives span quietly the gasping transition that evolution made millennia ago, bringing life out of the sea. The manatee, a sea mammal with white breasts (the creature on which the fiction of the mermaid is based), is sometimes caught here.

A slender spatula of land runs out from the mangroves at the shining gape of the river's open mouth. On it is a strip of a town, so narrow that you can see through the gaps between the rows of coconut palms and the smart little villas to the water on the other side. There are no blocks of buildings; the only objects of height and bulk are the ocean-going ships moored off the jetty. This town is Banana, an old slave port and the oldest white settlement on the Congo. It looks like a bright prefab; no memory, here, of the ships that passed, heavy with human cargo, taking Africa to the rest of the world – a world that lived to see a new nation in Brazil, a Negro 'problem' in the United States, riots in London's Notting Hill. I could not believe that those extraordinary beginnings could have been wiped out entirely, but all I could find was a neglected graveyard by the sea. Dutch, French, Portuguese, English and German names were on the headstones, and the earliest was dated 1861. Nobody stayed in Banana unless he died there; nobody built a house meant to last; there were no solid monuments to community pride among slave traders.

Perhaps, while I am writing, the new past, so recent that it is almost the present, is disappearing without trace as the older one did. The white personnel from the Belgian naval base, and the comfortable hotel where Belgians from the stifling interior used to come to swim and lounge in the harlequin garb of resorts the world over – will there remain, soon, much sign of their passing?

A few miles up the same – and only – coast road that led past the graveyard, there was a fishing village that was unaware not only of the past but even of the passing present.

On swept sand under coconut and Elaeis palms the bamboo houses of the village had the special, satisfying neatness of fine basketwork; big nets checkered the shore and a flotilla of pirogues lay beached. Squat monsters of baobab trees, fat-limbed and baggy, sounded tuba notes here and there among the string ensemble of the palms. In the hollow trunk of one of the baobabs was a chicken house, reached by a little ladder. Two old men sat making nets in the sunlight sliced by the poles of palms. One was rolling the thread, using the reddish bark fibre taken from a baobab not ten feet away. A woman came out of a house and took in a basket of flame-coloured palm nuts, ready to be pounded for oil. Under the eaves of her house hung the family storage vessels, bunches of calabashes engraved with abstract designs. These people had none of the aesthetic deprivations I associate with poverty. They walked between classic pillars of palm, and no yesterday's newspapers blew about their feet. They were living in a place so guileless and clean that it was like a state of grace.

A fast motor launch took me in five hours from the West African Coast to the cataracts that kept the white man out of Central Africa for three hundred years. The mangroves were left behind at once, the river continued so wide that the distant banks seemed to be slipping over the horizon, and islands appeared faintly as mirages and then came close, shapes extinguished beneath a dark cloth of creepers. The undersides of the clouds were lit by sunlight shaken glitteringly off the purplish-brown storm-coloured water that heaved past us. As we took the highway against the main current, far off, Africans moved quietly on the verges of the river, their slender pirogues threading the darkness of overhanging trees.

Ocean liners come this way up the Congo to Matadi, the town at the foot of the cataracts, and it has the air of a nineteenth-century seaport. The steep, twisting streets that lead down to the docks are sailors' streets; there is even a notice in the hotel: No parrots allowed. The Congo here looks as I was never to see it anywhere else. It has just emerged from the skelter and plunge two hundred miles down a stairway of thirty-two cataracts in a total drop five times the height of Niagara Falls. It is all muscle, running deep between the high confines of granite hills, and straightening out in swaths from the terrible circular pull of whirlpools.

I saw the rock of Diego Cão, naval officer and Gentleman of the Household to Dom João II, King of Portugal, who reached the mouth of the Congo in 1482. He set up a stone pillar on the southern point of the six-mile-wide mouth of the estuary, and so the river got its first European name, Rio de Padrão, the Pillar River. Diego Cão came back twice. On his third trip he sailed 92 miles up the river until he was turned back by impassable cataracts. He left an inscription carved on rock to show how far he had got; for more than three centuries this was the limit of the outside world's knowledge of the river.

On the face of volcanic rock above the powerfully disturbed waters of the first cataracts, a mile or two above Matadi, was the cross, the coat of arms of Dom João II of Portugal, and the names of Cão and his companions, cut in the beautiful lettering of an illuminated manuscript. The inscription had the sharp clarity of something freshly finished instead of nearly five centuries old.

The place of the rock, where Diego Cão turned back, is a dark place. No earth is to be seen there; only great humps of grey-black rock, and, like rock come to life, tremendous baobabs (those anthropomorphic, zoomorphic, geomorphic living forms, always less tree than man or beast or stone) with their wrinkled flesh that looks as if it would cringe at a touch, their token disguise of brilliant leaves, and their mammalian fruit pendent from long cords. I took one in my hands; it was fully a foot and a half long and must have weighed five pounds. The light-green velour skin was fuzzy as a peach. There came to me, through my hand, all the queerness of the continent, in the strange feel of that heavy-hanging fruit.

There is a road bypassing the cataracts that once barred the way into equatorial Africa, and a railway. Without that railway, Stanley said, all the wealth of Africa behind the cataracts was not worth 'a two-shilling piece'. Stanley himself hacked and dragged his way on foot, sometimes following hippopotamus trails, over the hills and through gallery forests – the dense tunnels of green that cover water courses. The black men dubbed him – with grim admiration, since many of their number died portering for him – *Bula Matari*, 'Breaker of Rocks'.[2] But it is easy, now, to come upon the splendid sight of Stanley Pool [Pool Malebo], the 360-square-mile river-lake above the cataracts, and the beginning of a million square miles of accessible river basin.

On the south bank of the Pool is Léopoldville [Kinshasa], one of the few real cities in Africa, if one of the most troubled, where last year the splendid celebrations of Congolese Independence Day gave way at once to riots and political chaos.[3] Ever since the first agitation for independence, in 1959, there have been riots from time to time, and worse, the fear of riots all the time. When trouble does come, city people white and black flee in their thousands across Stanley Pool to Brazzaville until things cool down again. Brazzaville stands on the north bank, the capital of another Congo Republic, a slightly senior and entirely peaceful independent black state that was formerly part of French Equatorial Africa.[4]

Many big airlines alight here, beside Stanley Pool, at Léo or Brazza, migrant birds always on their way to somewhere else; they bring the world thus far, with their thin filaments of communication they touch thus lightly upon the vast and lazy confidence of the great river that opens an eye of dazzling light beneath them as they take off and go away: the river that carries with ease the entire commerce of the deep Africa through which it is the only highway.

The Pool has always been the point where all the trade of the river, and that of the interior that comes down the river, logically converges, and life there since ancient times must have been a little different from that of the rest of the river. Life on either side of the Pool today is dominated by the presence of the new African – the young men with Belafonte cuts and narrow trousers. One sits behind a teller's chromium bars in an air-conditioned bank, another may only sell lottery tickets in the streets, but they are all *évolué* – for good – from the old African, who sold his land and, as it turned out, his way of life to the white man for a few bottles of gin and some bolts of cloth.

On the south bank, Léopoldville's Congolese cities of 360,000 people shuttle with vitality night and day, while the 'white' city – no longer segregated by anything except old usage, new fears and the black man's poverty – is dead after the shops shut. On the eve of independence, 21,000 white people were living there; it is difficult to get a figure for those who live there now, for of the numbers who fled last year, some have quietly come back, and of course there is the shifting population of United Nations personnel.

The bloody foundering of the new state naturally has focused attention on what the Congolese have *not* got: not a single doctor or lawyer among them and not so much understanding of democracy as you might hope to find in an election of officers of a sports club. These are not sneers but facts. When you go about Léopoldville among the Congolese, you are reminded that if there are no Congolese doctors or lawyers, it is nevertheless also a fact before your eyes that the fishermen and warriors that Stanley encountered eighty-one years ago have become clerks, laboratory technicians, ships' captains and skilled workers. They also reveal an aptitude for spending hours talking politics, reading party newspapers and drinking beer – a way of passing time that is characteristic of some of the most civilised cities in the world, and that has been the beginning of many a man's political education. They stood small chance of making a success of governing themselves when independence fell into their clamouring hands; now they may have to pick their way through years of near-anarchy before they defeat tribalism, evade or survive foreign domination, and learn, a tragically hard way, how to run a modern state.

The city Congolese have the roaring capacity for enjoyment that looks as if it is going to be one of the pleasanter characteristics of the new African states. Dancing begins in the open-air cafés at two o'clock in the heat of a Sunday afternoon, only a few hours after the last cha-cha-cha of Saturday night has ended, and the influence of the weekend hangs over well into Monday, even in these lean times.

On a Monday morning I visited the Léopoldville market, that colossal exchange of goods, gossip and sometimes hard words. Two or three thousand vendors, mostly women, were selling fruit, vegetables, miles of mammy cloth as dazzling as the patterns you see in your own eyelids, patent medicines and nail varnish, and also several things you would never think of, such as chunks of smoked hippo meat and piles of dried caterpillars sold by the newspaper poke. At least five thousand people were buying there. Lost among them, I understood for the first time the concept of the values of the market place. For it was clear that these people were not just doing their shopping; they were expressing the metropolitan need to be seen at the theatre, the city instinct of participation that fills the galleries of houses of parliament and the foyers of fashionable hotels. They had come to hear what was going on in their world, and what a man's reputation was worth at current prices.

When I emerged from this vociferous and confident press, the Congolese taxi driver who drove me away remarked, 'Ah, it's a pity that you saw it on such a quiet day. No one comes to market on a Monday – all too tired after the weekend. You should have come on a Friday, when it's full of people.'

The Congo crosses the Equator twice in its 2,900-mile length, and it is the only river system in the world whose main stream flows through both northern and southern hemispheres. Some of its tributaries are on one, some on the other side of the equator. This means that the river benefits from both rainy seasons – April to October from the north, and October to April from the south – and instead of rising and falling annually, it has two moderate highs and two lows each year. It does not flood, and though navigation in times of low water is sometimes tricky, it is always possible.

The Congo is shorter than the Nile, the Ob, the Yangtze and the Mississippi–Missouri system, but only the Amazon exceeds it in volume of water discharged into the sea. Its hydraulic energy is estimated at a sixth of the world's potential, and there are a thousand known species of fish in its waters.

From Stanley Pool the Congo opens a way more than a thousand miles, without a man-made lock or a natural obstacle, through the centre of Africa. It leads to what Joseph Conrad called the heart of darkness; the least-known, most subjectively described depths of the continent where men have always feared to meet the dark places of their own souls.

No bridge crosses the river in all this distance. No road offers an alternate way for more than short stretches, and these always lead back to the river. The river alone cleaves the

forests and reveals, in its shining light, the life there. Sometimes, for hours, there is no break in the wall of forest.
Sometimes, beyond an open stretch of papyrus, a group of
palms stand like animals arrested in attitudes of attention. One
morning crowds of pale-green butterflies with black lacy
frames and veinings to their wings came to settle on the
burning metal of the jeeps that were tethered to the barge in
front of our boat.

This boat – the *Gouverneur Moulaert* – pushed a whole
caravan; two barges and another boat, the *Ngwaka*, for third-
class passengers – mostly black. The pace, night and day, was
six miles an hour; a little more than the pace of a man. We were
never out of touch with the life of the shore. All day long,
pirogues paddled out to hitch up alongside our bulky complex,
and the people came aboard to sell dried fish and palm or
banana wine to the passengers of the *Ngwaka*. Two huge
catfish, each with a mouth big enough to take a man's head,
were lugged aboard for sale to the crew, and once a basket of
smoked crocodile feet was casually handed up. For the wilderness was inhabited everywhere, though it often seemed empty
to our eyes, accustomed to landscapes where, even if few
people are to be seen, there are evidences of men having made
their mark in the way the country looks. These people, slipping
out of the forest into the sight of the river, didn't obtrude; their
flimsy huts, roofed with the fronds that the forest can abundantly spare, lay far down among the humus litter at the
forest's feet; their manioc and bananas were merely patches of
vegetation a little differently organised from the rest of the
wilderness.

There were many peoples, of course. Every day we saw
different faces turned to us from the visiting pirogues. North of
the equator, tattooing was no longer a matter of misplaced
vaccination scratches. There were patterns of serrated nicks
that sometimes made a bold second pair of eyebrows; there
were round engravings like beauty patches on women's cheeks.
On some faces the distortion was beautiful; they were forma-
lised into sculpture in flesh. On the faces of the old, artifice had
given way to nature, and the imposed face was broken up by
the patient triumph of wrinkles.

Our water caravan did not halt for the first night and day,

but in the small hours of the second night I was awakened by the sudden stillness of the engines. There were muffled cries in the air; I got up and went on deck. Out of the darkness and dark warmth the two great spotlights of our boat hastily framed a stage setting. A few palm trees were the only props. Before them, on the twenty feet or so of water between our caravan and the shore, black pirogues moved, silent and busy. The third-class ship ahead of ours glowed with light as if it were afire; everyone aboard was up, and life was going on purposefully. I saw the whole scene as if I had carried a lantern into a cave. Once, twice, the non-existent land showed the incredible sight of the lights of a car, carving through it and away. The calls of men and women traders graceful as shades in some watery level of a Dantesque Lethe, came to me as the caravan began to move away. The pirogues showed tiny candle halos of orange light; there was silence. Then a long cry: '*Ivoire!*'

By daylight, these ports of call were signalled by a mile or two of bank tamed by occupation; the red-brick buildings of a mission set back on a grassy slope, a palm-oil refinery or coffee-plantation headquarters. As well as the river people, and the workers from the refinery village, whatever white people there were always came down to the shore to survey us across the water; an old priest with a freshly combed, yellow-stained beard hanging to his waist, a couple of jolly-looking missionaries in cotton frocks, a Portuguese trader's wife, with sad, splendid eyes and a moustache, who never waved back.

At Coquilhatville [Mbandaka], exactly on the equator, I went ashore for the first time. It was a small modern town with its main street set along the river, and an air of great isolation. There is a magnificent botanical garden there, with trees and plants from the jungles of the Amazon as well as nearly all known varieties native to tropical Africa. The Belgian director was still there, then, a happy misogynist living alone with a cat. He opened his penknife and cut me a spray of three cattleya orchids from the baskets blooming on his open verandah. When I got back to the boat, I found that cargo was still being loaded, so I put the orchids into a mug and crossed the road from the dock to the main street again, where I had noticed the *Musée de l'Équateur* housed in a little old building. Striped wasps droned inside, tokening the peculiar resistance of the equatorial forest to the preservation of material things; but if heat and damp threatened to invade the fetish figures and the carved utensils behind glass, it did not matter, because they were all in everyday use in the region, with the exception, perhaps, of a coffin, about twelve feet long, in the form of a man. It was an expression of *rigor mortis* in wood – angular, stern and dyed red. The face was tattooed, and in the crook of the left arm there was a small figure representing the dead man's wife. But I was told that people in that part of the country usually bury their dead in ant heaps, and certainly I never saw a cemetery near any village along the river.

Conrad romanticised the Congo; Stanley, for all his genius of adventurousness, had a vulgar mind. Conrad projected his horror of the savage greed with which the agents of Léopold II brought 'civilisation' to the river in the 1880s, into the look of the river itself. The inviolate privacy of the primeval forest became a brooding symbol of the ugly deeds that were done there, the tattooed faces became the subjective image of life without the organised legal and moral strictures with which the white man keeps the beast in himself at bay. Stanley sometimes saw the river as a potential old-clothes mart; the tattooed and naked people irresistibly suggested to him a 'ready market' for the 'garments shed by the military heroes of Europe, of the club lackeys, of the liveried servants'.

Neither vision fitted what I saw on the Congo, though some of the antiwhite and intertribal atrocities that have been committed since independence have matched in horror what white men did in the name of civilisation less than a century ago, and Conrad's vision of this part of Africa as the heart of man's darkness has taken on the look of prophecy. For myself, I had not been many days on the river when I stopped thinking of the people around me as primitive, in terms of skills and aesthetics. Their pirogues and all the weapons and tools of their livelihood were efficient and had the beauty that is the unsought result of perfect function. The pirogues were masters of the water, and like their gear, many of them were chased with carving of great restraint and discipline. The armoury of fishing spears, with their variety of tips and barbs, represented hand-forging and metalwork of a long skilled tradition, and a jeweller's eye for the beauty inherent in the strength of metals. Any paddle or bailing scoop – common articles of everyday use among riparian people – could have gone straight into an art collection; which is as if to say one could pick up a plastic spoon in a white man's kitchen, a spade in a suburban garden, and confidently put them on exhibition.

After Coquilhatville the river mustered such a day-and-night assault on the senses that you could not read. In the slowly passing forest were the halls and mansions of prehistory: great mahogany trees, ficus, and, out-topping the tallest palm, the giant kapok with its trunk like pale stone. There were times when the pull and contrast between the elements of land and water seemed to disappear altogether. On golden water, garlands of green islands floated. As the light changed, the water became smooth as ice; our length, our bulk skimmed it like a waterbug. Then the floating islands, with their hazy, lengthening reflections, coloured a surface like that of a mirror on which the quicksilver is worn; and perfume came to us from the forest. There were many flowering creepers – an orchid-pink one that spread itself out to the sun over a tree, an occasional red or orange one – but the perfume was the cold, sweet, unmistakable one of white flowers, and came from a waxy trail of blossoms, deadly poisonous, very beautiful.

A storm in the night brought tremendous rain hosing down on us. The sky swelled and thinned with lightning like the overblown skin of a dark balloon. In the morning, the jungle was dripping and brilliant, and an hour-long forest of trees suddenly appeared, covered with ethereal orchilla moss, their beards matted with water. Other trees had ant-heaps looking like spools of thread wound high up on their branches. When the boat drew near an island – there are four thousand of them in this stretch of the Congo – or passed close to one of the banks, the raucous gossip of grey-and-red African parrots was overheard. The Africans catch young parrots by letting a ball of latex, from the wild rubber lianas, down the hollow trees where the parrots nest; the claws of the young become entangled in the tacky ball, and when it is drawn up they come with it. They are caught to sell as white people's pets, unlike the monkeys, which are favoured as food. In a lonely stretch of forest, two men wearing nothing but loincloths of bark startled me by holding up a monkey they had just found and killed in one of the traps they set up along the river.

Not long after the caravan had left Bumba, its most northerly stop in the curving course of the river and the point at which the Congo–Nile road down Africa meets the Congo, we approached a village where a whole armada of pirogues came out to meet us. From our galley came a shower of jam tins; men, women and children leaped for them from the pirogues into the water. The men were naked; the women were wrapped in mammy cloth but they too seemed unencumbered. Some who boarded our boat did not leave it for several miles, when the pirogues had left them behind long ago; they simply stepped off into our swirling wake and swam back home. They are the only people I have ever seen who swim as others walk or run.

We passed, and sometimes made a stop at, places that were once the Arab fortresses of Tippu Tip, a powerful Arab slave trader whose help Stanley was ironically forced to seek in his journeys, although one of the professed objects of the association for which Stanley worked was to wipe out the slave trade. One of these places was Yangambi, which Stanley came upon in 1883 as a populous village in ruins, with its male population murdered and its women and children fettered by the neck or leg in an Arab slave camp built of the remains of their home.

The Belgians built a fine agricultural research station at Yangambi, the biggest in Africa, a garden town with its own shops, school, hospital, club and pleasant houses as well as laboratories and experimental plantations. It belonged, like everything else, to the new Congolese state, and it still had its complement of Belgian scientists when I was there, but the disorder that has since descended on nearby Stanleyville [Kisangani] may have brought its usefulness to a standstill.

Across the river, from a great village that stretched for several miles along the bank, Topoke people brought huge forest pineapples to sell us. The tribesmen were intricately tattooed, with the attentive eyes of merchants, though they grow bananas and catch fish. Many of them are followers of what is known as the Kitiwala – an African corruption of the name as well as the character of the Watch Tower Society, which (like a number of other harmless religious sects in a country where Christianity, traditional animism and black nationalism provide a heady inspirational mixture) has become a subversive secret society. So much so that the Belgian colonial administration outlawed the distribution of those apocalyptic pamphlets familiar on street corners all over the world.

At Stanleyville the river's great right of way through twelve hundred miles ends; the Stanley Falls [Boyoma Falls] break it — they are rapids, really — and the equator is crossed again. On the other side, in the southern hemisphere, is the stretch of the Congo that leads to its source near the copper belt of the south; it has another name, Lualaba. Livingstone 'discovered' it (for Europe) but did not dream that it could be the distant Congo, known far away in West Africa.[5]

Stanleyville lies just below Stanley Falls, as Léopoldville lies just above the lower Congo rapids. But the river at Stanleyville is of a size the eye can encompass, and in fact the town is on both sides of it. Here is a place deeply of Africa, sunk in Africa. In Léopoldville the tropical vegetation is not dwarfed by, but a match for, the giant modern buildings; the modest colonial buildings of Stanleyville make no challenge to the towering fecundity of the tropics. There is a lofty feeling that comes from living things, not buildings; palms, whose trunks are covered with a cool compress of moss, bright as seaweed and feathered with ferns, hang above the avenues, and the Traveller's Tree — an exalted relation of the banana palm that stores cool water for the passer-by at the base of fringed fronds arranged like the spread of a peacock's tail — is common.

Stanleyville is — or was — the late Patrice Lumumba's[6] town, and it has become a place of terror for white people. From time to time, now, it is cut off from communication with the rest of the country, and the world; planes cannot land there, and the river convoy service from Léopoldville, carrying food and other supplies, is disrupted by unrest. But the *Gouverneur Moulaert* and its water caravan reached the end of their journey at Stanleyville during an interval of calm. There, I was even able to have one last experience of the river before I left it to continue my journey by land.

I went with the Wagenia fishermen to visit their fishing grounds in the rapids of Stanley Falls. I found them at home in an ugly 'Arabised' village a mile or two from the town. It was a poor collection of low mud houses like a heap of sand-castles that a tide had lapped over; the extent of its Arabisation seemed to consist of the one mud hut, daubed with white and a line of shaky Arabic script, that served as a mosque. African villages such as this one on the riverbank are relics of the proselytising for Islam that was a side line of Arab slavers from the East Coast.

It was just five in the afternoon when I got to the Wagenia village, and I had to wait while the crew mustered, struggling out of the patchy decency of the white man's cast-offs that they wore to work in Stanleyville, and emerging from their dark mudholes in shorts and loincloths. There were twenty-five paddlers and three musicians, and we took to the water in a big pirogue that held us all comfortably. A coxswain stood in front of me where I sat in the middle, and another, a lean and handsome old man, stood up aft. He was the leader of the chanting; sometimes this accompanied the drumming, sometimes followed on the beat of the drums, and sometimes was beaten into silence by the master voice of the drums. The pirogue skidded and shot across the rapids, the bodies of the paddlers jabbing and rising, and as the water became wilder the drums hammered up the energy of the men, deafening and dramatic.

We crossed the river and landed among reeds where rocks jutted out half-hidden by very fast and evil-looking rapids. Giant cornucopias of fish traps hung from an incredible catwalk of huge logs and lianas strung over the dreadful waters. Three of the fishermen shinned over the lianas and logs and, balancing like high-wire artists, pulled up the traps full of slapping fish. I found myself in a scene I recognised as identical in every detail with the sketch reproduced in Stanley's account of the Wagenias when he founded his first river station at the Falls in 1885; they fish the wild, twisted water exactly as they did then.

Returning downstream towards Stanleyville, the going was smoother and the paddlers made a great show of speed, rhythm and drumming. We cut across the path of the ferryboat that plies between the 'black' town on one bank and the 'white' town on the other; the cranes on the dock were at work on their slow devouring and disgorging. It was an odd feeling to be the centre of a kind of floating war dance in the middle of a modern port preoccupied with political fervour; while I enjoyed the show-off of the Wagenias, I felt something was fraudulent, and could not make up my mind whether it was the modern port or the old pirogue. Yet the Congo River was not demeaned either way. The Congo, like that other stream, of time, is neither past nor present, and carries both in an immense indifference that takes them to be one. There is no old and no new Africa to the great river; it simply bears a majestic burden of life, as it has always done.

While I was travelling on the Congo River I might have forgotten for days at a time that I was in a land suffering the great political crisis of its existence. Yet all through the thousand-mile river journey from Léopoldville to Stanleyville, while the banks of the Congo showed a life regulated by other mores and even other gods than those of the contemporary world of history, a scribble, chalked by an idler in Léopoldville on one of the barges in the water caravan in which I travelled, remained: '*Vive le Roi M. Kasavubu[7] et l'Indépendance*'. In all the traffic of the caravan's progress, the scribble was not rubbed off. And whenever it caught my eye there was brought home to me the realisation that Africa, however troubled it may be, has never been more interesting than it is in this decade; it may never be so interesting again. The Africa the nineteenth-century explorers found – the jungle and the scarified faces that I myself was seeing on the river – and the Africa I had seen emergent in the city life of Stanley Pool are in living coexistence though centuries apart. These are the two great periods of the continent; the colonial Africa that came between them was the dullest, despite its achievements and historical necessity.

When Stanley was busy opening up the Congo River to trade in the name of Léopold II of Belgium, he met in the wilderness Pierre Savorgnan de Brazza, who was equally busy staking out rival claims for the French. Opposite Léopoldville, which Stanley founded, across the great width of Stanley Pool is Brazzaville, which de Brazza founded. Four years ago the Pool was French on one bank and Belgian on the other; now Brazzaville is the capital of one Congo Republic, and Léopoldville is the capital of another. The new definitions are only a little less artificial than the old colonial ones; for the people on both banks of Stanley Pool are the same people – the Bakongo – who had a kingdom of their own in the fifteenth century. The definitions are less artificial only because the people of the right bank and the people of the left bank have entered into community with the modern world under two different influences – the one French, the other Belgian – and certain approaches to life characteristic of the French, and others characteristic of the Belgians, will probably distinguish the two African peoples forever, despite the fact that the Congolese of the former Belgian Congo have shown a fanatic revulsion against the Belgians.

On a Saturday night I took the ferry across Stanley Pool to what used to be the French side, and went to an open-air café in the Poto Poto district of Brazzaville, a vast black slum that is the real city, although its swarming existence in shacks and unlit streets goes on completely buried under an extravagant growth of creepers and palms, while the pleasant colonial town built by the French shows up more prominently through the tropical green.

Chez Faignon lay behind a dirty alley full of amiable hangers-about, a barber's stall doing good business, and an old, blind house. Yet it turned a face to the sky as a moonflower; there was a raised dance floor, a marvellous band panting out to the night the triumph of its return from a Left Bank engagement in Paris, a pungent atmosphere of cats and spilled beer, and a collection of women whose blatant gorgeousness is the only grand style of beauty I know of in the world today.

These ladies of joy – as many of them were – suggested all the wickedness of courtesans of the great age; they also giggled and whispered in each other's ears like schoolgirls. They were wearing – carried to the nth degree – the form of dress that the modern women of the Congo basin have evolved for themselves, and that, though it goes by the humble French word *pagne* – loincloth – combines the grace of the sari with the revelations of the bikini. It consists of a décolleté, almost backless tight bodice, a bandage-narrow skirt from pelvis to ankle, and some yards of material draped to cover the gap between bodice and skirt. The ladies dance the *paso doble* in this outfit, and the gesture with which they unhitched and rearranged the drape recalled the business of the cape before the bull and also revealed, for quick glimpses, smooth, bare belly.

I sat at a table with French friends and pointed to various people around us: 'Who would they be?' There were a few white couples among the gay ladies and town bachelors. 'Just people who like a good band to dance to on a Saturday night.' 'And that man over there?' He was a white-haired white man with a smooth, pink jaw, impeccably dressed in quite a different way from that of the Congolese bachelors, who were elegant in the manner of young Americans trying to look like young Italians. I was told he was Monsieur Christian Gayle, Minister of Information at the time — the only white man in Africa holding a cabinet post in an independent black government. A little later the Minister of Information left his party of African friends — which included the Minister of Finance and also a spectacular six-foot Senegalese lady in turquoise chiffon *pagne* and diamonds — and joined us. He was a calm, charming man who wore the ribbon of the Légion d'Honneur and was once a member of the French Chamber of Deputies. The finish of Europe lay upon him invisibly but effectively; he was serenely unaware of any temptation to Africanise himself. He told me that he had come to Brazzaville seven years ago on a stopover between planes, and had lived there ever since. 'The only way a white man in Africa keeps his self-respect now is when he is working with independent Africans. Last year, when I was Speaker, the leader of the opposition knocked me over the head with a portable radio. I remained calm. That is one of the important things left to do in Africa — to keep the peace between Africans, who don't really understand the principle of loyal opposition — of putting the country first.'

A few weeks later Léopoldville, on the other side of the river, was a place of brutality again, with the Congolese battering a bewildered assertion of their freedom on the heads of one another, as well as on white heads, and the size of the task

M. Gayle had foreseen became clear. Since then, even the United Nations has seemed less than equal to this important thing left to do in Africa.

When the river had taken me halfway across the continent to Stanleyville, I continued by road north and east through other parts of the centre of Africa, a spread of more than 900,000 square miles that was colonised by the Belgians. It is eighty times the size of Belgium itself – indeed, the whole of Western Europe could be contained within its borders. Almost the whole of the Congo River basin belongs in it, the Mountains of the Moon, many thousands of miles of tropical rain forest, and beyond the forest, rich copper, diamond and other mineral deposits. Men and animals extinct or unheard-of anywhere else still live in the equatorial jungle, and the uranium for the bombs of Hiroshima and Nagasake came from the mine at a tiny place called Shinkolobwe in the savannah.

Vive l'Indépendance. There was no mud hut so isolated, no road so lost in this wilderness that the message of that scribble on the river barge had not reached it. On the way north, in a country hotel on a lonely road where men carry bows and arrows just as we carry umbrellas and newspapers, and pygmy women run like shy deer twenty yards into the forest before they turn to pause and look at you looking at them, a huge yellow American car brought a couple of party politicians to put up for the night in the room next to mine. They were urbane young black men, and after drinking French wine with their dinner, they set off to address a meeting in the village. The people round about were the Mangbetu, whose artistic sense has led them to the elegant distortion of their own skulls; they have artificially elongated heads as a result of the custom of binding them in babyhood, and the taut skins of their brows give both men and women the look of women who have had a face-lift.

I had seen one of their beautifully decorated courthouses that day. Its mud walls were covered, inside and out, with abstract designs incorporating the figures of animals and weapons in terracotta, black and white. The court was in session and a group of women were listening to the drone of somebody's grievances and passing silently among themselves a bamboo water pipe, also decorated. They were unsmiling women who wore the *negbwe*, a concave bark shield, on their behinds, and little else. But their near-nakedness wore the forbidding expression that my limited experience is familiar with only on faces. Among them, I had the curious impression that I was not there.

Early next morning I passed the open door of my neighbours' room and saw the two politicians, in shirt sleeves and bow ties, sitting on their beds counting a great pile of currency contributed to party funds by the Mangbetu, who had attended in full force at the meeting the night before.

And there was no part of the country, however remote, where you might not be startled by the sudden appearance of a group of ragged children, yelling at the car as it passed. Speed whipped the cry away; but it was always recognisable as the same one: ' *'dépendance*!' Perhaps, deep in the forest they had never left, they did not realise that they had got it; perhaps only when the cotton crop was gathered, and there was no one to buy it, and they were hungry, would they realise the change had come.

Once my companions and I met with an older form of African confidence, and one that belonged to a different kind of independence – a kind safe from disillusion. We had stopped to quench our thirst on warm soda water on a road that led through a neglected palm grove, old and taken over by the jungle. A Congolese with a demijohn of palm wine came over the rise toward us, his wavering progress given a push by gravity. A lot of the wine was inside him instead of the demijohn, and when he drew level with the car, he stopped, greeted us and then stood a minute, watching us with a fuddled amiability that presently turned to amused patronage. He pointed to the soda water. 'That's your drink,' he said. Then he lifted the demijohn. 'This's ours.'

For years travel maps have shown the continent of Africa populated apparently exclusively by lions and elephants, but these maps are out of date now, and will have to be replaced with something ethnographic as well as zoogeographic. For the people have come back; they are no longer discounted by the world as they were for so long. The people have come back into their own, no matter how strife-torn they may be; and the animals have not gone yet. This, if he can dodge between riots and avoid the crash of toppling governments, is a fascinating combination of circumstances for a traveller.

Gangala-na-Bodio – the hill of Chief Bodio – is high up in the Uele district, the north-east corner of the Congo, out of the equatorial forest and lost in the bush near the Sudan border. On the hill, in the middle of the home of the last great herds of African elephants, was the only African elephant-training station in the world. I write 'was' because I must have been one of the last visitors to go there, and in a matter of weeks after that, all news from this remote corner of the Congo ceased. The few white people in the district fled to the Sudan, and I imagine that the Belgian commander of the station – the only white man there – must have been among them. It is doubtful if the Congolese – even those who treated their elephant charges with such loving care – will be able to look upon elephants as anything but potential food, now, with the country's economy in a state of collapse, and hunger general.

I arrived at Gangala-na-Bodio two weeks after the capture of two wild young elephants. Each was attended by a pair of monitor elephants, old, wise and immensely patient, who hustled them gently but firmly through the routine of the day; but there was a nightly crisis when they were led off to be bedded down in their stockades. On my first afternoon at the station I was charged by Sophie, the wilder of the two. I was standing with a couple of other visitors, watching her being eased into her stockade by the trunks and tusks of her monitors and the shouts and prods of cornacs – trainers – armed with pronged forks. Suddenly she broke through the legs of one of her monitors and hurtled straight for me, her eyes mean with infant rage, her trunk raised for battle and her ears flaring. I lost my head and ran – the wrong way, right among the immense columns of the monitors' legs. They trumpeted, but though the sound was alarming, it was, in a manner of speaking, a mere tut-tutting – a mature deprecation of Sophie's behaviour and mine. I scrambled up into a fodder cart, quite safe.

The majestic charm of elephants creates a wonderful atmosphere to live in. In the morning, their great shapes constantly detached themselves from and merged with the heat-hazy shapes of the bush, where they were out to pasture, or they would appear, with the pausing momentum of their gait, suddenly blocking the bright end of a leafy path at the station. Harnessed to clumsy carts, they did all the hard work of the camp. At four in the afternoon all thirty-one of them were led to the river for their daily bath. Each day I watched them career slowly past me down the riverbank and into the brown water. Some had cornacs on their backs, and they were careful not to dunk them; the men scrubbed luxuriously behind the beasts' ears with handfuls of grass. Some linked trunks and played well out in the river, and rolled each other over with a whoosh that sent four great stubby feet waving in the air. As they came out, in strolling twos and threes, they plastered their foreheads with sand from a pile dumped there specially for them. The cornacs shouted, the laggards broke into a heavy trot to catch up, and the whole procession (wild Sophie with her tail a stiffly held aerial of alarm) trailed home through the trees while the cornacs broke raggedly, then more surely, into *Alalise* or *Dina Dina*, two Hindi elephant songs the Indian mahouts left behind them long ago.

From Gangala-na-Bodio I went out into the bush on one of the station elephants. A cornac in a smart trooper's hat was up in front, and I sat behind on a hard little seat strapped to the elephant's back. We were accompanied by another elephant and his cornac. The cornacs and I had no common language (they belonged to one of the Sudanese tribes of the north-east Congo) but they seemed to have one in common with the elephants, and as we swayed regularly through the early-morning air, first wading across the river (our elephant filled his mouth as he went, like a car taking petrol), my cornac kept up a nagging, reproachful, urging monologue in the elephant's enormous ear. A family of giraffe crossed our path, and though I admire them, from the vantage point of an elephant's back I felt less impressed than usual by their loftiness. Then we stopped within a few yards of a herd of bushpigs, who showed no sign of wanting to run, and passed before the serene eyes of a Thomas's Cob – a lovely antelope – without startling him.

We saw a herd of elephant in the distance to the east, and slowly swung off toward them through the trees. I held my breath as our two elephants moved right up to mingle on the fringe of the herd of five cows, three calves and a monumental bull. But the wild elephants seemed unaware of the two who bore men on their backs, and the tame elephants showed no remembrance of the freedom from which they once came. I have often seen the wild animals of Africa from a car, or even on foot, in game reserves, but I have never expected or felt myself to be anything but an intruder among them. On elephant-back, they accepted me as one of themselves; it was a kind of release from the natural pariahdom of man in the world of the beasts – an hour, for me, that early morning, which was the reverse of that hour at midnight on Christmas Eve when it is said that beasts can speak like men.

From Stanleyville, at the end of the thousand-mile main navigable stretch of the Congo River, a road follows the old slave and ivory caravan trail through the Ituri Forest, the primeval jungle through which Stanley walked for 160 days, almost without seeing the light.[8]

The life of the forest is an internecine existence; completely enclosed, each step, each minute sealed off from the next by a conspiracy of leaves, lianas and deadening mosses. The trees are host to all sorts of other living forms. Some are held by lianas in a deadly embrace that eventually hugs them out of existence, so that only the lianas remain, locked soaring upright; through them you can see the space where the tree used to be. Shell-shaped wasp nests stand like platforms on the tree trunks. Bunches of swordfern and fungus are stuffed in every crevice. On the floor of the forest, stiff waxy lilies are hatched out by the ancient humus.

The forest creaks like an enormous house. In the silence of the day, showers of small leaves fall from so high up you cannot see where. But most of the things that lie fallen are tremendous; pods from the beanstalk Jack might have climbed, huge silky seed cases, green on one side, silvery fur on the other.

At night the forest is as noisy as a city. Among the barks, grunts and cries there was one Greek and immortal in its desperate passion, gathering up echoes from all the private wailing walls of the human soul. It turned out that it came from an outsize guinea pig of a creature called a tree hyrax; I saw one in captivity in one of the villages where, like parrots, monkeys and pythons, they are popular pets of the few white inhabitants.

Most of the animals of the forest do not show themselves, but on the Epulu River, deep in the jungle, I visited a trapping and breeding station where I had a chance to see the rarest and most timid, the okapi, the forest giraffe. The station was simply a part of the forest enclosed, and I came upon the okapi in the cathedral light for which their being has evolved. They were the most luxurious-looking animals imaginable, as big as horses, with legs striped waveringly in clear black and white as if they were standing in rippling water, and a rich sable sheen on the rump shading into glowing auburn that changed in movement, like a woman's hair tinted different colours at different levels.

The pygmies, who belong to the forest just as the okapis do, venture out of it hardly more. They are the only autochthonous people of the forest, and in parts they live a nomadic life, hunting, and are at home wherever they twist together the few branches and leaves that provide shelter for a short time. (These huts are not much more elaborate than the gorilla nest I saw later on an extinct volcano.) But many pygmy groups have attached themselves to other African communities, who live where the forest has been cleared for cultivation, and these have adopted a more permanent way of life and live in the villages. Pygmies have interbred, too, with full-size people, and in many villages there is a confusing variety of sizes that don't necessarily correspond with ages. A boy of seven can be as big as his grandfather, and what looks like a man's small daughter turns out to be one of his wives.

Driving along a road one morning where the forest had been pulled down to make way for coffee and banana plantations, we heard drums in one of these villages. A child had just been born; a small tam-tam and biggish beer-drink were in progress as a celebration. Two fine young men stood at long drums suspended over smouldering logs to keep the skins taut. Around them a company of men, women and children shuffled and sang. There were several gnomes of men with the huge eyes that pygmies have, like the eyes of some harmless night-prowling creature.

There was a tall man, small-featured and handsome, who wore at an angle, in drunken parody of his own natural dignity, a straw and parrot-feather toque exactly like the one in a sketch that Stanley reproduced, as an example of dress in the region, in one of his Congo exploration books. There were people with filed teeth and others with tattooed navels. Young girls and old crones who wore only small aprons of beaten bark were the most enthusiastic dancers, the crones inspired by drink, the girls perhaps by the wonderful intricacy of their coiffures – corrugated, helmeted, deeply furrowed as if the very cranium had been cleaved in two.

Pygmies and other forest Congolese use the road to walk on, but there is no feeling that it connects them to anything. They are complete, in and of the forest. The women peer from under the forehead band that supports a huge, papoose-shaped basket filled with bananas, wood or palm nuts; often a baby sits on top of it. The men carry their bows and arrows, pangas and hunting spears, and the great bark-fibre nets with which they trap animals. Sometimes they have with them the little Basenji dogs that look like mongrel fox terriers with wide pointed ears, and cannot bark. Often there are people playing musical instruments as they walk; harps with resonators of stiff buckskin, and the *likembe*, a small box with metal tongues that is heard, plaintively plangent, all over Africa.

The landmarks here are giant red sand-castles of ant heaps, carefully covered with palm leaves over a stick frame; the cover prevents the winged grubs inside from flying off, by suggesting a night which ends only when the Africans open the heap to eat them. Cars that falter on the way provide, for a while, other landmarks; the hulks of recent American and Continental models lie abandoned here and there, the creeping plants beginning to cover them within a year or two of their announcement as an innovation in motoring. Soon they disappear under the green.

Stanley almost gave up hope of emerging from the forest into the light, but after five months the day came. 'Instead of crawling like mighty bipeds in the twilight, thirty fathoms below the level of the white light of the day, compelled to recognise our littleness, by comparison with the giant columns and tall pillar-like shafts that rose by millions around us, we now stood on the crest of a cleared mount.' The end of the forest is just as dramatic today, from the road that leads east. Perhaps more dramatic, for you can drive in one day from the equatorial forest to the sight of snow.

At four in the afternoon, the trees fell away before us, the green land fell away beyond that, and a great blue ghost of a mountain hung across the horizon. It was an infinity; a palm or two stood up clear in the foreground against swimming blue. Then the cloud at the top of the blue shape shifted a little, the outline neared and hardened; we saw the white glitter, the soft contour of snow on the jagged peaks of a whole range. It was the Ruwenzori – Ptolemy's Mountains of the Moon. And we came upon them, remote as the moon, from out of the close warm forest and the pygmies burrowing there.

Across the Semliki Plain we drove toward the mountains through elephant grass, spiked acacias and companies of royal palms. There were banana and paw-paw plantations, too, down where we were; and, up there, the alps. At the foot of the mountains there was a hotel that seemed to float in the radiance that came up from the plain. A water garden of three swimming lakes held, upside down, the snow flash of the mountains' highest peak, 16,795-foot Margherita; and between hotel and peak there was a five-day climb, for the hardy, through every type of vegetation from equatorial to alpine.

This part of the Congo – the Kivu province – and the neighbouring territory of Ruanda-Urundi (still under Belgian trusteeship),[9] is unlike any other part, not only of the Congo but of all Africa. From the Mountains of the Moon driving three days to Lake Tanganyika, the car seemed to be pulled from side to side by mountains and lakes that reduced most famous drives to the stature and duration of a scenic railway in the painted canvas of a fairground.

Tourist pamphlets, with their passion for making everywhere sound like somewhere else, used to call this the Switzerland of Africa, and no doubt will again when the country is once more open to pleasure travel, but it is not much like Switzerland, and if it were, who would bother to seek in Africa what is so handy in Europe? It is unlike the rest of Africa because it is the high reservoir − watershed of both the Congo River and the Nile − of a continent, seared through by the equator, which is largely baked dry where there is any altitude to speak of, and steaming wet where there is none. It is unlike Switzerland because many of its green mountains are volcanoes (two are still active); its strange pale lakes have floors of lava; its cattle (my first sight of a cow in all the Congo) are long-horned beasts like the cow-god Hathor in Egyptian tomb paintings; and on the roads behind the villas that the Belgians built on Lake Kivu you see brown giants and pygmies. The giants are the Hamitic Watusi of Ruanda-Urundi, and the pygmies, not the pure forest breed, are the Batwa.

In the middle of this mountain and lake-land, enclosing three-quarters of the shores of Lake Edward [Lake Rutanzige] and reaching to Lake Kivu, is Albert Park, a wonderful game preserve on the floor of the Great Rift Valley. I drove straight through it, for I was on my way over the border of the Congo into Uganda − the frontier runs over the Mountains of the Moon, through Lake Edward and over three volcanoes − because of an animal that can only be seen outside a game preserve − the mountain gorilla. There are many on the Congo side of the volcanoes that cross the Great Rift Valley from West to East, but, under Belgian administration at least, no one was allowed to go up after them. At the Uganda frontier post of Kisoro, there is a tiny country hotel whose proprietor had permission, and himself provided the guide, to take people up the side of the extinct volcano, Muhavura, where gorillas live.

I set off up Muhavura early in the morning and climbed to ten thousand feet, well into the bamboo belt. The gorillas do venture up the full fourteen thousand feet of the volcano, but bamboos provide their beds − a fresh one each night − and a favoured food, and the guide felt that if we were to come upon them at all, it would be there among the bamboos that enclosed us like the bars of a vegetable prison. Progress was a matter of squeezing between them, usually on hands and knees because the glassy-wet earth gave no foothold. We were within a degree of the equator − but it was dripping cold, up there; where there was no bamboo, there were leafless, lichen-scaly trees spun all over with a floss of moss that came against your face like a wet sponge.

A broken stalk of wild celery, a huge, knobbly-surfaced mushroom, nibbled and discarded, made a trail read by the guide. Soon he showed me five fresh gorilla beds, that had been slept in the night before. They looked more like giant nests than beds; the stout bamboo poles were bent together five or six feet above ground, and then roughly thatched with leaves. There was fresh dung, and in the wet earth, huge knuckle-marks — like us, the gorillas use hands as well as feet to get along on the mountain. This deserted bedroom had an odour that curiously matched the gorilla's own place in creation; not quite man, not entirely beast, a compound of lodging-house back room and zoo enclosure.

I did not see the gorillas although we trailed them for four hours. Apparently people who do come upon them do so quite suddenly; the male, who may be a six-hundred-pound six-footer, then stands his ground, beating his breast and arms and giving a blood-freezing battle cry, while the females and young make off. How the exhilarating mixture of curiosity and pure funk with which I sought this experience would have stood up to it, I shall not know until I go back one day and try again; for this time, my sense of let-down was forgotten by the surprise when I turned my back on Muhavura for the climb down, and saw before me a marvel of a plain far below, with little volcanoes set in it like cup-cakes fallen in in the middle, and the grain and counter-grain of the scratchings of agriculture, and more volcanoes, ringed from base to summit with contoured planting in a pattern as ordered as the plaiting on the Africans' heads, and the pale moonstone gleam of yet another volcano that held, instead of fire and brimstone, a lake.

Climbing down, we sank slowly, like birds coming to rest, to the level of this plain.

The white man, as a power, is fast becoming extinct in Africa; it may be that the wild animals will follow him. Africans and animals have lived together so long that one is inclined to think of them as belonging together in a natural order, but the truth is that the domain of the beasts has long been a puppet kingdom, upheld by white governments not only by means of game preserves and sanctuaries, but, more important, by stringent hunting laws outside them. Once the greater part of the continent is ruled independently by the Africans themselves, it is unlikely that they will be able to regard the beasts as anything but a supply of meat and an obstacle to the expansion of farmland. By the time the Africans have secured confidence in their place in the twentieth century, it may be too late to remedy the sacrifice of the beasts. It is just possible that this sacrifice might be avoided if the African states would agree to let the game preserves be the responsibility of an international authority, such as the United Nations.

Whatever happens, the hour of man has struck in Africa. We have swarmed over the whole of creation; it would be humbug to pretend not to hear, simply because elephants often seem so much nobler than men, buck more beautiful and even lion less menacing.

I left the Congo with men's voices in my ears. It was in Katanga [Shaba], the rich province that was the first to secede from the central government.[10] Katanga, with its copper, uranium, diamonds, gold, cobalt and tin, is richer in minerals than any other part of Africa (with perhaps the exception of the Union of South Africa)[11] and once supplied more than half the national income of the old Belgian Congo. The Belgians in particular, and international mining interests in general, have managed to retain powerful influence in this prize territory, and its Congolese president, Moise Tshombe, is regarded in most other independent African states as a white man's stooge – a puppet animated by the old colonial strings.[12]

For the first few months after independence, in June 1960, the breakaway state of Katanga was the one part of the former Belgian Congo that remained peaceful. But later tribal fighting began there, and in certain mining and industrial centres the whites were subjected to a reign of terror just as bad as those that hit the late Lumumba's Stanleyville, or Kasavubu's Léopoldville.

On a Sunday morning the town square of the prosperous copper town and capital of Katanga, Elisabethville [Lubumbashi], was ready to receive President Tshombe on his return from the Brussels Conference at which the Congo had been granted independence.[13] The day before, I had seen chiefs in leopard-skin regalia lunching at the Léopold Deux, the most elegant hotel; they had arrived from the country to welcome him. And early on Sunday morning I had been wakened by the sound of ululating cries in the streets, as less exalted supporters came into town by lorry and on foot.

The scene in the square was one of dazzling, jazzing holiday joy. Twenty thousand faces looked from the branches of the flowering trees, from the top of buildings, from a solid phalanx in the streets – all black. There were boy scouts and religious sects in white-and-blue robes and chiefs in fur, feather and beads, and young men in forage caps and party uniform. There were several hundred women whose faces and arms were painted white and whose hair stuck out like pipe cleaners in tiny plaits all over their heads. There were drummers and dancers with tribal masks on their faces, and on their feet the issue boots they wear in the copper mines. While they stamped and sang, a white man in shorts held a microphone impassively before them.

After a two-hour wait, a party official leapt on to the red-and-white striped official stand, stilled the drums and the din, and held up a gentleman's overcoat, of discreet colour and the best tailoring. Like a thump on a gong, a tremendous cry rang out from the crowd and hung on the air: the coat was a sign, brought by dispatch rider from the airport, that their leader had truly arrived.

Soon Tshombe came in person, a beamish, very young-looking man, as many African statesmen tend to be, standing up in an open car, a very large pink one, as many African statesmen's cars tend to be. It had been announced that photographing of his person was forbidden: the reason – not announced – was that no one is yet quite sure that there may not be something in the old African belief that, by sticking pins into or casting a spell over an image, you may be able to bring harm to the person it represents.

He looked afraid of nothing, nothing at all, this young man in the blue lounge suit. Yet as I watched him up there on his platform of welcome I could see that he was surrounded by everything that Africa has to fear. The faces of white men – men of prey or good will, who could tell? – were there, few and ominous, close beside him before the black crowd. And, just behind him, there was a mountainously fat chief, holding a fly whisk with the authority of a sceptre.

Madagascar

(1969)[1]

A four-letter word brought me to Madagascar. Not the usual sort. A single word in the local tongue. I read that in the Malagasy language the world 'lolo' means both 'soul' and 'butterfly', identifying the chrysalis with the shrouded corpse, and the butterfly that emerges from it with the soul from the body of the dead. A people who could express the concepts of resurrection and the eternal renewal of life in a single image conjured up by one short word – they took a hold on my mind. That was why I went to their island in the Indian Ocean, which otherwise had attracted me neither more nor less than the dozens of others floating about the warm seas of the world under the general heading of Island Paradise: a time-spotted Gauguinesque romanticism that seems to survive for all except the inhabitants themselves, now flying the flags of their doll-sized independent nations and hoping for the discovery of off-shore oil or on-shore uranium.

Island Paradise sources of information labelled Madagascar the Great Red Island; home of the gryphon; fourth biggest island in the world. Flying over it at last, I was not surprised to find that it was, of course, not red at all: a deep, contused glow in the skin of mountains and hills cosmically wrinkled below, a flush the colour of purplish jasper that came up under the thinning grass of the dry season. Amber rivers opaque with mud moving strongly in U-curves along the valleys, roads (where there are any at all) following the same line of looping low resistance, the colour of powdered rust. As for size – while I zigzagged about the island either on land or by air (a thousand miles from end to end, three hundred and sixty across at the broadest point) with climate and landscape constantly changing, what became a reality for me was a pocket continent. And as for the poor giant gryphon bird whose last known egg, holding more than two gallons of omelette ingredient, was taken to Paris for exhibit in 1850 – the present wild-life population of lemurs proved so elusive that they might just as well have been extinct along with her. But the people were there. The Malagasy, of whose language I went knowing just one word, were not at all elusive and very much alive in the tenth year of their independence both as one of the former French colonies still under the skirts of the French Community,[2] and as a member state of the Organisation of African Unity.

Wherever you fly in from, you alight on Madagascar at the capital, Tananarive [Antananarivo], four thousand feet up on the high plateau among the ribbed shapes of shining rice paddies. The island lies 250 miles across the Mozambique Channel from the south-east coast of Africa and was once probably joined to it; no one really knows. No one knows either where exactly the inhabitants came from and when, although ethnologists presume it was from the south-west Pacific in the succession of migrations from some centuries before the birth of Christ until the fifteenth century. The first thing you notice in Tananarive is how strikingly Polynesian as opposed to African their descendants, the people in the streets, the Merina, look, and the Merina's language, which over the centuries and through their long political dominance has become the language even of the coastal tribes who have an admixture of negroid and Arab blood, is a Malayo-Polynesian dialect full of repeated syllables and long names beautiful to look at but hellish to remember. The first Merina king recorded by colonial history has a prize one: Andrianampoinimerinandriantsimitoviaminandriampanjaka. Known now as Andrianampoinimerina, it was under his rule in the eighteenth century that the Imerina kingdom began to extend its sovereignty over lesser tribal kingdoms of the island. Among the portraits of the Merina dynasty I saw hanging in the palace complex that is still perched above Tananarive city, his picture is the only one that shows a 'native' king – naked except for a loin-kilt, feather in hair, spear in hand. When he died in 1810 his son Radama I welcomed the English and French, primarily in the hope of using the white man to help him complete the

Merina conquest of the island. The portraits of all succeeding monarchs show dark-skinned queens and princes in Napoleonic satin and Victorian hour-glass velvet: the white man, in the form of the rival influences of France and England, had begun to use *them*.

Of course the riff-raff of the white world – pirates such as John Avery and William Kidd – had found the Madagascar coast a useful base, the Portuguese had discovered it in 1500 and abandoned their trading posts there two hundred years later, the Arabs had made foot-hold settlements as early as the seventh century and the French chartered companies of Louis XIV's reign had unsuccessfully attempted to colonise the southeast coast. But on Madagascar just as on the continent of Africa itself, it was in the nineteenth century that Europe's acquisitive scramble for colonies really began. France and Britain bristled at each other half-heartedly for years over 'influence' with the Merina; neither seems seriously to have wanted to take on the place. Their fortunes at the Merina court rose and fell, often promoted unofficially by eccentric individuals like the extraordinary Jean Laborde, a shipwrecked blacksmith who became Queen Ranavalona I's favourite and taught the Merina to make cannon, textiles, paper and sugar, and Cameron, a Scot, who is responsible for having fossilised the charming wooden palace in its present stone carapace. The French and English were alternately welcomed and rebuffed. Which power would take over the island finally was decided in the casual way European powers handed out other people's countries among themselves in those days of piously-professed concern for the poor heathen: England swopped her chances in Madagascar in exchange for a hands-off Egypt on the part of France.

Nobody asked the Malagasy how they felt about being disposed of by this gentlemen's agreement; there were several Franco–Malagasy wars before France annexed Madagascar in 1896.

> *Tsihy be lambanana ny ambanilanitra*
> – Men form one great mat

For nearly a century before the French conquest, the Merina had ruled the greater part of the island from Tananarive. Now that the French have gone, unlike so many capitals on the African mainland it is not a white man's town from which the inhabitants have decamped; it's what it always was, long before the white man came — the island's own metropolis. It has grown more in the last ten years than in the preceding fifty, and in the new quarters of Ampefiloha there are the big apartment blocks of international middle-class living, but the life-style of the city radiates from the daily market — the *zoma* — of the Analakely quarter to which the splendid boulevard of the Avenue de l'Indépendance leads theatrically, overlooked by the *haute ville*, the hill faced with tall houses in smudgy pastels all the way up to the Queen's palace. A wide flight of steps debouches into the blue and white umbrellas of the market from either side of the city; walking down the Escalier de Lastelle from my hotel on my first morning, I felt I was making an entrance of some sort. Indeed, it was Friday and the show was on. Every Friday the *zoma* bursts out and spreads down the entire length of the Avenue de l'Indépendance for the full width of the sidewalks and the arcades of the conventional shops.

No wonder the Merina — those makers of enviable imagery — visualise human interdependence in terms of weaving. Although the *zoma* stalls sell everything from furniture to horoscopes and rose quartz, from delicious oysters to dried octopus like stiff old gloves, and medicinal ingredients that looked as if they might quite possibly be the tongues of newts, what most people were selling was made of straw. Impossible to catalogue so many different objects woven in so many ways out of different kinds of straw — rice, maize, palm, banana-leaf, raffia. There's nothing more satisfying to buy than something made of straw; it's beautiful, cheap, and cannot last — thus gratifying the eye, the desire to get something for nothing, and leaving one free of the guilt of laying up treasures less ephemeral than the flesh.

And picking a way through the weavers' stalls was also to become threaded into the great mat of people who were trading or buying. A quarter of a million live in Tananarive; most of them seemed to be in the streets, but it was not noisy and nobody jostled — if anyone did, nobody lost his temper. The Merina, whether or not they have adopted western dress (all the women have), still wear the *lamba*, a long cloth, usually white but sometimes a surprising saffron, draped Mexican-style across the shoulders. It looked very fine with ordinary pants-and-jacket, and on women with babies enveloped the baby head and all against the mother's body. Malagasy babies must feel extremely secure in this intermediary stage between the womb and the world.

Every man was wearing a hat, and everyone who wanted to look a man — that is, every little barefoot urchin. A straw hat of course, and usually sombrero-shaped. The sombrero and the poncho are a dashing combination: but the Merina are not dashing at all, on them this outfit confers a sombre dignity. If there is anything definitively un-African about them apart from their looks, it is this quiet demeanour. In place of black ebullience, brown calm.

I was in a taxi one day when it was almost run down by another. The two drivers, eye to eye through glass, paused for a long moment. No word, no gesture from either. We drove on. Are there no curses in Malagasy? Even if there are not, neither driver resorted to the riches of French invective. In place of temperament, withdrawal.

Zanahary ambonin'ny tany — Gods on earth

It turned out that the one word *I* knew was a key one. For the Malagasy, both the Merina of the high plateau and the *côtiers* — the coastal tribes — the dead are part of life. *Lolo* is dead soul ghosting the earth, and living butterfly. The *lamba* is precisely the same garment as the shroud. In ancient times there was a civilisation stretching from the Indian Ocean to Melanesia, based on the cult of the dead and the cultivation of rice. The ancestors of the Merina brought from the Pacific the art of cultivating rice in irrigated paddies, and possibly the cult of the dead along with it. Both have survived into the present day. The dead are believed to be the sole source of happiness, peace, and above all, fertility. The greatest virtue for a Malagasy lies in actual physical contact with the corpse; during the dry season from May to September, as often over the years as they can afford it, the family gathers, sometimes from great distances, at the family tomb to exhume the bodies, give them fresh shrouds and a breath of air, and celebrate their presence with drinking and feasting. Christian conversion (about 40 per cent of the population practise Christianity) and conversion to Islam (about 5 per cent are Moslem) have been accommodated to the custom by the Malagasy instead of resulting in its abolition. President Philibert Tsiranana's democratic government, which would prefer people's energies to be directed to raising production as a means of attaining peace, happiness, fertility, etc., has to tread delicately in its efforts to discourage it.

I wasn't sure whether I wanted to join the party at an exhumation. But I did want to see the tombs, whether the occupants were taking the air or not, because the cult has given rise to an extraordinary religious art – grave sculptures in wood. I knew that the best examples were to be seen far from Tananarive, in the south, near the west coast ports of Tuléar and Morondava. The charming and helpful Malagasy in Tananarive were unexpectedly discouraging when I said I would go by car – why not fly? I would settle for Morondava, then, if Tuléar was too far to drive. I was a bit puzzled when it was calculated that Morondava – only 250 miles – would take as long to reach, but didn't want to listen to any more objections, and set off in a new hired French car with a skilful Malagasy driver on a route marked as a national highway. We did get there – after two days, the second a knuckle-whitening climb over the spine of the island and down through the mountains by way of stony gullies, carrying our own petrol and always hoping the next bridge wouldn't be down. My apprehension was put to shame by the fairly frequent appearance of small shoe-box-shaped buses, marked *Taxi Brousse* (bush taxi) that rocked by, crowded with serene faces. Anyway I had jolted into me unforgettably that the greatest need of the island is roads. It has one of the best networks of internal air services in the world – used by foreign businessmen, government officials and visitors. Air tickets are far beyond the pocket of the average Malagasy, and apart from the line connecting Tananarive with the principal port, Tamatave, there are only a few strips of railroad. If half the country's 1963–73 development plan funds have been earmarked for the improvement of transport, there's not much to show for the money so far on Highway 24.

Down on the other side of the mountains was flat country with the peculiar hot silence of the bush invested, like power, in the monolithic growth of baobab trees; forms from the sophisticated imagination of a Miró, planked down in the nowhere. Morondava was a one-street town of Indian and Chinese shops, an old colonial hotel enclosed by jalousies, and a lovely beach with the Indian Ocean rolling in. I set off for the grave sites. First a visit to the chief's village at Maravoay; this part of the island was once the kingdom of Sakalava and is still inhabited by Sakalava tribes, who are negroid, so the old man in a loin-cloth was unmistakably African. He refused permission to view the graves: recently somebody had sawn off grave figures and taken them away. While the driver protested my honest intentions, I was watching a woman making-up in a cheap store mirror, drawing a dotted pattern in white clay across her cheekbones and down her nose. Better housewives were occupied threshing rice. We had to return to Morondava to buy a bottle of rum; then the chief stiffly relented. We drove through dry winter bush from the village of the living to the village of the dead. In a clearing among paper-bark trees with livid trunks sloughing tattered parchment, were the small fenced allotments the dead occupy. These were all about six by eight feet, and the shoulder-high palings were decorated with finial carvings of birds and humans, and tall, totemic geometrical cut-outs, so that the place seemed peopled above ground as well as below. It was very quiet; I saw that butterflies were hovering everywhere...

The tombs I had seen in other areas were blind cement or stone structures, some with a kind of doll's house on top, and the form that grave sculptures take also varies according to region. The Mahafaly sculptures farther south are totems, sometimes surmounted by miniature tableaux from the dead man's life – his cattle, his house, his family; the horns of sacrificed Zebu cattle are part of the monument. The Vezo (a Sakalava tribe) sculptures around Morondava are unique in their eroticism. At Maravoay, among the representations of colonial messengers in de Gaulle caps, ladies in European blouse-and-skirt complete with high-heeled pumps and dangling handbag, there was a single couple shown in The Act, he, still wearing his messenger's cap, peering rather nervously from behind her intimidatingly female body as if caught in an irresistible indiscretion while on duty.

But at Ambato, a site a few miles up the coast among deserted sand dunes within view but not sound of the sea, the first sight of the village of the dead was of a village petrified in orgy. On the fifty-odd graves, couples − and an occasional threesome − are represented in almost all the common and uncommon variations of sexual intercourse. In this desolate place the sight comes as a *statement* rather than a spectacle: through the moment of man's most intense experience of his own body, the assertion of his fecundity against nothingness. It has the audacity of a flag stuck on the moon.

Of course, for a non-believer (in the context of ancestor-worship) it's tempting to see the fierce joy of coupling as defiance of the loneliness of the grave, Andrew Marvell's fine and private place where none embrace. But this is as subjective as my driver's explanation that these dead had been 'very fond of women'. Apparently the truth has little to do with either the grave occupants' sexual capacity or resentment against death; the skilful lovers symbolise the fertility that, like all good things, comes to the living from the dead.

While the clothed and painted figures are naïve in conception and execution, and the partly-clothed couples lean toward caricature, many of the naked couples are works of extraordinary beauty and technical achievement. Since they are embellishment first and faithful representation only second, artistic licence is dictated by the necessity to show all positions as vertical. The way in which the sculptor has solved problems of form and volume in dealing with the interplay of limbs and bodies is often masterly. Some of the sculptures have a classical tenderness rather than the expressionism or symbolism associated with other 'primitive' sculpture. And there was one grave in particular where the total conception showed a complex creative vision: human couples were alternated with pairs of mating birds, the sacred ibis with their slender beaks affectionately intertwined, one pair linked by a small fish, its tail in the one beak, its head gripped by the other.

Malagasy sculptors often hand down their art, not only from father to son but also from mother to daughter. A family tree of the sculptors of Iakoro hangs in the ethnological museum in

Tananarive. But the artistic tradition is dying out, the grave sites are not protected, and not one of the magnificent grave sculptures from Morondava is preserved in a museum in Madagascar. I righted a grave-post topped by a lovely bird that was being ground to dust by the jaws of ants; there were so many others, powdering into the sand. I suppose soon the only ones left will be those that appear, mysteriously (export is forbidden) in the rich art collections of Europe and America. There was that story of the old chief at Maravoay: 'some people had sawn off figures and gone away ... '

Out of the cult of the dead, the oligarchy of the Merina, the oligarchy of the French that followed – the *lolo* of the Malagasy Republic that emerged in 1960 has had time to dry its wings in peace. President Tsiranana and his PSD (Social Democratic Party) – extremely conservative, despite the name – stay comfortably in power while on the mainland of Africa coups and counter-coups come and go. Tsiranana (of the Tsimihety tribe) and many of his top men are *côtiers*, and although they are anxious to prove that they stand for a democratic, non-tribal government and have largely succeeded, they represent the final defeat of the aristocratic Merina as well as independence of white rule. Yet the Merina with their monopoly of the capital province, their lingering caste system, their educational superiority and natural aloofness remain an overwhelming presence when you are on the island – their palace may be empty, but they *are* Madagascar as no other single element is. The French presence also remains in evidence, particularly in Tananarive: the governor's rose-coloured, tin-roofed palace becomes the French Embassy, the work of Boris Vian and Malraux being presented at the *Centre Culturel Albert Camus*, French food and wine in every restaurant (if you have to be colonised at all, how lucky to be colonised by the French). French culture 'takes', and survives political bitterness in her former colonies. Jacques Rabemananjara, Minister of Foreign Affairs, once one of the famous rebels exiled from Madagascar after the bloody 1947 uprising against France,[3] is a Malagasy poet who writes in French, just as Senghor,[4] poet and President of Senegal, belongs also to French literature. Whether due to French influence or the traditional oral culture of the Malagasy with its *ankamantatra* (riddles), *ohabolana* (proverbs), and *anatra* (good advice), often combined in short, sometimes erotic poems called *hain-teny*, Tananarive publishes more newspapers than any place I've ever been. On the Escalier de Lastelle, among the booths selling cheap sunglasses and the island's semi-precious stones, I counted fourteen Malagasy newspapers pegged up for sale round a cigarette stall; but there are, in fact, about 155, some in French, for a total population of six million people. Writing poetry seems to be a prestigious pastime; among the papers were privately-printed booklets of amateur verse with the dim picture of a bespectacled teacher or civil-servant author on the cover.

President Tsiranana, who needs only a lei round his neck to look like a welcoming Polynesian host in a travelogue, was a particularly close friend of General de Gaulle and no doubt will now embrace Pompidou as warmly. France remains the island's main source of economic aid and biggest customer for its products, mainly stimulating, nourishing, sweet or fragrant – coffee, tobacco, rice, manioc, sugar, cloves and vanilla. The United States is next best customer; the trade began in pirate days when an American buccaneer vessel introduced Malagasy rice to North Carolina. The Malagasy I talked to were disappointed at the smallness of American investment and aid, though. In five years after independence the US gave only $13 million.

The island can feed itself abundantly, but apart from nickel on the eastern side – and of course there is the inevitable oil-prospection going on – has none of the important mineral discoveries that bring the white world flying in to promote development. For this reason it is making a late and hasty entry in the Island Paradise lists, and has begun a jet service that links it with the regular tourist run down Africa. Nossi-bé, a tiny island off the north-west coast of the main one, has been decided on as the main draw outside Tananarive itself. And no wonder – you don't have to drive to get there, and a short flight lands you in a place that really does seem to have escaped debased Gauguinism. Brilliant sugar cane lying stroked back, silky, in the breeze, sudden dark walls of tropical forest, coffee bushes flowering white rosettes, ylang-ylang perfume trees weirdly espaliered, great glossy-leaved mango trees ivied with pepper vines – the whole island rustles softly and breathes sweet. The government-owned hotel in a coconut grove on one of the beaches has a tiny casino under a banana-leaf roof where you can play baccarat (why is it presumed that at the end of getting away from it all, as at the end of the rainbow, there's got to be a pot of gold?) but the real action was down the beach on Sunday morning, when two busloads of Sakalava arrived for some occasion I'm sure was more important than a mere picnic. On this shore of Madagascar, nearest to the East Coast of Africa and African and Arab influences along the ancient trade routes of the Indian Ocean, the *lamba* becomes a brilliant cotton robe worn by women – I could see the restless pollen-yellow, purple, red, orange, from afar. They wore elaborately-filamented Arab-style jewellery on ears and necks, turbans, flowers picked from the forest that shaded the edge of the sand, and some used lipstick as well as sophisticated variations of the clay-patterned maquillage I had seen down south, at Mara-voay. Drums, flutes and clappers entertained the company. They drank and ate from enormous black boarding-house pots that were then scrubbed clean in the sea by the painted ladies with their robes hitched up. The men put on smart nylon trunks from France and went in for a swim. Then the whole party was drummed, piped and clappered back into their *taxis brousse*.

At the inauguration of the Organisation of African Unity in Addis Ababa in 1963, President Tsiranana hopefully suggested that the Organisation's title should include the words 'and Malagasy' after 'African'; he was curtly told that if the Malagasy didn't consider their state African, they had no place in the Organisation at all.[5] But Merinas and *côtiers* alike, the islanders privately don't really regard themselves as Africans even now, when for political and economic reasons as well as ancient geographical ones, their destiny is lumped in along with that of the Third World. Tsiranana, in addition to his natural conservatism, fears the proximity of the Chinese-communist-controlled island of Zanzibar, and places Madagascar 'without any bad conscience' among the moderate African states in the OAU and not the revolutionary ones; but he also allows himself to have no bad conscience over the fact that the new jet service is run in collaboration with South Africa, and Madagascar is receiving trade missions from there, while the OAU condemns any contact with the country of white minority rule and colour bar. Of course, the agricultural machinery Madagascar buys from France would be so much cheaper, imported from nearby South Africa . . .

It was only in my last two hours on the island that I went up to the queen's palace that I had seen from my bathroom window in Tananarive every morning. One of those neck-dislocating rides to see the sights: here the Presidential Palace (once the Royal Prime Minister's) with its onion turrets and central glass dome of a steam-age exhibition building, there the old Royal tribunal, a Greek temple of pillars and pink stone – and then the group of strange mansions, large and small, that crowns the town and is known collectively as the *rova*. Beside the Manjakamiadana, the palace that Cameron turned to stone, is the Tranovola, the Treasury Palace, an enormous Victorian wooden doll's house, its white verandah arches of cathedral proportion, and inside, delightful naïve murals in which fruit, flowers and people's eyes have the same open gaze. Beside the Tranovola, two tiny yellow-and-green pagodas on a stone platform – the royal tombs, to which the last Queen, Ranavalona III, was brought back from her exile's grave in Algeria in 1938. *Her* palace is like a country house built by one of those decadently Europeanised Russians in Turgenev: partly English, partly Swiss cuckoo-clock, with an Italianate touch.

Hidden among the decorative and architectural mannerisms of nineteenth-century England and Europe is Andrianampoinimerina's original royal Great Place; I use the African term for a king's quarters because 'palace' is too cheaply grandiloquent for this lofty shelter with tall crossed lances at either end of its steep roof. A dwelling like a tent made of thick black wood, divided internally only by the differentiation of the hearth from the rest of the tamped-earth floor. Round the walls are his carved wooden shields, his spears and muskets, and his drinking vessels made of clay given a pewter patina with graphite.

The museum curator (we showed off to one another, agreeing that some of the palace murals were pure Douanier

Rousseau) apologised for rushing me, but there was a Japanese trade delegation in town, and she was due to escort them through the palaces any moment; they arrived just as I left, very small and neat and alert with the magpie curiosity they carry everywhere. What had they come to Madagascar to sell? What had they come to buy?

An hour later, waiting for the plane to take me away, I bought a newspaper and read an announcement that work had started in Tananarive on the Madagascar Hilton. I remembered reading how President Tsiranana had once said, expressing the detachment of the Malagasy as well as a sly dig at Africa's troubles, 'If the *Bon Dieu* proposed to me that Madagascar should be rejoined to the African continent, I would ask him to let it remain an island.'[6]

Well, we all know that no man is an island; but no island is an island, either − not now. Can't afford to be. From among the corpses and butterflies, the crook'd finger is beckoning, and sooner or later, for one reason or another the continents will close in.

Pula!

Pula. In the middle of Southern Africa there is a country whose coat-of-arms bears, instead of some Latin tag boasting power and glory, the single word: *rain.*

On the map Botswana appears as a desert big as France. And sometimes, in Botswana, looking at the figures of men, the bole of thorn-tree or palm, a single donkey, breaking the white light, it seems a vast sand-tray in which these are lead toys stuck upright. But they are rooted there. This Kalahari sand nourishes them – grasses, thorn bush, *mopane* forest, birds, beasts, and 600,000 people. They live on it, in it, and off it. In places it hardens into a crust of salt; it swallows, in the north-west, the waters of a great delta. But even the final desiccation of the south-west provides harsh sustenance for those – beasts and men – who know where to find it, and for those who know how to space their thirst, there is water if you dig for it.

A desert is a place without expectation. In Botswana there is always the possibility of rain. The hope of rain. Rain *is* hope: *pula* means fulfilment as well as rain. As a political catchword, the cry has a less muffled ring than the many variants of the word 'freedom'.

From the days of the late-nineteenth-century conquest of southern Africa by whites until 1966, Botswana was the British Protectorate of Bechuanaland and, except for parties of anthropologists for whom it was a trip back to the Stone Age culture of the Kalahari Bushmen, it meant the 'line of rail' connecting the Republic of South Africa with Rhodesia that ran up inside its border along the strip of fertile farmland settled by whites. The Line of Rail is still there, the two or three frontier towns – one street with hotel verandah and shops facing the railway station – but as a way of life it no longer sums up the country, only the colonial past. Botswana's railway was – and is – owned and operated by a neighbouring country, Rhodesia,[2] and Botswana's capital was until recently a town just outside its borders, in South Africa.[3] The brand new capital, Gaborone, is only just inside; the pull of economic gravity remains unavoidably towards the south, where are based the international mining companies whose discoveries of copper, nickel and diamonds beneath the sand will mean, ten years from now, the doubling of the per capita income, at present on the poverty line. Gaborone is set down on the Line of Rail but not of it, complete and ready-to-use: an Independence Expo in whose pavilions, after the celebrations, people stayed on. Flag-waving consular Residences, a national museum, churches with contemporary bell-towers, the hotel/cinema/national-airline/shopping complex which even includes an American Embassy – one-stop urban civilisation. In the piazza of the shopping mall a few thorn trees have been left to assert the empty savannah outside, but the barbers, beggars and vendors of an African town are too overawed to set up business under them. Emancipated black girls drink beer among the men in a hotel bar, now, at mid-day. Out of the cheerful exchanges in the Tswana language there comes suddenly, in English, the authentic tone of Gaborone: 'I give it three years, and I buzz off.'

More than twenty years ago Seretse Khama, Chief-designate of the Bamangwato and Paramount Chief-designate of all the Botswanaian tribes, married a white girl while studying law in England and was exiled by the British colonial administration from his ancestral home in Serowe.[4] It was one of the biggest political scandals in Africa, with all the private intrigues of an African dynasty, the Khama family, to complicate the issue. Sir Seretse Khama, knighted by the British, elected by democratic vote, is now first President of Botswana; the Bamangwato remain the biggest and most distinguished tribe; Serowe remains the seat of the Khamas as well as the capital of the wealthiest province and probably the last nineteenth-century African – as opposed to colonial – town south of the equator.

In their Great Place where the Khamas lie when they die, they are not so much buried as set on final watch over the Bamangwato. You reach the Great Place by a steep walk up behind the swept, stockaded *kgotla*, the open-air tribal court and meeting-place beneath a big tree, and the silos where communal water or grain are stored. On a hill that gives out upon the whole town and beyond is a pink stone terrace of graves – the Grecian urns, marble scrolls and infant angels of 'funerary art'. The real monument is the one the earth has spouted and tumbled in an outcrop to one side, Thataganyana Rock. Little humpy *dassies* dart fussily in and out its petrified burst-bubble holes.

Thataganyana is a superb vantage-place for the living as well as the dead; we leant upon the warm wall of the terrace and looked down over the entire life of this town like no other town, a town ordered garland by garland, not in streets or blocks, loop after loop of green rubber-plant hedging circular houses grouped round cattle stockades made of stony grey tree-trunks. Far away, the square of a sports field marked in the same green, and then the fuzzy plain overlaid, by the eye, with thickness upon thickness of blond grass and grey bush until it laps a few hills, one flat-topped, that are exactly the single woolly hills drawn on ancient maps of Africa. A God's-eye view; you can also see into everyone's clay-walled, decorated backyard. A woman whirrs at her sewing machine. Gossiping men lean against walls. A baby staggers about in a G-string; an old man in a parson's black suit, with hat and stick, pays a visit. You can hear everyone's life as well: it is Saturday afternoon and those people who have decided to kill a goat, brew some maize beer and throw a party – a popular way of making money, since an entrance fee is charged – amplify African jazz above the hollow knock of wood being hewn. We stayed on while the moon came up and only the little bronze buck, symbol of the Bamangwato on top of the grave of Khama III, stood out clear. Just before the light went, a tiny girl ran from the houses and squatted to relieve herself in the security of the Great Place's shadow.

Down in Serowe in a gaunt cool house with the drinks and the guns ready on the verandah lives Sekgoma Khama, graduate of Dublin University and cousin of the President. He is a princely young man, almond-eyed and handsome, with a strangely fateful laugh — when a gun went off among us while we were jolting in a truck over the veld after eland, the bullet searing the ear of his close friend, he broke the shock with that laugh, not in callous amusement but as a kind of baring-of-teeth at the hazards of life. The hunt itself was in the nature of a quest: as Tribal Authority (the democratic title for Chief; he is acting in that capacity in place of an elder brother studying the problems of developing countries, abroad) he has the right to bag himself a single head of the rare species a season. He set off early with us among a house-party of friends — a Jamaican, an African geologist (rarer even than the eland), a pretty Swedish girl who was helping to found a cottage textile industry in the town, and a whole entourage of gun-bearers. Half an hour out of Serowe the red hartebeest with their tarnished copper coats stood, not recognising death when one among them fell, but a small herd of eland were as elusive as any unicorn. Their broad light flanks always seeming to be presenting themselves one-dimensionally, just the way they look in ancient Bushman paintings, they led us a dance from the grassland into the scrub forest, where they threaded away between screens of trees while even Sekgoma's crack shots fell short.

When his brother returns, Sekgoma Khama will take up again his full-time occupation of managing the Khama family's lands and cattle, and serving on the Land Boards that, as much as the switch to a money economy, will change the structure of Botswana society. He sees change not as abandonment but transposition of traditional institutions: cattle-as-wealth not capital — which was the basis of the economy — becomes 'a ranching operation'; the tribal monopoly of land loosens as allocation becomes a matter of applying to a government board instead of the local chiefs. He felt at home in Joyce's Dublin; lucky man, it has not made him feel any the less at home when he sits under the tree at the *kgotla*, settling some dispute among the 36,000 people of Serowe. He shows disquiet over only one thing: 'The mineral discoveries so far are all in our Central Province … it could be a delicate situation, politically …'

The Bamangwato, it seems, cannot escape being a favoured

people; for them, the cry *Pula* does not go unanswered.

Like the ownership of cattle, hunting has always been the way
of life of the people here, whereas in other parts of Africa in
colonial times it quickly became only the privilege of whites. In
a country without billboards (or even road signs) a pair of
horns on a tree marks a turn-off or the way to a cattle post, and
in every place of habitation bones and the skins of game pegged
out to dry are homely as a front garden in the context of other
lives.

In spite of this, Botswana is one of the few countries in Africa
that still has great herds of game left, not only in reserves but
living alongside men. The Kalahari, hostile to agriculture, is
what has saved the animals, and they have learned to subsist
sleek-coated through the dry months upon the heavy desert
dew condensed on tough vegetation. There is conflict now
between, on the one hand, the Government's reflection of the
Western World's concern to preserve wild life in the Third
World and, on the other, the curious unconscious alliance of
interest between the Africans who've always shot for the pot
and whites who have shot for trophies and fur coats. The
fashionable vocabulary of environmental studies is invoked
these days by people in the skin-and-bone trade. In Francistown on the Line of Rail, while walking through a 'game
industry' past mounds of lopped-off elephant feet and vats of
impala and zebra skins soaking, we were given an erudite
lecture on the ecological viability of the whole R3-million-a-
year business − indigenous people continuing to live off
indigenous animals, rather than the development of agricultural and industrial employment for the people and protection for the animals. The very balance of nature was being
preserved, our cultured white informant said, by buying from
Africans the skins of only plentiful species, and utilising every
scrap of the product − and by this time we had left the sickish
smell of the curing sheds and were in a workshop where
beautiful and noble creatures like those we had pursued on the
plain outside Serowe were emerging finally: as elephant-foot
umbrella stands, ostrich-foot lamps and zebra-skin bar stools.
In the taxidermy department, some white safari hunter's lion
was being tailored into his skin, with little strips of cosmetic

tape to hold it in place over the stuffing.

There is only one road to the west and it leads three hundred miles from Francistown to Maung, the last place on the map that signifies more than a store, a well, and a mud village. Early on the way the earth gives out, the Kalahari begins, then the road skirts the rime of the Makgadikgadi salt pans and the heads of ilala palm stand up like broken windmills. As if all their sundered parts had flown together again, we encountered along the road impala, gemsbok crowned with antennae-straight horns, kudu bulls with elaborately-turned ones, ostriches with legs like male performers in ballet drag.

Maung reached has the unreality of any oasis; no relation between the deep blue and green of the Thamalakane River shining between towering wild fig trees and the monotonous village of grey huts on endless grey sand not a hundred yards away. Riley's Hotel (the old London Missionary Society mission station converted by an Irish pioneer adventurer, now dead and legendary) and Riley's Garage are the fount: the big pub behind mosquito-screening where white-collar Africans have taken up darts among hefty white habitués, the grease pits where trucks and Land-rovers are relieved of the sand that clogs their innards. Lumbering four-wheel-drive vehicles are to Maung what ships are to a port – their image of power and freedom not only demarcates road from sand by the impress of their tracks, it also dominates the imagination of the black children: their toys are model trucks home-made of bent wire on condensed milk-tin wheels.

Walking through the village we read a 'Wanted Man' notice of a new kind. R5 reward was offered for Diphetho Monokrwa, 'last seen following a herd of buffalo'. We came upon, at nine in the morning, a party of women in Victorian dress embellished with jewellery and eastern turbans, sitting like telephone-cover dolls in the sand, making a leisurely meal of tea and porridge. Before the 1914–18 war Herero people fled from German genocide in South West Africa [Namibia]; here they live still, their extraordinary women peacocking it among the Tswana hens. These are the women who played the Lysistrata act without ever having heard of her – they refused to bear children while the men submitted to German oppression. Only that sort of female spirit could sustain a vanity colossal as this, trailing wide skirts through the sand, boned up to the throat in the heat, ironing flounces with a flat-iron filled with burning coals, creating in poverty a splendour constantly remade out of bits of what has worn out. After the meal they passed round a cup of salt and a pocket mirror; each cleaned her teeth with a beringed finger, and took a critical look at today's face.

Maung is the last place you can buy a loaf of bread for many hundreds of miles. It is also the plenitude of the Okavango delta and you can skip the desolation and fly there in a few hours to canoe and fish and bird- and game-watch. The Okavango, misnamed a swamp, is really a vast system of clear bayous created by the Okavango River and seasonal flood-waters that come down from the highlands of Angola each May. At least one of the safari camps that are setting up business has its own air-strip. Just outside the Moremi Game Reserve, in a self-styled 'game kraal'[5] built of reed and thatch to house a wealthy species of tourist, each suite has its pastel-coloured portable thunder-box and each guest his personal servant. For the hard-living Francis Macombers[6] are being replaced by wildlife worshippers, and the white hunters, pushed as far south as Botswana, have gone about as far as they can go, and many are themselves turning for survival to leading photographic safaris and mugging up ornithology to please bird-watching clients. Derek 'Kudu' Kelsey is one of the adaptable ones, as ready now to aim the amateur photographer's camera so that he may bring back the trophy picture as once the white hunter was to put his client into the position where his gun couldn't miss. But while Mr Kelsey is a perfectionist, filing the wicked cat's-nail thorn off every knob of the magnificent *mukoba* trees of his 'kraal' lest a guest might suffer so much as a scratch at Africa's hands, he retains a dash of endearingly uncalculated zaniness from wilder, colonial times. In the morning he took us by canoe expertly along the water-paths made by hippos through papyrus that lead on for many days journey up the Okavango; in the evening he appeared in dinner jacket and trousers worn above bare ankles and *veldskoen* shoes, and had arranged for 'dinner music' to be provided by the grandfathers, wives and babies of a nearby village, who sat round the fire clapping and singing their narrative chants. Later, there were dancing girls, in the form of the six- or seven-year-old daughters of the waiters, abandoning a sweet bashfulness to shake their little bodies frenziedly in grass skirts.

We bought that last bread in Maung.

Carrying our water and petrol as well as food we struck out west again, into the Kalahari. There are roads marked on the map, but a loose hank of tracks ravels the sand out of Maung and it doesn't much matter which spoor you choose, provided it fits the wheel-gauge of your vehicle, and you stick to it.

We arrived at Lake Ngami at night, put down sleeping bags on anonymous sand in an anonymous dark. Our headlights showed weirdly that the cabs of trucks had worn topiary tunnels in thick thorn trees. We didn't know which side the lake was, only that the few lights in the bush were the village of Sehithwa. One cannot always be sure if the lake will be there at all: when Livingstone saw it in 1849[7] it was seventy miles long, but there are years when it disappears altogether; it is one of the farthest points where the delta is quaffed by the desert.

This year it is there, about eight miles of it, in the morning. Like a long gleam seen between the slit of eyelids, at first. No trees on the banks; there are no banks. Sometimes for minutes, when nothing is flying, it looks empty of life. But again, from a certain angle, the skimming birds and the crenellations of the water are the same, so that the whole surface is made of grey wings. What appear to be verges of water and ooze are thousands of gliding duck, quiet and close; a white sand-bank in the distance is really solid flamingo. The bush stands withdrawn, half a mile from the water. Suddenly I see silent explosions of dust puff from it, and as I watch, herd after herd of cattle, black, russet, white, and dappled, stippled and shaded variations of these colours, burst out of the bush and advance in slow motion, because of the heavy wet sucking at their hooves, across horizontals of grass, sky and water. Herdsmen on horseback with skinny dogs pushing rodent noses into every scent ride by now and then; among all these cattle, one of the men comes up and asks me for milk. Horses, knee-deep, shake their manes like vain girls bathing. Pelicans on the water turn the lake into a child's bathtub filled with plastic toys. The flamingoes will not stir until late afternoon, when the colour under their wings as they rise seems to leak into the water like blood from a cut finger. As the day moves on heat hazes interpose – between land and water, between one layer of birds or beasts and another – new glassy surfaces of a water that isn't really there. The peace, born of the passive uncertainties of this beautiful place, one year a lake, another a dried bed of reeds! Over the trembling horizon you can just make out two nubile hills – The Breasts of The Goat. In shallow years, they say, you can drive across through the lake and pass straight between those hills. It is the way to Ghanzi, where the great cattle drives going south pass; and on, deep in the desert, to the non-places where the Bushmen withdraw from the threat of other men.

No one had been able to agree where petrol or potable water would be available on the two hundred miles to the Tsodilo Hills. But then no one had told us, either, of the existence of Marcos's bar, suddenly come upon in the ash-pale desert of Sehithwa village, where we sat disbelievingly drinking iced whisky and arguing over the mathematical problem in a correspondence study course the young village barman was following.

Villages were more austere even than uninhabited stretches, scoured down to shadeless mud houses, a single store, in an emptiness cleared of thorn by the appetites of goats and the need for fuel. Austere but not desolate: the store was always full of people buying scoops of sugar and maize meal before wire-netted shelves offering blood tonics and gilt ear-rings, and racks where dusty dresses were chained together. There was no green thing to buy; only the chestnut-shiny fruit of the ilala palm, arranged in frugal pyramids on the sand. When I ate an orange from our supplies, I found myself tasting each suck and morsel down to the pith; the bright skin cast away was an extravagance of fragrance and colour.

The road as a total experience filled each mile and hour, whether you were the one swirling the wheel in split-second decisions and slamming to lower and lower gear, or were simply bent on keeping your balance in the passenger seat. In parts the sand was bottomless, bedrock-less: pits covered with broken thorn and branches looked to be and were traps — the wheels of other vehicles had dug them. The company of the road was that of the marooned: great trucks beached, helpless, their passengers philosophically brewing tea and suckling nfants in their shade. The code of the road, quite apart from its condition, made it impossible to say when you could hope to reach where, for you stopped to help, whether with water and cigarettes, or a tow-rope and whatever heaving man-power you could muster. There is a bush *panache* about the way the Batswana set out over this desert of theirs without a pump or spare wheel, calmly doubling up the human burdens of one truck upon another as they break down.

It becomes true that it is the journey and not the arrival that matters; we forgot we had a destination. Yet at the village of Sepopa we picked up a guide from the headman and were told there were only fifty miles more to go. An unidentified track turned off abruptly left, from nowhere to nowhere. For miles we found ourselves displaced, out of Africa, still lurching over sand, yes, but through a European beechwood, flaming with autumn — we were in a *mopane* forest. Behind it, the first sight of a hazy blue back; and then, as the forest thinned on to a pale plain, a whale-shaped hill came out of the bush, the Male hill of the Tsodilo.

The Tsodilo are called hills but whether a mountain is a mountain or a hill a hill is not a matter of height but presence. After hundreds of miles of the horizontals of sand, that mastodon of rock is the presence of a mountain; and the emotion one feels standing in the cold dark shadow it casts across the afternoon is the uneasy one engendered by the primeval authority of a mountain. Behind Male is Female hill, the sheer and fall of soft chalky colours, stone flanks that are olive, rose, smoke-mauve, and behind her are a series of hidden amphitheatres, bays of heat and quiet. And as you climb in the last real luxury left, a boundless silence, years thick, you come with a strange contraction of perception upon paintings made upon the rock. It is as if, out of that silence, this place speaks. There are rhinoceros, zebra; on an umber battlement — quite clear of surrounding blocks of rock spangled with livid fish-scales of lichen — an eland and giraffe. In a cool cleft we lay on our backs (as the artist must have done, at work) to see a line of dancing men with innocent erect penises that have no erotic significance and persist as a permanent feature of Bushman anatomy, even to-day. Among the animals, schematic drawings and men, there were terracotta imprints of the hands of the artists, or perhaps of others, less talented, who wanted to assert their presence. They were the size of a child's hand; inevitably, I measured mine against them, clumsily touching across the past. Nobody knows exactly how old these Bushman paintings are, but the Bushmen have wandered this part of Africa for a thousand years and the surviving ones have long lost the art and have not been known to paint within living memory. The paintings were discovered to the world only in the 1950s; new ones are found by anyone who has a few days to spend looking. But very few people have seen even those that are known; by August, we were only the eighth group of travellers to come to Tsodilo that year.

There was a village of twenty-five or thirty people just beyond the reach of the afternoon shadow of the Male hill of Tsodilo. They were a little clan of Mbukushu, the home of whose creation-myth the Tsodilo Hills are. *Nyambi* (God) let people and animals down to earth from heaven on a rope to the Tsodilo, and so the world began.

We went over to visit with our guide, who had a letter for one of the villagers. Beyond Maung there are no post offices and a letter will be carried by whatever truck happens to be making for a point nearest its destination. No one in the village could read; the old woman for whom the letter was intended handed it back to our guide and settled on her haunches to listen while he read aloud to her. It was from her son, working on a gold mine near Johannesburg, more than a thousand miles away in the Republic of South Africa. Our guide had also, as a young man, been far away to the mines; one of the changes that Sir Seretse Khama's government is most determined on is the end of Botswana's necessity to export her men as contract labour, but the experience of going to the mines is one that has entered profoundly into remote lives and changed forever ancient patterns of existence – that is the furthest reach, in consequence far beyond its military might, of the White South. The letter from the mines was read through again so that — one could see the vivid concentration of response wincing across the old woman's face — she would remember it precisely as if she could refer to the text.

Meanwhile, the women and children had gathered and I had doled out the remains of a packet of sweets I happened to have. Not enough to go round; but the asceticism bred of a begrudging environment has its own pleasures. These babies who never get sweetmeats exhibited the very opposite of lust for them. One sweet fed four, scrupulously divided from mouth to mouth. The wrapping paper was sucked. Fingers were licked so lingeringly that the pinkish-brown skin came through the dirt. A young Tannekwe Bushman girl and her small brother got their share — a shy yellow pair with oriental eyes and nostrils delicate as shells. They were probably the children of a family enslaved by the Mbukushu.

The black, round, pretty Mbukushu mothers had a queen among them, standing tall and a little apart, with a turned-down amusement on her sardonic mouth. She perversely wore an old striped towel half-concealing her kilt of handmade ostrich shell beads and hide thongs, and her long legs with their calf-bracelets of copper and hide, but her slender, male youth's shoulders and the flat breasts her body seemed almost to disdain, the assertion of her long neck and shaven head, resolved all aesthetic contradictions. The prow of Male hill rose behind her. Sometimes one comes across a creature, human or animal, who expresses that place in which it has its being, and no other. In the Kalahari, she of the Mbukushu was such a one.

When her ancestors migrated from the north in the early nineteenth century they gained among the Tswana tribes the reputation of great rainmakers. They practised human sacrifice to make rain; today rainmaking is being replaced by water conservation schemes, such as the Shashe River one in the south, and plans to water the desert from the Okavango, but the Mbukushu still speak for Botswana when their rainmaker asks of *Nyambi*, in the old formula: 'Do not make too much lightning; just give us quiet water so that we can have food.'

Merci Dieu, It Changes

Ghana five years after Nkrumah.[2] I didn't ever see it in his time, but his presence has been so omnipresent in the consciousness of contemporary Africa that one approaches – at last – the physical reality of Accra in terms of a place where he once was. Black Star Square. The first of those vast independence celebration stadia that were built in country after country, and now stand, grandiose and deserted, eternally gouged of an occasion whose historical immensity, of course, can never come again. This one is backed by the huge rough seas that ride up the coast of West Africa. The empty arena looks lonely as power is supposed to be. The famous statue of Osagyefo[3] isn't there; some harmless Unknown Soldier enthroned in its place. What about the victims, said to be Nkrumah's sacrifices to witchcraft, supposed to be buried there? Did they dig them up for decent burial, after the coup? Did they dig anyway, and find nothing? Is that what such legends are: the same nothingness, whether filled by the malice of white foreigners branding Africa eternally savage, or by the projected fears of bewildered Africans themselves?

Going about the town, every day I pass Flagstaff House (army headquarters), the broadcasting station, and police headquarters. Colonial-looking entrances with white walls, flags, sentry-boxes, and that ivy of Africa, splurgy bougainvillea, lounging over all. But it was here the coup took place, the young Major Afrifa and his soldiers marched in, those in power fired back or escaped out of windows, there was a few days' confusion, a little blood, and it was done.

The airport is renamed after Colonel Emmanuel Kotoka, a maker of the coup and victim of an abortive counter-coup a year later – he was taken there and shot. Accra is a lusty warren where the pressure of humanity overruns mere bricks and mortar and one hardly notices the buildings whose batteredness certainly predates the coup, but here and there are nameless edifices in Independence baroque whose expanse has no life behind it. In one, a window open, a piece of clothing hung out to dry; someone is perhaps camping within the shell. This was once the headquarters of the powerful United Ghana Farmers' Council, which, along with the women's movement, became the only expression of the people's will — and it seems he made sure their will was his — Nkrumah consulted once he had become both the Head of State and chief executive, Life Chairman and General Secretary of the governing Convention People's Party, and no longer even held party congresses. Other landmarks interest me in a detached way; this one stops me short, with a private melancholy. There are so few African countries where the people who live off the land become a power and have a real say in the direction of government policy: it was a noble beginning, even if it went badly wrong, this time. I want to accost someone, anyone, in the street and tell him: as a Ghanaian, as an African, it must be tried again. And again and again.

But to be white in the streets of Accra is to feel oneself curiously anonymous and almost invisible; one is aware of one's unimportance, in terms of what a white face has meant and now means to people. To be white is to have been rendered harmless: a rather pathetic centuries-old monster the source of whose power-myth has been revealed to be mumbo-jumbo.

Tema is a Sunday drive up the coast from Accra. It's Nkrumah's city in the way that a city is the possession of the man who has a beautiful scale model, tall buildings, perfect cloverleaf flyovers, miniature trees and gardens, cars and people — just as if it were real. Nkrumah must have had such a model somewhere in Christiansborg Castle. The half-realisation of Tema — the city has never been completed — shows that it would have been like all those Brasilias that have to go through a process of attrition by humans, in accordance with obstinate local styles of life that keep making nonsense of 'international' architecture. Meccano giants step up at every change of the car's perspective. They climb down to the port, carrying power from the Akosombo Dam — in terms of surface, the biggest man-made lake in the world — to the Kaiser aluminium smelter. From a long green plain away, industrial towers proclaim a new faith in place of the single steeple among the huts that used to proclaim that other white man's religion in African towns. The splendid roads loop and bend according to plan, but often debouch into a bank of weeds. There is a slope covered with good neat houses; against the walls of the refinery a shanty town made with packing cases has cooking fires smoking away – that's underdevelopment, it's a way of life dictated by necessity and as difficult to put an end to as to put out the grass fires that burn up Africa.

The famous deep-water harbour is very fine, with every bolt on its straddling cranes carefully vaselined against rust, but there are few ships and no one about, the quays so neat that I notice some spilt peanuts as the only evidence of cargo. Perhaps it's because it's Sunday; the figures show that Tema handles more traffic than the old harbour of Takoradi. As for the aluminium smelter, the government would like the American consortium to finance the exploitation of local, if low-grade, bauxite deposits at Kibi, instead of using raw material brought in by Kaiser from Jamaica and Australia. That's the present situation – a variation of but hardly emancipation from the colonial role in which Africa produced the raw materials and the processing into profitable finished products was the preserve of others.

On the way back to Accra, I drive down to the promontory where Christiansborg Castle has stood for three centuries. Blinding white, looking through palm trees at the sea, it appears Arab rather than Danish. If what one can see *is* the castle at all; it has been much built around and to various purposes through various occupancies. Now it is nobody's castle, an administrative block. You cannot enter, but you can walk round part of the thick white walls with stopped-up cannon in their embrasures. Nkrumah, whose palace this became, passed through this gateway in state one day and did not dream he would not come back. Following the walls towards the sea, I suddenly find a grave. Dr W. E. B. DuBois, American Negro, father of Pan-Africanism, came home from his race's long exile from Africa to die, and he lies here forever.[4]

Peace to the huts; war on the palaces.

The pennant that is hoisted over every revolution and every coup. Nkrumah spent £8 million to build State House for an eight-day OAU conference. When he left for Peking and Hanoi on his last journey as President of Ghana, he took £45,000 of the £51,000 left in the state treasury. The present regime, avowed as well as forced to economy by Ghana's national debt — estimated at $850 million — has been able to build no road or bridge since 1967. While I was in Accra there was a strike of sanitary workers because they had not been issued with gloves and protective clothing, and when some formality took me to a local police station, I saw that the policemen did not have complete uniforms, either. One of the issues taken up by a fiery little Accra newssheet, the *Spokesman*, was the elaborate house being built by President Kofi Busia[5] in his home village. While lack of foreign exchange means that all sorts of essential imports must be forgone, thousands of cedis worth of luxury fittings and material for Dr Busia's house are being imported. It is no State House or Christiansborg, yet certainly it will be a palace in comparison with the yards of Accra, where children, chickens and rubble seem awash on open drains, and people are paying 20 pesewas (100 pesewas to the cedi; the cedi worth roughly a dollar) for two plantain bananas.

Although the government has just published a pamphlet on the subject of President Busia's willingness to open a dialogue with South Africa, stressing that the Ghanaian stand differed from that of the other main supporter of dialogue, the Ivory Coast, in that Ghana intended to continue to support the Liberation Movements at the same time, most people seemed more embarrassed than anything else by the idea of the first of the independent black states talking to one of the last strongholds of white power. The issue that was preoccupying the press in general and the members of the Opposition party was the government's proposal to change the chairmanship of the Regional Councils from an elected to a government-appointed position. Nkrumah abolished the Regional Councils; they have been reinstated and are the most important move, outside free elections, away from wholly centralised power and back to genuine contact with the needs and wishes of ordinary people.

Of course, the very fact that there is an Opposition to walk out of the House in protest over such matters, and a *Spokesman* exists to attack the nature of the asceticism of Dr Busia's regime, says something for that regime. As another visiting foreigner remarked to me – 'At least no one's in jail.' There are no political prisoners.

The faces in public office, like the façades of the buildings stripped of their original designation, carry still the Nkrumah image, in reverse. They are almost all men whom he denounced and discarded; the pedigree for high position is exile or imprisonment under Nkrumah. But the faces of the junta which ruled the country from 1966 to the first post-coup elections in 1969 are strikingly absent. Members of both the government and Opposition are vague about the present activities of these army (and police-) men, and meet stiffly the reasonable question: why has none of them come forward to serve, in politics, as a civilian?

So far as I could gather, all have relinquished their army careers. Ex-Colonel Afrifa is running that old West African money-maker, a transport business; nobody seemed to know what General Ankrah himself was doing these days, and at least one dignitary said with asperity that he didn't care, either. 'They promised to hand over to civilian government after a specified time, and they had to keep that promise.' Only Afrifa, under forty, had gone so far as to remark that the provision that the new president of Ghana must be over forty was an insult to the youth of the country; interpret that as frustrated political ambition of the highest order, if you like.

Everyone has heard of the mammy wagons of Ghana, a chaotic unscheduled bus service that gets people dangerously where they want to go without the dreary queueing and frustration inseparable from ordinary bus services. Everyone knows that these trucks bear sayings or slogans. There is something evangelistic about even the most hedonistic of them, something exhortatory and moral, that suggests their original inspiration must have been missionary: those texts on love or sin chalked on boards outside churches. What I didn't know before I went there was that Ghana taxis have their statements, too, in the form of stickers on the dashboards. One gets into the habit of looking for omens – a private text-for-the-day, a warning? – as one moves around in Accra. Perhaps there will be a message to be interpreted only by oneself (like letting a hotel Gideon Bible fall open where it will), in the next taxi one climbs into. One afternoon there was. Just two words that were the last word on everything I had seen and heard and done. 'It changes.'

Ivory Coast from the Accra–Abidjan plane had a brocade texture, the crowns of thousands of palms in plantation pattern.

Abidjan: like all cities built on water it has the extraordinary quality of perpetually looking at itself. Even the stream of evening traffic, seen twice over from across one of the lagoons – once on the road, once reflected in the water – is hypnotic, narcissistic, silenced and calmed into a flow of liquid darkness and floating flares. Why haven't I read it was like this? I decide it is one of those places you have to go to, that perhaps really don't exist at all unless you are in them. It certainly doesn't exist in any comparison I might try.

Abidjan is full of flowers you cannot and have no wish to identify – not merely that apoplectic bougainvillea and coarse hibiscus trumpeting 'tropical paradise', but huge trees pollened with yellow and pink, and verges knee-deep in delicate lilies like just-struck match flames. There are unexpected scents; not only the whiff of 'Femme' or 'Je Reviens' from one of the passing white French ladies, but the delicious sweat of warm flowers. The highrise architecture is outstandingly imaginative, anyway, slender buildings standing on stork legs that emphasise the relation of the city to water, but the real reason why these blocks are so much more successfully rooted in their environment than is usual, is because for once the *scale* of natural growth within it matches them. There are trees, here, that are not dwarfed by a skyscraper. They look as if they had been waiting through centuries for men to learn how to build in the proportions of the tropical forest.

The hotel I live in, across the water from the city in the 'diplomatic' suburb of Cocody, has a swimming pool where wives of French businessmen spend the day watching their children; occasionally, in the outdoor bar overlooking the lagoon, a white couple entertain a rich or distinguished black man and his lady, in the way of business or diplomacy, with an air of exaggerated ease. Opposite the craftsmen's market in town, a coffee-shop-cum-bar-restaurant is filled with Frenchmen eating a businessman's lunch and reading the Paris papers, while pestering Senegalese traders, quick to recognise a tourist face among them, parade snakeskin sandals and indigo-dyed caftans along the terrace. In arcades and side-streets, Lebanese sit entombed by the rolls of wax-print cloth whose market they traditionally corner. Outside boutiques showing the current *fantaisie* of the Boulevard St Germain, black boys have their home-made stalls selling cigarettes and gum. Down in their big market Africans congregate endlessly round small purchases from the numerous petty traders, seated before a pyramid of a few tomatoes or eggs, dried fish or cola nuts, who all seem to make a living, in Africa.

In a bar where I go to escape the mid-day heat, the blonde *patronne* in hot pants and boots is making up her eyes before a mirror and the indifference of a very tall Latin wearing a handbag, while a black barman plays a worn Georges Moustaki record over and over. The tall man shoulders his handbag and leaves, and the *patronne* at once turns prettily: 'What can you do, Madame? – I love him. He's Italian, he has to go back to Rome. But when you fall in love – eh?'

Yes, Abidjan is a beautiful city. A beautiful colonial city, despite its ten-year independence.[6] With all the colonial pre-occupations, comforts and diversions. There are twice as many French here as there were before independence. In Accra *you* – the visitor – can't get a decent bottle of wine or find a taxi whose window handles aren't missing so that you can close up against the rain. But dirty Accra on a Saturday – the dinner-bells of traders ringing, the vast chatter and surge of the streets, the sense not of people on their way through the streets but of life being lived there; the bars and hotels of Accra, the female tycoons of trade and transport with flesh and finery piled up splendidly, ringed hands round glasses, voices holding forth to men puny by contrast, the dancers sauntering to the lazy pluck and thump of highlife music, the little velvety-faced tarts with narrow hands, assuming bored solitude on a bar stool or taking over the ladies' room to adjust already exquisitely-arranged turbans or hitch the angle of a breast under cloth – the

Ghanaians are living their own life and all quarters of their shabby capital are theirs. Accra belongs to them in a way that Abidjan doesn't seem to belong to the Ivoiriens.

This remains valid although in the days that follow I go to Treichville and Adjamé, the African quarters, and see for myself that the Ivoiriens are materially better off than Ghanaians. Everywhere new housing schemes have been realised, and the houses, though basic as subeconomic habitations must be, are decent and imaginative. There are schools with lacy brick walls to let in the air; and market-places covered against the sun and provided with facilities to keep them clean. These are the things that the people need; it is something of a surprise to find them here, instead of the black slums which, in Africa, usually lie behind the white men's air-conditioned shops and bars.

Ghana and the Ivory Coast started off similarly endowed with natural resources – Ghana is the biggest cocoa producer in the world, Ivory Coast the third biggest producer of coffee – and geared economically to the provision of raw materials for the industrial powers of the developed world. For the rest, the neighbours could hardly have been more different: Ghana under Nkrumah one of the most radical, the Ivory Coast under Félix Houphouët-Boigny[7] the most conservative of new African states. While Nkrumah has had his stool kicked from under him, Houphouët-Boigny, who has put down whatever discontents may have shivered from time to time across the lagoons of Abidjan, still lives in the tall pagoda-shaped residence among the palms and flowers of Cocody whose lack of any suggestion of a fortress surely reflects confidence. Ghana, the richer country to begin with, is hobbled by debt; Ivory Coast had a trade balance of 32 million Central African francs in 1969. She is the *enfant chérie* of France, showered with loans and French capital that have helped her diversify her economy, in return for President Houphouët-Boigny's loyal promotion of French influence and interests within such important groups as his Conseil d'Entente (Ivory Coast, Dahomey, Niger, Upper Volta) and ocam (Afro-Malagasy Common Organisation) all the way up to the OAU, where he leads the call for dialogue with apartheid Pretoria[8] while French arms sales to South Africa are difficult to explain away to African states.

Those African states dedicated to radical change in the life of the masses rather than broadening the base of a black élite have so far achieved less for the masses than conservative states who have been content to foster a black élite, perpetuate foreign private enterprise and foreign investment, and finance social uplift out of the fringe benefits of capitalism, so to speak. It seems ironic. But it is not conclusive. It's a blessing to be given decent sub-economic housing, schools, hospitals and markets. But will the people, particularly the people in the interior – always so different from the capital, in African countries – get any further than that, under Africanised but colonial-style capitalism? In West Africa more than 80 per cent of the people still live on the land. Will they ever be more than the beneficiaries of the charity of the élite?

There is no impudent *Spokesman* published in Abidjan; in fact, French journalists must take care, when reporting local issues to Paris, not to annoy the French government by criticising the Houphouët-Boigny regime. Apart from Houphouët-Boigny's there is a palace there, though of a curious kind – indeed, a whole 100,000-acre Versailles is under construction. The part-state, part-American-owned Hotel Ivoire, with its thousand rooms, casino, theatre and ice-skating rink, was just along the lagoon shore from my modest hotel. I wandered there one day by way of a path made by servants' and fishermen's feet, following the shore. Someone's little patch of maize was being cultivated; high grass touched my cheeks on either side. Once inside the movie-labyrinth of the hotel, I was still wandering – along soaring, carpet-muffled corridors, glass galleries, through lounges that reduce the human figure to a small stroke, past bars buried like Chinese boxes. There was a model of the total plan of which this place is only part: an 'international tourist area', 'garden city environment' for 120,000 people, that will encompass whole existing African villages for the diversion of those tourists for whom the attraction of golf clubs, convention halls and an Olympic sports centre palls. To 'see' Africa, natives and all, it will not be necessary to stir from this environment of grotesque home comforts created by the Californian architect and urban planner William Pereira and Mr Moshe Mayer, an Israeli millionaire whose family-portrait face is displayed along with a letter from President Houphouët-Boigny, welcoming the project and referring to Mr Mayer as 'my dear friend'. This part of Africa was once known as the White Man's Grave; now he sees it as his pleasure-ground. A shift in the angle of a timeless subjectivity? Hardly more, and little enough.

There are not many mammy wagons in Abidjan. Those that exist generally have no identification except their registration plates. But when I went to the bus station in Adjamé with a professor of philosophy who had sat marking *baccalauréat* papers in the open-air bar of our hotel, there was a message for me. While we talked, a mammy wagon was being loaded with passengers and bundles. It had a worn text, decorated with painted flowers, half-legible; I could just make out the words, '*Merci Dieu*'. Since I am a white South African and the professor was a black Ivoirien, it was natural that we should be discussing the idea of dialogue between our two countries. What was perhaps a little less predictable was that I was arguing against dialogue, because – as I was quick to illustrate my point – the kind of contact between two enfranchised individuals he and I were having was what was needed within my country, rather than talk between the white establishment of that country and black statesmen from other countries – and he, on the basis of how well *we* got on, if nothing else, was prepared to give dialogue a trial. Well, yes – thank heaven for small mercies, not everything is predictable in Africa these days – whatever else has happened, the old equations, the defined roles, national and personal, good and bad, are all in question.

A Vision of
Two Blood-Red Suns

(1977)[1]

Coming into the new 'black republic' of Transkei* from the
north, I was out of it again almost at once and then in again.
The road leads through an area and town 'excised' for whites.
On the map these blobs and trickles of black and white,
marking off the 87 per cent of the Republic of South Africa
reserved by 4 million whites for themselves from the 13 per cent
offered to 18 million blacks,[2] are an ethnic Rorschach test
whose logic is to be understood only by initiates of the political
ideology of apartheid; from the road, it's suddenly easy for
anyone. Passing before one's eyes, the perfect contours of vast
lands ploughed and crops reaped by machine, the barns full of
bright farming equipment, the pedigreed stock, the privacy of
trees and gardens drawn round the fine farmstead of the white
area change abruptly to the black area's uneven strips cultivated by hand-plough, the bare hills with their discs of mud
huts and squares of spiky agave enclosures for motley beasts
herded by children. The only machinery is the occasional
wrecked car, dragged off the road and picked clean.

A torch-light procession of hundreds of winter-blooming
aloes – red-flame, blue-flame, white-flame – passes a church
upon a hill in an infinity of empty hills. A range of shadows –
the Drakensberg Mountains that form Transkei's north-east
border – fades with the light that is leaving a feminine
landscape of classical curves broken here and there by ravines
intimately furred with virgin forest. Where this has been
replaced by afforestation already there is the inappropriate
European dusk gathered by Northern pine. A slope is a football
field because racing youngsters are using it for that purpose,

* Where I have used 'Transkei' – the term for the so-called 'independent homeland' –
instead of 'the Transkei' – denoting the region – it does not imply any recognition on
my part of this integral area of South Africa as a separate country.

221

and marks one of the 'rehabilitation' villages established to control landless people and soil erosion caused by random grazing: several hundred rounds of mud and thatch instead of hilltop crowns of two or three, the new tin flash of a windmill, kilometres of wire fencing. Many women carrying across their heads loads of wood twice their height, and one or two elderly men in old business suits on horseback are making their way along concourses undefined as the football field. Broad tracks made by ox-drawn sleds lead only to sources of firewood and water. For me, on the way to places with onomatopoeic names, *Tabankulu, Lusikisiki*, there is the one fierce road. Stones and ruts; no signposts. As if to confuse an invader − but the invader is merely one who doesn't know the signs of the terrain so firmly staked within the lifetime range of the people who live here that they walk alone, in the dark, old, female, as surely as and much more securely than western contemporaries find the way home from a suburban bus stop.

Great space; and human intimacy. To think one has found it even here is an illusion, so far as the sense of space is concerned. This 1976 creation of a country[3] (4.4 million hectares) larger than Switzerland is so overcrowded in terms of agricultural potential that it cannot survive unless enough industry can be established to take half the people off the land.

But the human intimacy is no illusion. These people are innocent; innocent of alienation, our crime against ourselves. One mid-day I was received in the empty round mud room that was the home of a woman so poor there were not even any of the usual home-made utensils to be seen. Her children had the peculiar, still sad air of malnutrition. She apologised with social grace for not being able to offer food to her white guests, as if home freezer supplies just happened to have run out − but no, I am projecting my own kind of situation on one I couldn't conceive of: she assumed, without loss of pride or self-respect, perfect understanding of shared circumstances. Like the majority of families, hers had no adult male living at home − the men are away working on the mines or canefields of South Africa − but three youths had dropped in to visit. She was animated and charming in her rags. The youngsters shared a cigarette rolled from a piece of newspaper none of the company could read, but tranquil communication was strongly present as the smell of grass-thatch and woodsmoke that comes from the skin and hair of these people as you sit among them.

On a mountain-top with a view no multimillionaire could secure to himself in Europe, I found three little girls alone in possession of two huts, a tethered calf, a hen-coop made of woven branches and a field where mealies had been reaped. A figure out of Grimm climbed into view with a load of wood and a bunch of wild asparagus fern she had cut to make a broom. A child ran off reverently to fetch a tin of water. The quizzically-intelligent old woman quenched her thirst: What did white people want to visit a dirty homestead like hers for? A confident, welcoming joke. To submit at her invitation to the dim, wide, conical engulfment of her hut was to find the order of good housekeeping. Apart from the grindstone and pestle for maize and the huge clay pot for brewing maize beer that are the standard furnishings, there were gourd dippers and enamel store plates; the careful luxury of a bottle of paraffin hung among the hoe and scythe hooked under the eaves of the thatch. Around one curve the base of the wall extended to make a low clay bench like a windowseat, and there were a couple of stacked carved stools: the men's side of the house. The grandmother and the children sank at once into a calm unit, close together, on the sleeping mats of the women's side. In place of the ticking of a clock, in these houses silence is the piping chip-chip of chicks whose tiny blur carries the light from the single source of the doorway as they pick grains of meal from the smooth mud-and-dung floor.

The old woman's son is on the mines; she provides and cares for the grandchildren out of her yearly R144 old age pension. What about the money her son earns? That pays taxes and supports his wife and their smallest children. A relative comes to plough the grandmother's steep field; she cultivates and harvests herself, just as she walks the mountains to fetch wood and water. The ideal love between women and children I see everywhere here — that is what it is made of: that great burden of toil. The sturdy little girls each find some surface of their grandmother's body to make tender contact with; this thin woman with the blue-black darkening of age in the wrinkles of capability is their bedrock. Grimmest facts of economic hardship are the ugly secret of such love.

The biggest contribution to the national income of Transkei is still the sale of men as migratory labourers. In the first elections that symbolised independence, 55 per cent of the people at the polls were women. After 300 years of white rule in South Africa the men of Transkei cannot earn a living at home. The land allotted them under the division of South Africa into white and black areas of occupation is not sufficient to support their families, and the cities and industries they have given their labour to build over generations, the gold and coal mines they have manned, are hundreds of kilometres from the poor portion they have been persuaded to accept of South Africa, which could not have realised its rich potential without them.

Govan Mbeki is a man of the Transkei, educated, politically capable, but not honoured by any chieftainship or cabinet appointment in the new black government. He is imprisoned for life on Robben Island off Cape Town for political activities that asserted the right of South African blacks to share non-racial government over the whole of South Africa. I keep remembering how he has written of the Transkei as a 'breeding camp' where the men come home for three months a year to procreate, in these round huts, the next generation of cheap labour for whites.[4]

The white man had hardly set his spoor of boot and wheel upon this part of Africa before visions of how to rid themselves of his overlordship began to come to the indigenous people.

A hundred and twenty years ago a black Jeanne d'Arc saw and heard the African ancestral dead. To Nongqause they foretold that if her Xhosa people gave up witchcraft, killed their cattle and razed their maize crops in sacrifice, on the 18th February 1857 two blood-red suns would rise and a hurricane would sweep the whites back into the sea by which they had come. New fields of maize and new herds of cattle would appear, and Xhosa warriors dead in frontier wars would live again.

The Xhosa were fighting a battle that could not be won. Not only was it the oxhide shield and assegai against the gun, but ultimately man's masterful technological attitude to his environment – acquired in Europe's nineteenth-century industrial revolutions – against the compact with his environment that is the ancient pastoral society's solution to the problem and mystery of our place in creation. The need of a miracle was the Xhosa reality: they did as Nongqause's vision bid.

On the 18th February 1857 the two blood-red suns did not rise, and the whites were not swept into the sea. Sixty-eight thousand Xhosas starved to death and those who survived did so by making their way to the Cape Colony to beg food and work from the white man.

In Transkei's capital, Umtata, among the rows of traders' stores and under the glass and steel mirrors of fine administrative blocks built with the South African government's money, there is a building unique in the history of all that was and is South Africa. The Cape Dutch-style colonial stateliness suggests perfectly what it was intended it should: a parliament just like the white man's. It was here that the vision of driving the white man into the sea underwent a transformation to become the constitutional vision of getting the vote and direct representation for blacks, along with whites, in the government of South Africa.[5]

In the mid-nineteenth century the British of the Cape Colony controlled the Transkei through magistracies, and blacks had a qualified vote in the Cape legislature.[6] The paring-down of the black franchise was successive until 1894, when the annexation of all chiefdoms of the Transkei to the Cape Colony was completed. Then Rhodes, the Empire-builder who wanted to see all Africa draped in the Union Jack, introduced an Act that established a system of African representation *outside* a common society of black and white.[7] A pyramid of councils, part elected, part white-government-nominated among chiefs, conveyed the Transkeians' needs to the white government; the black councillors had no powers of legislation and the government had no obligation to act on their advice.

The South Africa Act of 1909, which unified the country in the wake of the Boer War, took away from those blacks who still managed to qualify for the vote the right – never yet exercised – of electing a black to parliament.[8] While that same Act entrenched the African franchise in the Cape,[9] the long-term process was clear. In the early thirties an unqualified franchise was given to all whites; by 1936 black voters in the Cape were removed from the common voters' roll.[10] The Transkeian supreme council had moved into this elegant doll's house of power where, on a budget that ten years later did not yet amount to more than half the money spent by the South African government on printing and stationery, the council was allowed to deal only with local education, roads, agriculture, limitation of stock, and tribal law.

The quaint 'natives' parliament' was called – both institution and building – the *Bunga*, derived from a Xhosa word meaning 'a discussion'. Apart from placating chiefs for their loss of authority to white magistrates, the *Bunga* incidentally gave educated Transkeians a chance (unique for South African blacks) to learn by frustration the workings of Western government administration.

The *Bunga* asked for direct representation for blacks in the South African government year after year; at the same time, it asked for greater administrative powers within the Transkei. These aims were never accepted by the Transkeians as mutually exclusive. In the 1950s apartheid made them so. The 'self-government' the new laws prepared for applied only to the eight 'Bantustans' – nascent black statelets – of which the Transkei was one. 'Self-development' was carried out by government-appointed and even government-created chiefs (the present Prime Minister was made a Paramount Chief) functioning as 'Tribal Authorities' whose decisions could be vetoed by the white government in Pretoria.[11]

The *Bunga* as an institution dissolved itself in 1955. In 1976 the *Bunga* doll's house with its solemn panelling and gilded citations of democracy became Transkei's National Assembly, in return for the surrender of any claim for Transkeians ever to sit in the parliament of South Africa, or take any part in the central government of South Africa, where more than a third of the Transkei's people live and work.

Both private reception rooms at the Umtata Holiday Inn are called the Kaiser Matanzima Room. If this is caution, it isn't lack of imagination. Prime Minister Kaiser Matanzima gives no chances to rivals who might qualify to have their names honoured. One of the new administrative blocks is named after State President Chief Botha Sigcau, rewarded with that high office for his politically-strategic importance as Paramount Chief of the rebellious Pondo people; but President Sigcau's portrait does not hang in the Cabinet Chamber with Kaiser Matanzima's, and Matanzima has not repealed the preventive detention Act that, under South African rule, kept the leaders of the Opposition party in jail during elections for the country's first independent government. (The leader of the opposition was jailed again, by Matanzima, while I was in Transkei.) George Matanzima, Minister of Justice, now, but once struck off the lawyers' roster for professional misconduct while practising in South Africa, seems content to be the closest of siblings. The Brothers Matanzima have the same Roman senator heads. Their family name means 'strong saliva'; the taste of power turns venomous when Kaiser Matanzima attacks those who call him a stooge of the white South African government, a man who has betrayed the black man's right to share all South Africa. From time to time, venom flickers even at the government that set him up.

Kaiser Matanzima's cousin, Nelson Mandela, and his other compatriots Walter Sisulu and Govan Mbeki are serving life sentences. The constitutional vision has receded further and further. It is not difficult to see why Nongqause's vision of ridding the blacks of white overlordship would be transformed, yet again, into a third avatar. To some blacks, 13 per cent of the land seems better than nothing; a beggarly black state within South Africa could be regarded as a Trojan horse from which liberation could overrun white domination.

Matanzima is the man, as well as the opportunist, of his time. He carries within his personality the contradictions of the vision transformed. He has opted for tribal nationalism, accepted and approved apartheid; on occasion he lifts the black power fist and declares solidarity with blacks in South Africa who reject apartheid and hold out for full rights in a unitary state. He pledged he would not take independence until the South African government fulfilled Transkei's claims to additional land and guaranteed such citizenship rights as there are for blacks in South Africa to those Transkeians living and working there. He has got part of the white-owned land he

claimed – some of it as a gift of farms to the Brothers
Matanzima personally. But he has given up the right to South
African citizenship of the 1·3 million Xhosa-speaking people
who do not live in Transkei. Thousands of them were not born
in, nor have they ever seen Transkei. The language they speak
is declared by the South African government as proof of
Transkei nationality; in this way apartheid 'keeps South Africa
white' by making 'foreign' sojourners of the majority of South
Africa's urban black population. If they refuse to accept
Bantustan citizenship, they become stateless. While I was
in Transkei a vast settlement of squatters near Cape Town
was bulldozed[12] and 70 per cent of the inhabitants, Xhosa-
speaking, were ordered to go 'home' to Matanzima, who had
neither welcome, land nor work to offer them.

No foreign dignitary attended the Transkeian 'independence
celebrations' in 1976: the countries of the world have not
officially recognised the existence of this one.

The single gain Transkei made in the independence deal is
the abolition of South Africa's lower standard of schooling for
blacks.[13] A scholarly Transkeian of the missionary college old
boy network castigates UNESCO for refusing educational aid,
now: couldn't I influence *anyone* – the Americans, West
Germans – to give young Transkeians scholarships abroad?
Even Amin's Ugandans get them! 'Everyone sneers at us for
taking orders from Pretoria – why won't they help us train
people to make our independence real? Orders ... it's not true
... Well, what can we do? D'you know that the library here in
Umtata was opened to blacks only after the celebrations in '76!
We're not stooges ... we need teachers, librarians ...'

His eyes move about his government office as if to catch out a
filing cabinet listening and observing. Yet he gabbles indis-
creet asides. His son has 'disappeared'; I know what that
means? – yes, from South Africa where he was studying – fled
abroad after detention during the riots in 1976. These young
people want nothing to do with this independence ... Out in
the street he accompanies me courteously but I am merely a
presence from which his preoccupation echoes. *Pretoria*,
Pretoria, he murmurs – a ringing in his ears.

In the bar at an Umtata hotel a group of attractive black

men wearing young executive clothes meets heartily every evening: a lawyer, an insurance man, 'reps' (travelling salesmen) from South African firms, and functionaries in the paragovernmental Development Corporation, financed by South Africa. The Corporation is concerned with getting blacks into business as well as attracting white foreign industrialists by the inducement of tax remissions, no minimum wage and no trade unions. A game of cards is slapped down among the beer bottles, banter flies in a mixture of Xhosa and English, a tray of fried fish goes round in place of peanuts. The insurance man has just won his company's citation for the month's highest average of life insurance sales; the cosmetic 'rep' swaggers: 'A gold mine, I'm telling you, this country's a gold mine.'

To whom does one sell life insurance here?

To the grandmothers whose worth could not be compensated by any premium? To the men who tell me they don't know where to find the new R2·50 livestock tax payable on each head of cattle – their only capital?

In two years Umtata's population has risen from 25,000 to 31,400. Apart from imported skilled workers and administrators employed on the R20-million university, the hydroelectric scheme, the industrial and housing developments, the new affluent class is a bureaucracy and its hangers-on. R37·5 million invested in the country by South African and foreign industrialists, and R59·5 million from the South African-financed Development Corporation have provided only 12,500 jobs for Transkeians. Unless he works for the government or has the minimal education and maximum good luck to be able to take over a white store on finance borrowed from the Corporation, the Transkeian has little choice but to labour for low pay at home or hire himself out to the mines across the border.

The Umtata Town Hall clock has stopped and not even independence sets it measuring a new era. At noon by my watch old women in their tribal petticoats and turbans settled like huge black snails on their heads are watering the public gardens from cans; cheaper for the municipality than the outlay for a hose, I suppose. Life down the road at the end of York Street remains the reality of the capital for most people. Taxi drivers tout custom along the bus queues; some vodka 'rep' has been zealous: all buses bear the huge legend — SMIRNOFF, THE SPIRIT OF FREEDOM. In the market a medicine man dressed like a respectable farmer sells potions from bead-covered gourds which are his apothecary's jars, and among business women sewing braided print skirts there is one who sells teaspoons of snuff from a tin which she also uses to mark out the circumference of the women's anklets she cuts from the tubes of old tyres. And all along one side of the street are the recruiting offices, with their neat and cheerful, fresh-painted façades like white suburban houses, and their cajoling signs. The older ones tell a picture-story: assegais and shields invoking manliness, the homecoming of the beaming miner stepping off the train into a company of admiring women and children. The latest recognises that tribal black men have entered the kind of contemporary world offered them, abandoning hope of anything but money: no human beings, no smiles — a miner's helmet, shown as a cornucopia filled with notes.

In the yards of the offices are small buses and Land-rovers that pick up recruits from their villages. Men are waiting about with their cardboard suitcases and blankets. Some look very young; there is an atmosphere of detachment and silence in the stoicism of an unavoidable destination, very different from the strutting confidence of government officials running up the broad steps of new ministries, and the free-riding pleasure of the Rotary Club candidates on their nightly spree in a hotel bar their colour would have excluded them from in South Africa.

'If I were to get a telex from Johannesburg asking me to send a thousand men this week, I'd have no difficulty.' The white recruiting officer for South Africa's biggest gold-mining company, a group of coal mines, a construction company and a sugarcane growers' association, says that more men than ever are prepared to go off for a nine-month stint as a contract labourer. Black miners' wages have been raised considerably lately; but the wage gap between white and black average monthly earnings on the mines continues to grow — at present it is a staggering R700 in favour of whites. Blacks are housed in barracks and nutritiously fed, free, as units of labour, in the interests of efficiency that take no account of further, human needs.

In most old trading villages there are no whites now except those left behind under marble angels in the abandoned European cemeteries (the Xhosas mourn elaborately but plough and plant over their last season's dead). The trading stores, the butchery and the single hotel have all been taken over by blacks, and so have the recruiting concessions that used to be as much part of the white trader's turnover as the sale of sugar and blankets. In one of these villages I watched young black men in ear-rings, sniffing and hawking against the early morning cold, led into the magistrate's office by the local recruiting agent – a brisk black girl loud on platform shoes. The magistrate read to forlorn closed faces the terms of the agreement whereby they would go to the mines; the men touched a clerk's ballpoint in symbol of the illiterate's signature to the document. The girl wrote bus and rail passes for the journey. They were led out, launched on their career in a place where they are not permitted to stay longer than nine months at a stretch, and are forbidden to have wife, child or family come to live and make a home with them.

The Transkeians are people of twelve tribal clusters, each with its strong sense of identity and named terrain, although they all speak Xhosa dialects.

In the 1880s Pondoland was still an independent country governed by its own chiefs when a colonising party of Germans from South West Africa (Namibia) – then already annexed by Kaiser Wilhelm I – landed on its wild coast and obtained grandiose concessions for mineral and commercial exploitation from an ancestor of the present President of the Republic of Transkei, Chief Botha Sigcau. In return, two sons of the tribe were taken to Germany to be educated. It would have been a good bargain for the Germans if the British had not ridden in to remind the Pondos, with a military escort, that Pondoland had *already* been given away – to the British, by Sigcau's father. The Germans left; no one can tell me if the two young Pondos achieved their *Abitur*.

Pondoland was the last Transkeian territory to come under white rule and it seems it will be the last to accept the apartheid dispensation of independence. In the fifties at a meeting called to persuade Pondos to accept 'Tribal Authorities' as a form of self-government, a man literally turned his backside to Botha Sigcau, its protagonist-in-office, and was cheered: *Umasiziphathe uya Kusubenza sifile* — Bantu (tribal) authorities will operate over our dead bodies!

They did. A vast popular movement of resistance arose in Pondoland in 1960, concurrent with the general uprisings in South Africa that culminated in the police massacre of blacks at Sharpeville. Thousands of Pondos came down from their mountains on foot and horseback to demand, among other things, the removal of Paramount Chief Botha Sigcau. Tanks and guns from South Africa met them. Thirty Pondos died for their part in the revolt, 4,769 were held in preventive detention.

All this is not entirely in the past. Everywhere, burnt-out huts, baked to rough pottery by fire, stand among occupied ones: oh yes, I am told, it happened last year, in 'the fighting'. Vendettas between chiefs and their people opened during the revolt continue, in forms dictated by the new status of the country. Every time the subject of the new livestock tax is mentioned there is, in the company of ordinary men smoking their pipes and women sorting grain from grit for the next meal, a flash of resistance taken for granted — 'No one will pay.' An interpreter extrapolates: 'They want to kill Sigcau.'

If it's true it would not be the first time he has had to flee for his life in this exalted landscape. Pondoland is at once peaceful and dramatic beyond reconciliation. On high terrible roads you move through the sky by way of mountains that set you down only when they reach the sea. Looking from mountains on to mountains: dark ploughed land cast like nets, there; velour of light on contours of rose, blond and bronze grasses. Where the grass has been burnt, coal-blue shapes; where the first rains have fallen on these, stains of livid growth spread as the shadows of the clouds do. The lovely chimera's torso of the earth reclining; black, gold, brown, green markings of its pelt; and down into the broad flow of a valley that is scratched by reaped mealie fields where red cattle are stumbling, the great paws of mountains stretch and flex. Rivers searching through to the sea are too far below to be heard. They disappear for kilometres behind mammoth slopes; suddenly, when it is almost night, shine up from the dark clutches of the land.

The Pondos seem always to be seen in silhouette against the sky. At a high snake-bend near the Umzintlava River, young men are come upon, gathered on a rock. Behind them valleys fall sheer and they live somewhere in what, to them, is the neighbourhood: this or that mountain-top group of blind-backed huts whose doors – and windows, if they have any – all face the same way, not at some town-planner's dictate, but out of the older logic that a habitation must turn its back to the direction from which bad weather blows. Goats are shaking out their cries across space. There's a tiny store balanced near by but nobody is buying. The young men are not going anywhere. They are merely out to be appreciated by each other and anyone else who comes along. My inventory of what they were wearing will be extraordinary but there is nothing outlandish about it, here. Not only because this is as much local men's gear as blue jeans and T-shirts are elsewhere in the world, but also because Pondos have mastered an esoteric law of aesthetics, along with dandies and Dadaists – style is a combination of incongruities.

They wear some of the endless varieties of headgear devised among Transkeian men and women – a striped towel can be as intricate and dashing as a piece of hand-beaded cloth or a beaded diadem and locks. They wear long skirts not stitched but draped skin-tight. Their midriffs are bare and suck in and out with sexually self-confident male laughter. All carry knob-kerries (home-carved truncheons) and the pointed staffs that are a thinly-disguised substitute for the spear of warrior days, and still can and do kill, if used in anger. One has glittering expanding watchstraps all up his slim black arms; another wears dangling ear-rings. All wear golfer's sleeveless cardigans with the air of starting a fashion. One has a flowered tablecloth knotted nonchalantly round the wrist of the hand he gestures with, and when the sun goes down he flounces the cloth loose and it becomes a cloak arranged to fall in Grecian folds from his shoulders. It's taken his fancy to carry a child's plastic handbag. No matter. What is tribal dress? Something in a constant state of change since Africans began to wear anything. A plastic handbag is no more inauthentic than a turban introduced by Arab slavers. You just have to know how to make it your style.

These young men have the Vogue model's saunter. But names of mines they have worked in come quickly to their tongues: Stilfontein, Grootfontein, Durban Deep. On their mountain-top *piazza* it is difficult to imagine, crouched under a weeping rockface, enclosed in dank dark with several kilometres of earth above them, their steel-helmeted heads.

The centres from which life is ordered for the people living in the round huts that seem to have come spinning to rest, like counters in a game, everywhere round the mountains, are not made out at first sight. But each airy community has its chief's Great Place. The weekly court is in session in one. Horses are tied in the traditional clearing under trees which was the original form of an African court where chief and tribal elders deliberated; there is a little schoolhouse-type building, broken panes patched with cardboard, an assembly squeezed close on benches and the floor, the well of the court demarcated by a barrier and witness stands of imposing carved wooden solidity certainly representing the justice of the early British magistracy.

The prosecutor is the only fat man I encounter in the Transkei, a black Orson Welles, skilled in sarcastic showmanship. Before the court are two striped blankets. The case is a charge of adultery, and these the husband's evidence that another man came to sleep with his wife and forgot his blankets when he left. The tribal elders of the jury pass remarks about the cuckold that need no translating. When the next case is called I find that the composed, handsome woman whose Maillol feet beside mine jingle columns of brass anklets, whose profile and long hair braided with clay and beads I have been aware of close to mine, is the plaintiff in a divorce. Her husband up in the dock is much older, with irritable veins raised in sunken temples. The jury take snuff and go in and out as their attention waxes or wanes. The young magistrate in sports jacket and shined shoes – a Tribal Authority appointee – who takes down his own court record in longhand, asks how many children the couple have. The woman says ten. The husband: 'I see eleven.' Her blanket hides that evidence. Now I understand the secret source of her confidence; a woman with a lover. She is unembarrassed and unrepentant. The husband wants her back to take care of the children, anyway. Her brother is there to tell the court that not only will she not return but the husband must pay her family a debt of bride-price still outstanding.

Now a witch-doctor takes the stand. Barefoot, a dark raincoat; and all I can detect that is not entirely unremarkable in this face is deviousness. He claims he cured an epileptic child by a herbal inhalation and cuts in the skin, and was not paid the cow that was his fee. He has a shrewd, loyal, consciously modest wife who knows how to please the court but then contradicts a vital piece of evidence and loses her husband's case for him.

Lawyers are not allowed to plead in a chief's court and criminal cases are heard in the common law courts in trading towns. In this Great Place a one-eyed headman prods witnesses to attention with either malice or humour — he has a different expression on each side of his face, and it depends from which side I see him. The reason why the prosecutor is so well-fed may be because people holding this position, I am told, can 'arrange' a verdict at a price. Yet for me something of the intangible truth about our lies has been arrived at in his cross-examination...

The sea into which the Xhosa's ancestral dead promised whites and their world would be swept is the southern boundary of Transkei. A long coastline has at every river-mouth a small resort created by the patronage of ordinary middle-class white South Africans who enjoy the luxury of nature not yet polluted by themselves.

The bungalow hotel at Umngazi River Mouth has been taken over by the Transkei Development Corporation, but it employs a white manager, and for the time being the habitué bird-watchers and fishermen still come. The dining-room walls are collages of glued paper fish recording catches. Oysters are 60c a dozen. You sleep in a thatched hut and don't need to lock the door for fear of any intruder, yet you have a private bathroom. The rush-hour heard in the night is the splendid traffic of the Indian Ocean tide coming in. The pure, single sound at the bottom of the well of sleep at dawn is the ferryman's oar-locks as he rows to work from across the wide Umngazi; he will take hotel guests back and forth to the beach at their pleasure throughout the day. Like him, all the people who work as hotel servants come from the village on the hills on the other bank of the river. White resort and black village face each other. Sitting on the hotel terrace under coral-branch flowers of great erythrina trees people drink beer and follow without moving, like an idle tune they don't know their fingers are drumming, the rhythm of other lives, over there; the procession of bowed oxen under the whip of the boy taking the three-cornered sled to gather fuel from the beaches' sculpture-galleries of driftwood; the women setting out and trailing back with on their heads the sacks of mussels, black as their wet legs, that change their gait. At night, dart games and after-dinner liqueurs in the bar; crowns of fire are suspended in the thick darkness – over there, the people are burning their steep pasture.

I went across with the hotel's night-watchman going home in the early morning. Kingfishers squabbled a cock-fight in mid-air and the tide was so far out the huge Indian Ocean rollers were the sea's horizon, smoking like a waterfall. It was a long walk to his house in the village; over riverain fields, then through a forest of yellow-wood and milk-wood trees laced by butterflies, up a path it would have been easier to swing through, from branch to branch. Mussel shells littered the way like peanut husks cast by people nibbling while they walk. Friends of the watchman caught up with us; I was reminded that all my life, in Africa, has been lived among people who apologise when you trip and stumble.

The watchman's family was not put out by the early intrusion of a stranger. Always the same question: From *Egoli*? – 'place of gold', Johannesburg's African name, but to Trans-keians it means the gold mines, anywhere over the border. The hut door is open before the black pigs belching by, the tattered dogs still stiff from the night's cold; it breathes quiet smoke. Inside, two women, both young and beautiful, are suckling babies – his wives. His mother, another one of those spare, authoritative old women who never give up the femininity of some adornment, sups tea from a saucer and the young mothers sip theirs slowly above the babies' heads. There is no food set out. No furniture in the hut except an iron bedstead and a small kitchen dresser, made of boxwood in crude imitation of one someone has seen in a white man's house. The wood fire that never quite dies in the shallow hearth round which everyone centres, smells sweet. A day has begun in poverty, without the alarm clock, radio, coffee and eggs, commuter's train that doesn't wait. It won't do to romanticise, but there is something here I have to formulate for myself: respect and wholeness. The watchman takes out a very small mandarin (he must have filched it from the hotel garden) and presents it to his elder child. The tiny fruit is brilliant and luxurious, in this house.

About 27,000 new jobs a year have to be found for Transkeians. Agriculturally, there are two irrigation schemes under way which could help to feed the people a little better, but there will be no surplus for export. Unless traces of nickel, copper and platinum, of which geologists so far have no great hopes, turn out to be extensive deposits, the region has none of the primary products the world needs. Coffee, tea, pyrethrum, nuts – beginning to be grown and processed under state schemes – and forestry with its corollary development of sawmills and furniture factories, provide an opening into modern productive activity that has some relation to what the country has and the people know. Most of the new factories in Butterworth, the nineteenth-century town designated the most important 'growth point' for the establishment of industry, have no relation at all. Factories owned by South African industrialists manufacture products such as those derived from coal, rubber and plastics imported duty-free from South Africa under conditions of a new domestic colonialism. These plants have their cut-rate workers living literally outside their gates; row upon interchangeable row of identical brick cabins in barrack formation without any architectural reference-points to community – add or subtract a row here or there, nothing would be noticed. I recognise the model at once: Soweto, the dreary paradigm of black segregated townships in South Africa. With all the world's experience of humanising low-cost housing at their planners' disposal, Transkeians are passing from their round thatched huts to this.

In the end, you have to look for people in their times of release
— festivity or sorrow — in order to approach their identity with
yourself. It comes while you stand back from the mystery of
exotic mores: rooted, like your own, in myths without which
the inevitable progression from birth to death would be a
chain-gang of mortality.

The people of the Transkei do not debar an outsider from
places where their ceremonial rites still heavily underscore
adaptation to those of church, court, and industrialisation. In
the dimness of huts, I had made out the Cross painted or the
miner's badge nailed on the wall; but there were also circumci-
sion retreats all over the countryside if one knew how to recognise the sign, a ragged yellow flag on a stick. I was allowed to
enter one in Bomvanaland, although only mature men and
pre-pubertal girls may visit the initiates who, for three months
after being ritually circumcised, are isolated there; as a white
woman whose sexuality is not codified under the same sanc-
tions as blacks, I was to all intents unsexed, I suppose.

Two men rolled in blankets smoking at the roadside were
doing their shift of the twenty-four-hour vigil kept over the
retreat. The hills they led the way into on foot showed no
human being or house; then there, in a groin of forest where I
guessed there would be a hidden stream, there was also hidden
a large, blind, woven grass hemisphere at the bottom of a clearing ringed by stakes fluttering scraps of coloured rag and
plastic. There was something quietening about crossing that
symbolic boundary. But from the lair of contorted trees their
movements over months had hollowed out, three or four young
men burst, sociably painting their faces with the gestures of
women and actors. The cosmetic was *ngceke*, ground from a
chalky white stone and mixed with water from the stream in
the little gourd each wore dangling braceleted from his wrist.
Each clutched a drab blanket around himself against the wind.
There is nothing much to do all day for three months except
keep repairing this make-up of white that covers the whole
body from head to toe, as well as the face. The feminine gestures and the rough fooling-around and showing-off of any
group of young males were confusing — an atmosphere of a

harem and army camp, combined and yet out of place in this context for which I had no precedent or name.

Inside the grass shelter (not a hut or house; its feeling was unlike that of any habitation I have known) the frivolous mood fell away with the blankets discarded. These beings were naked except for the paint and a little sheath over the tip of the penis from which a long straw tassel hung stroking thighs as they moved. White lips made for oracles and the liquid dark of eyes, eyes so movingly, overwhelmingly alive in ghostliness and gloom suddenly asserted the yearning faculties of communication and comprehension – spirit and mind glowing against the presence dominated by bodies. If I was not a woman, among them, we were so fully human, there together.

Four of the eight young men had already been to the mines. They lay on the primitive shelf of branches that had been their communal bed for many weeks; there was a log to which they bent to light cigarettes; the fighting-sticks that recall old conflicts and the cursed-at dogs who have been companions through them all. No other possessions. Nothing in this straw cave but the shadows, in these beings' minds, of the world outside they will emerge into when their time is up and they wash off the white paint and burn, with the straw, the era before they were qualified to enter into the fullness of life, as men. What is that going to mean, what will be open to them in the third avatar of Nongqause's vision?

Living in the
Interregnum

The Unkillable Word

(1980)[1]

Both this and the following essay concern censorship, and some explanation of the new circumstances applying when they were written is in order.[2] In 1974 the Publications and Entertainments Act (which Gordimer had attacked in 'Censored, Banned, Gagged') was replaced by the Publications Act. This set up a tripartite structure as far as censorship was concerned. A Directorate of Publications would administer the system as a whole; committees appointed by the Directorate would consider publications submitted to them; and there was an Appeal Board which would deal with challenges regarding any particular decision. Anyone could submit a publication to the Directorate for consideration, but the right of appeal was limited to those with a financial interest in the publication; the person or body who submitted it in the first place (usually the police); and the Directorate itself. The right of appeal to the Supreme Court (explained by Gordimer in 'Censored, Banned, Gagged') was abolished.

It might not have been expected that the Directorate would appeal against the decisions of its own committees, but in fact this began to happen, and Gordimer was the first writer to undergo this extraordinary experience. In June 1979 Burger's Daughter *was published in England. By the end of that month it was embargoed in South Africa, and on 11 July banned by a censorship committee. There was widespread international publicity and Gordimer received letters of concern and protest from leading writers the world over. In August the Director of Publications appealed against the decision of his committee, not giving any reason for the appeal, though this was required by law. A special committee of literary experts as well as an expert on state security was appointed to report on the novel to the Publications Appeal Board. The state security expert found there was no threat to the state from the novel. The literary experts concluded that the original censorship committee, in banning the book, stood 'convicted of bias, prejudice, and literary incompetence. It has not read accurately, it has severely distorted by quoting extensively out of context, it has not considered the work as a literary work deserves to be considered, and it has directly, and by implication, smeared the authoress (sic).'3 Nadine Gordimer maintained that the decisions of all these committees were a matter of indifference to her, since they were all involved in the censorship system.*

Soon after, other books were 'reinstated' in this way, including André Brink's A Dry White Season,4 *while Etienne le Roux's publishers appealed successfully against the banning of his Afrikaans novel,* Magersfontein, O Magersfontein!5 *In April 1980 Gordimer was awarded the CNA Prize (one of South Africa's top literary awards) for* Burger's Daughter. *At the dinner at which the award was made she took the opportunity to take some sweet revenge on a system which had dealt so viciously with her novel. Her speech — given here — must have had some effect: one honoured guest left the main table 'visibly irate'.6*

The organisers of the CNA Award have honoured me with a large gathering at this dinner. So many faces I recognise — but there is one I don't seem to find.

Is Judge Lammie Snyman7 out there anywhere?

Has anyone the pleasure of his company at table?

He's the man, you know, who told a reporter from *Die Beeld* that his Appeal Board had decided to release *Burger's Daughter* from ban because it was so badly written that nobody would bother to read it anyway.

Well, that was Lammie Snyman's swan-song; we now have Professor Kobus van Rooyen — who will probably give us no chance to laugh at *him*. He has promised that Lammie Snyman's grey man, the ordinary average South African, will be replaced, as the censors' criterion, by another hypothetical species, cited by the Directorate of Publications as the 'probable reader'. *But the censorship laws remain the same.* The Censorship Act is still on the statute book. And even that hard fact does not satisfy the *Aksie Morele Standaarde* [Action Moral Standards] group that wants Etienne le Roux's novel *Magersfontein, O Magersfontein!* re-banned, and splutters that if this work cannot *stay* banned under the Publications Act, then the Act is useless and should be scrapped.

And so we have reached a point we never expected could ever be: we writers find ourselves absolutely at one with the *Aksie Morele Standaarde* group – we *all* want the Act scrapped, never mind our reasons.

Beneath the absurdity of this situation there is something highly significant happening. It is not that, in the end, censorship stands revealed as a senseless act, since it cannot even satisfy those whose moral standards it is supposed to be upholding. I am not one who has ever regarded censorship as senseless in its *aims*; I can see perfectly the logic of it, however idiotic some of its manifestations. Censorship is the weapon of information-control, thought-control, idea-control, above all, the control of healthy doubt and questioning, and as such as much a part of the arsenal of apartheid as the hippos [heavily armoured cars] that went through the streets of Soweto in '76. Censorship is as essential to the suppression of the realities of life here as the prisons where people are held in detention. Censorship is necessary for the daily maintenance of racism – and the laws of our country are still racist, whatever fancy names we give them; the very changes that are being made to ease the chafing of those laws round the necks of the masses still reflect racist differentiation in the assessment of people's needs and self-respect, from the comparative amounts spent on black schools and white schools and pensions to the special arrangements that have to be made, on occasions such as this dinner, to have blacks as guests in a white club. For these reasons, the Censorship Act is still with us. We shall never be rid of it until we get rid of apartheid, even if – for complex political and highly cynical purposes – a few books are 'reinstated' after a thorough mauling at the hands of the Directorate and Appeal Board; and even if the *Aksie Morele Standaarde* people and the *Nederduitse Gereformeerde Kerk* [Dutch Reformed Church][8] are incensed by the Board's reluctant, grudging, selective tolerance.

The significance that runs beneath the absurd situation in which proponents and opponents of censorship find themselves calling for the abolition of the Censorship Act, surfaces among us tonight. For here we have a literary prize being awarded to a book that was banned, and if you look at a list of works that have received the major awards in South Africa in recent years, you will see that these have gone frequently to books that have been under embargo, are banned, or have been banned and released. Now these awards, from the Hertzog Prize[9] to the CNA prizes, are not given out by organisations involved in political agitation against the government. The donor organisations have no desire – to put it mildly – to provoke officialdom. They cannot be suspected of subversive tendencies. I doubt very much whether any one of them would even subscribe to the idea of a counter-culture. Yet it so happens that often works chosen by independent judges, whose mandate is a literary one and who are well aware that the fact that a book is banned does not necessarily mean it is a well-written and genuine creative achievement, are not works that measure the 'standard of fit reading matter' for South Africans as set up by the government and set out by the Censorship Directorate. This is particularly marked – indeed, there are oozing battle-scars – in the case of the most pres-tigious Afrikaans prize, the Hertzog. For there has been a formal and distinct, national literary establishment in Afri-kaans as there never has been for English-language literature – perhaps because English-language literature has had the good fortune (even if it hasn't always acknowledged it) to be created eclectically by both black and white South Africans in a mixture too varied to settle down in any academy.

That the Mofolo-Plomer Prize,[10] linked neither to state cultural institutions nor big business, can be won by Achmat Dangor,[11] a young man who has done a lot of his thinking in preventive detention, is not a matter to register a quake beneath the feet of the South African cultural establishment; but when the Hertzog Prize goes to Breyten Breytenbach and to Etienne le Roux's novel, the latter described as 'septic art' by Dr Koot Vorster[12] even when finally released after a weari-some history of bannings and unbannings; when the CNA Awards go successively to the le Roux novel, and to André Brink's *Rumours of Rain*, and Gordimer's *Burger's Daughter* – when these things happen, what is the cultural establishment of South Africa standing on? If one were able to turn and point to a body of literature upholding what is known as 'the traditional way of life' there would be some *koppie* [hill] for that establishment to scramble to. But when the vigilante corps of that average, ordinary South African Lammie Snyman was always so fond of citing as an arbiter of excellence and relevance in the arts, complains bitterly that the Censorship Directorate fails to uphold the sacred morals and mores attributed to that average ordinary South African, the indignation echoes in a void. Where are the imaginative works that reflect implicitly, as literature does and propaganda does not, the images of a life being lived in these terms?

Where are the poems whose ethos is separate development? Where are the novels in which the visit of a Chief Mangope[13] to Cape Town is seriously presented as the visit of a foreign head of state to our country?

When the Moral Standardists and the Koot Vorsters cry out at their own institutions and the very institution of censorship that guards those institutions, one thing is clear − so far as literature is concerned, the 'traditional' South African culture does not exist any longer. It is not just a white dodo; it is extinct.

We writers in South Africa are so close to the hot breath of our problems, we seldom take time to stand back a little and note the movement of ideas in the outside world. They seem a luxury, to many. Yet sometimes we miss ideas that are not only pertinent but vital to our problems, and objectively supportive of our means of struggle. If we look today into a certain movement of ideas concerning the nature of man, we will find that, without putting a name to it, we ourselves are acting out a principle that is being established theoretically. Psychoanalysts in France, structuralists in the United States and France, conservative, liberal and left-wing thinkers in contemporary schools of linguistic philosophy agree about one thing; man became man not by the tool but by the Word. It is not walking upright and using a stick to dig for food or strike a blow that makes a human being, it is speech. And neither intelligent apes nor dolphins whispering marvels in the ocean share with us the ability to transform this direct communication into the written word, which sets up an endless chain of communication and commune between peoples and generations who will never meet.

The old biblical mystery of the Word, its transcendent power, is ours. And we know it instinctively, we writers here in South Africa. Professor Opperman brings it back literally from the dead.[14] John Miles, Mtutuzeli Matshoba, Ingoapele Madingoane, Miriam Tlali, Sipho Sepamla, Jack Cope, James Matthews, Sheila Roberts — all the writers who have had books banned — we go on to write the next book. New South African publishers have come into being who publish what they think of worth and take the risk of bannings and consequent financial loss as an occupational hazard. Lionel Abrahams and Robert Royston were the first to publish what no big publisher would: Oswald Mbuyiseni Mtshali's *Sounds of a Cowhide Drum*, nine years ago.[15] Ad. Donker published Mongane Wally Serote and got away with it; Sheila Roberts, and didn't. Ampie Coetzee, Ernest Lindenberg and John Miles calmly set up Taurus as non-profitmaking publishers whose policy is to print imaginative work, mainly in Afrikaans, without exercising any cautionary pre-censorship. Ravan Press is a phenomenon in terms of the old South Africa and the old South African concept of publishing: when its innovative founder, Peter Randall, was banned and debarred from working as a publisher, there appeared the poet Mike Kirkwood to make a fanfare success of a beleaguered beginning. Many wealthy commercial publishing houses would be happy to sell five thousand copies of a title by a new writer — Mike Kirkwood did it with Mtutuzeli Matshoba's *Call Me Not a Man*[16] in the few weeks between the publication of the book and its banning.

Old literary magazines die, new ones walk the tightrope with zest and verve, and if one issue takes a tumble into the censors' net, are quite ready, as *Staffrider*[17] has shown, to begin preparing the next number for publication. For the word, which we writers have in our possession and our keeping, is ours. It is not only protest, it is affirmation. The unkillable word. There are writers in prison and detention who, as young Jaki Seroke did, memorise the poems they are not allowed to write and thus carry them out in their heads when they come back into the world again. The primacy of the word, basis of the human psyche, that has in our age been used for mind-bending persuasion and brain-washing pulp, disgraced by Goebbels and debased by advertising copy, remains a force for freedom that flies out between all bars. A cultural counter-establishment is on the move beyond the government's control, no matter how many writers' telephones they tap, how many manuscripts are taken away in police raids on black writers' houses, no matter how many books they ban. The cage is empty. The keepers are beginning to notice; God knows what they will do next. But the writers are singing in the words of Pablo Neruda: *This is the song of what is happening and of what will be.*[18]

Censors and Unconfessed History

(1980)[1]

As Gordimer's CNA address implied, there were new censorship strategies in the air round about 1980. This had less to do with any change of structure than of personality, particularly the incumbency of Professor Kobus van Rooyen as the new Chairman of the Publications Appeal Board. This was also a time when reforms on the part of the state began to be touted in South Africa. Like the reforms, however, changes in censorship needed to be scrutinised carefully. Books were being unbanned; the Directorate was appealing against the decisions of its own committees; the appeals were being upheld. But was this really 'reform', a new enlightenment on the way? Or was it merely a more sophisticated form of repression? In South Africa nothing seemingly positive can be taken at face value. Gordimer's CNA address had been a kind of barbed flourish, perfectly suited to its occasion. Now, in a paper delivered at a conference on censorship — and much in the spirit of her 'Relevance and Commitment' address of the previous year — she considered these questions much more deeply and analytically; especially the issues of how censorship was dealing differentially with white and black writers and readers, and what this implied for South African literary and political culture.

Many of you will already have sat through a whole day's discussion by writers on censorship in relation to writers and readers, and will have debated your own views on the subject. I was not present, unfortunately for me, and so I cannot hope entirely to steer away from ground already thoroughly trampled, charged and snorted over — blood spilled there, perhaps! — since I share the preoccupations of my fellow writers. Indeed, I was the first to express the conviction, now become a general stand, that the release from ban of a few books by well-known white writers is not a major victory for the freedom to write, and that the action carries two sinister implications: first, those among us who are uncompromising opponents of censorship with wide access to the media can be bought off by special treatment accorded to our books; second, the measure of hard-won solidarity that exists between black and white writers can be divided by 'favouring' white writers with such special treatment, since no ban on any black writer's work has been challenged by the Directorate's own application to the Appeal Board.[2]

I don't claim any prescience or distinction for early arrival at this conviction: *Burger's Daughter*, my novel, happened to be the first released as a consequence of the Directorate's new tactics. It was natural for me to examine the package very carefully when my book came back to me — apparently intact, after all the mauling it had been through. It was inevitable that I should come upon the neat devices timed to go off in the company of my colleagues. It was not surprising that they should recognise for themselves these booby-traps set for us all, since a week or two later André Brink received the same package containing his novel, *A Dry White Season*. And then, in time for April and the seating of the new Chairman of the Appeal Board, came Afrikaans literature's Easter egg, all got up for Etienne le Roux with the sugar roses of the old Appeal Board's repentance and the red ribbon defiant of *Aksie Morele Standaarde*, the *Nederduitse Gereformeerde Kerk* and Dr Koot Vorster — of course, *Magersfontein, O Magersfontein!* was not released as the two other books were, as a result of the Director's own appeal against his Committees' bannings, but its release on an ultimate appeal by the author's publishers transparently belongs to the same strategy in which the other two books were 'reinstated'.

I am one who has always believed and still believes we shall never be rid of censorship until we are rid of apartheid. Personally, I find it necessary to preface with this blunt statement any comment I have about the effects of censorship, the possible changes in its scope, degree, and methodology. Any consideration of how to conduct the struggle against it, how to act for the attainment of immediate ends, is a partial, pragmatic, existential response seen against a constant and overriding factor. Today as always, the invisible banner is behind me, the decisive chalked text on the blackboard, against whose background I say what I have to say. *We shall not be rid of censorship until we are rid of apartheid.* Censorship is the arm of mind-control and as necessary to maintain a racist regime as that other arm of internal repression, the secret police. Over every apparent victory we may gain against the censorship powers hangs the question of whether that victory is in fact contained by apartheid, or can be claimed to erode it from within.

What exactly has changed since the 1st April 1980?

What exactly does the 'born again' cultural evangelism, staged with the positively last appearance of Judge Lammie Snyman and the previews of rippling intellectual musculature displayed by 37-year-old Dr Kobus van Rooyen, mean?

The Censorship Act remains the same. It is still on the statute book. The practice of embargo will continue. The same anonymous committees will read and ban; a censorship committee having been defined in 1978 by the Appellate Division of the Supreme Court as 'an extra-judicial body, operating in an administrative capacity, whose members need have no legal training, before whom the appellant has no right of audience, who in their deliberations are not required to have regard to the rules of justice designed to achieve a fair trial, whose proceedings are not conducted in public and who are not required to afford any reasons for their decision.'[3] The enlarged panel of experts has some of the same old names, among whom is at least one known *Broederbonder*,[4] and the new ones are recruited from the same old white cadres. The powers of the Board are what they always were.

There is no change in the law or procedure, then. Nor is any promised, or even hinted at.

What we have is a new Chairman of the Appeal Board, in a position whose power we already know: although he does not make decisions alone, the Chairman of the Appeal Board is the ultimate authority and decision-maker in the whole process of censorship. We also know that the head of any institution – and censorship is an institution in our national life – interprets the doctrinal absolutes and directs the tactical course towards that institution's avowed objectives according to his own personal ideas of how these should be achieved. His flair – for which quality he will have been chosen, all other qualifications being equal – will influence procedure, make innovations in the way *the same things* are done, whether the institution is a bank accumulating capital or a Directorate of Publications controlling people's minds.

Therefore it can only be the philosophy and psychology of censorship that have changed. Why and how is something we shall have to delve into in the months to come, beyond a first snap understanding of what was plain behind the unbanning of a small group of books in quick succession – the hope to placate certain white writers, the suggestion of an attempt to divide the interests of black and white writers. These actions were surely already the product of Dr van Rooyen's thought, since he was running the Appeal Board for some time before he was appointed Chairman this month. They were the first show of the quality of mind, the concept of culture, the concept of the relation of literature to society, to politics, to economics, to class as well as colour, the new Chairman has, and on which – as we see – the nature of what we are up against now will be dependent.

Since he took office he has made policy statements – signification from which it will be possible to trace the grid of his purpose. Taking as given the ordinary motives of personal ambition and good pay in his acceptance of the job of chief censor, we need to know how he sees his particular mission. We need to know what his sense of *self* and *other* is. For that is the vital factor in the praxis of censorship, the phenomenon of censorship as a form of social and cultural control. Philosophically speaking, on this sense of self and other is the authority of censorship conceived. A *we* controlling a *them*. Dr van Rooyen won't tell us what his private, affective sense deciding his thoughts and actions is; but we have the right to find out. I'll ask you to look at the evidence of his statements presently; first I want to return to the evidence of his actions – or actions behind which his hand can be detected – the unbanning of certain highly controversial books.

André Brink has pointed out that the week that his novel, dealing with the death by police brutality and neglect of a black man in prison, was released from ban, Mtutuzeli

Matshoba's story collection, *Call Me Not a Man*, was banned. The reason for banning supplied to Matshoba's publisher was objection to *one* of the stories only, 'A Glimpse of Slavery', dealing with the experiences of a black man hired out as a prison labourer to a white farmer.

Death in prison or detention; the abuse of farm labour. Both are subjects whose factual basis has been exposed and confirmed in the proceedings of court cases and, in one instance at least, a commission of inquiry. Two writers, each of whom can make with Dostoevsky a statement of the writer's ethic: 'Having taken an event, I tried only to clarify its possibility in our society'; the work of one is released, the other banned.

Now, in preparation for the new regime, from which we are being persuaded we may expect a new respect for literature, and are asked to accept this as a new justification for censorship, there has been much emphasis on literary quality in recent decisions by the Appeal Board. It seems that Dr Kobus van Rooyen wants to substitute the silver-handled paper-knife of good taste for the *kerrie* [knobbed baton] of narrow-mindedness and prudery, as the arbitrary weapon. But although it was decided by a Censorship Committee that there was (I quote) 'not inconsiderable merit in much of the writing in this collection of short stories by the African writer Mtutuzeli Matshoba . . . with regard both to the quality of the writing and to the author's insight in the human situations which he interprets', although the Committee members found the stories 'generally of a high quality', they banned the book because of a single story. They did this — again I let them speak for their anonymous selves — ostentatiously from the new 'literary' angle, claiming that this particular story was flatly written and the accumulation of its events improbable. But what was hatched beneath the peacock feathers was the ostrich with his familiar kick. They banned the book on one seventh of its contents, to be precise. They returned, when dealing with a black writer, to the precept followed in the past, when a work was to be judged 'desirable' or 'undesirable' not in relation to the quality of the whole, but could be damned because of a single chapter, page, or even paragraph.

The sole basis for the ban on Matshoba's book rested ultimately on a declared calculation made in the imperatives of political repression, not literary quality, although literary quality is invoked — the Committee stated that the appeal to the reader of the story 'lies not in the *literary creation* but rather in the *objectionable nature of the events* which are presented ... even if all these situations ... had occurred in this context in which they are set in the story, *the presentation of these scenes in a popular medium would be undesirable*' (my italics).

The standard used by the censors here is that of political control over *reading matter likely to reach the black masses*. If this is not so, let us challenge the Directorate to act in accordance with Dr van Rooyen's statement that the banning of a book by the 'isolation method' would now be rejected, and therefore ask for the ban on Matshoba's book to be reviewed by the Appeal Board.[5]

My novel *Burger's Daughter* was released by the Appeal Board last year, although it had been deemed undesirable in terms of the Publications Act of 1974. Among the numerous examples which evidently gave offence, one — cited under Section 47 (2) (c) of the Act — was the remark by English-speaking schoolgirls mouthing prejudices picked up from their parents: 'Bloody Boers, dumb Dutchmen, thick Afrikaners'.[6]

Miriam Tlali's novel, *Muriel at Metropolitan*, in the version found inoffensive and left on sale for several years, was banned last year on the sole objection of three offences under the same Section of the Act, the principal being the reference by the narrator-character to an Afrikaans-speaking woman as a 'lousy Boer'.[7]

Well, these ugly racist epithets are not my personal ones, nor, I think, are they Miriam Tlali's; but they are heard around us every day, and there are certain characters whose habitual inability to express themselves without them is another fact about our society no honest writer can falsify. Yet Tlali's book, otherwise quite inoffensive from the censors' point of view, ultimately is banned while mine is ultimately released. Is it more insulting for a white South African to be abused by a black character in a book than by a white one?

What is clear is that the Censorship Committee regards it as necessary to prevent black readers from reading their own prejudices, their own frustrations, given expression in the work of a black writer; outside the considerations assiduously to be taken into account by a new and enlightened censorship there is an additional one, operative for black writers only, that nullifies most of the concessions so far as black writers are concerned – they may not say what white writers say because they are calculated to have a wider black readership, and to speak to blacks from the centre of the experience of being black, to articulate and therefore confirm, encourage what the black masses themselves feel and understand about their lives but most cannot express.

And with this trend taken by the Censorship Directorate in the period preparing us for the advent of a new Chairman, we come to the event itself, and the statements of policy made by Dr Kobus van Rooyen since April 1st.

He has not said much; and one of his statements has been to the effect that he intends to say even less: he has announced that he will take no part in public debates on censorship. As a Johannesburg newspaper editorial pointed out, of public debates – 'These insights to the workings of a censor's mind were what helped speed the retirement of his predecessor. They will be missed.'*

Indeed.

Dr Kobus van Rooyen would be unlikely to present the image that emerged from the public appearances and statements of his predecessor. Nevertheless, Dr van Rooyen does not intend taking any risks. What interests us more is that he does not want openly to proselytise his philosophy of censorship any more than he intends to be open to the influence of counter views. This is an autocratic approach – let us not call it an arrogant one. From it we can understand that here is a man whose view of culture is élitist, someone in whose mind, whether consciously or not, is posited the idea of an official cultural norm. The fact that his version of that norm is likely to vary, here and there, in emphasis, does not mean that it is any less fundamentalist than that defined implicitly, along with the law, in the Censorship Act. The shift in emphasis is a real-politik adjustment to catch up with the change in the relation of literature to life that has taken place in South Africa, and that a clever man cannot ignore. The concept – that there is a right for a single power group to decide what culture is –

* 'Censorship, O Censorship', *Star* (Johannesburg), 5 April 1980, p. 6.

remains the grid on which, like the most functional of contemporary business premises, all manner of interior open-space arrangements may be made to suit the tenant; but the overall structure must be accepted. The myth of this version of South African culture sustains a man who is so convinced of his approach to his job that he is not prepared to discuss it, let alone admit any necessity to defend it.

Roland Barthes points out that traditional myth explains a culture's origins out of nature's forces; modern myths justify and enforce a secular power by presenting it as a natural force.[8] Sophisticated officials of this government may be openly sceptical of some of the more ritualistic aspects of our societal myth – the Immorality Act,[9] the awful malediction of four-letter words, etc. – but sophistication must never be taken for enlightenment; acceptance of the concept of a culture based on an élite dispensation to the masses who cannot create anything valid for themselves, acceptance of the role of literature in life according to that culture, are still firmly based on a particular myth of power.

Only from within that myth could Judge Lammie Snyman have taken the cultural standpoint revealed when he said earlier this month that blacks are 'inarticulate people who, I am sure, are not interested' in censorship.* And what a lightning-flash lit up a whole official mentality for us when, summing up the entire five years in which it was his responsibility to decide 'what was likely to corrupt or deprave an immature mind, or whether it was likely to horrify or disgust' the people of South Africa, he added: 'Of blacks, I have no knowledge at all.'

His 'average ordinary South African' – whose standards of morality and literary judgment he constantly invoked during his term of office – was not to be found among the majority of the South African population. For this reason, Dr Kobus van Rooyen has abandoned the creature. But not the idea that he has the right to create another of his own, whose imaginary or rather conditioned sensibilities and susceptibilities will be the deciding factor in what shall and shall not be read by all of us. What is regarded as Dr van Rooyen's most important statement is his announcement that his creature will be the

* 'Lammie Snyman Supercensor', *Star* (Johannesburg), 8 April 1980, p. 3.

'probable reader'.[10] Important it is, but not, I am afraid, for reasons assumed by some.

The assumption is that sexual explicitness as an integral part of sophisticated literature written in the idiom of educated people will now be passed; that complex works dealing with contentious or radical political characters and events above the level of simple rhetoric will also be passed. And there the effect of the change apparently ends, and so can only be regarded as beneficial; after all if you have not the educational background and trained intellect to follow these works, that is hardly the responsibility of the censors.

Is it not? By putting on the top shelf, out of reach of those masses Lammie Snyman confessed he knew nothing about, imaginative, analytical presentation of the crucial questions that deal with their lives, is one not hampering the healthy cultural development censorship purports to be guarding?

We should like to be able to put that question to the new Chairman of the Appeal Board, who evidently does know a great deal about those masses. Does he see the justification of that hampering in a mission to adjust the strategy of the myth to hostile forces he well understands?

Why may intellectual readers handle inflammables?

Is it because this readership is predominantly white, and radical initiative by whites has been contained by imprisonment, exile, bannings and the threat of right-wing terrorism, while the moderate, let alone the revolutionary initiative for social change, has passed overwhelmingly to blacks, and is not contained?

Why may white writers deal with inflammables?

Is it because the new censorship dispensation has understood something important to censorship as an arm of repression: while white writings are predominantly critical and protestant in mood, black writings are inspirational, and that is why the government fears them?

The definition of the 'probable reader' can be arrived at by the old pencil-in-the-hair and finger-nail tests,[11] believe me. The criterion for reading-matter allowed him is not literary worth but his colour.

As a cultural and not merely a politically-manipulable prototype, the 'probable reader' is a creature of class-and-colour hierarchy. He cannot be visualised, in our society, by those of us sufficiently free-minded to see that culture in South Africa is something still to be made, something that could not be brought along with mining machinery in the hold of a ship, nor has been attained by the genuinely remarkable achievement of creating an indigenous language of our European ones. He cannot be visualised by anyone who understands culture not as an embellishment of leisure for the middle classes, but as the vital force generated by the skills, crafts, legends, songs, dances, languages, sub-literature as well as literature – the living expression of self-realisation – in the life of the people as a whole.

Behind the 'probable reader' is surely the unexpressed concept of the 'probable writer'. The new Chairman of the Appeal Board has assured *him* that 'satirical writing will be allowed to develop'. To most of us this is an élitist concession. Of course, nobody stops anyone from writing satire, whatever his colour. But in the relation of literature to life at present, satire is unlikely to appeal to black writers. It requires a distancing from the subject which black writers, living their lives close within their material, are not likely to manage; it requires a licence for self-criticism that loyalty to the black struggle for a spiritual identity does not grant at present. So effective weapon though satire may be, as a social probe in certain historical circumstances or stages, it will not, so far as it is a concession by this government to freedom of expression, fall into the hands of the 'wrong' probable writer ...

There is a new directive which accepts that the writer may be a critic of his society and therefore often in conflict with its accepted moral, religious and political values. This just might benefit writers of work in the critical and analytical mode, but it will lift no barriers for the inspirational. Yet there is no ignoring the fact that the inspirational is a dynamic of our literature at present. Franz Kafka's standard, that 'a book must be an ice-axe to break the frozen sea inside us,'[12] is not the censors. Neither is there any sign of acceptance that in South Africa we writers, white and black, are the only recorders of what the poet Eugenio Montale calls 'unconfessed history'.

That has been made, and is being made every day, deep below the reports of commissions and the South African

Broadcasting Corporation news; it is the decisive common force carrying us all, bearing away the protective clothing of 'probable readers' as paper carnival costumes melt in the rain.

In the final analysis, censorship's new deal is the pragmatic manifestation of an old, time-dishonoured view of culture, already dead, serving repression instead of the arts, and its belated recognition of literary standards is its chief strategy. This recognition is shrewd enough to see what Lammie Snyman did not − that the objective validity of literary standards as a concept (there *are* works of genuine creation, there *is* trash) could be invoked for a purpose in which, in fact, they have no place and no authority. The criteria by which the quality of literature can be assessed have nothing whatever to do with calculation of its possible effect on the reader, probable or improbable. The literary experts who are instructed to take this factor into account, and do so, are not exercising any valid function as judges of literature.

In affirmation of freedom of expression, which is the single uncompromised basis of opposition to censorship, the literary worth or otherwise of a work is not a factor − what is at stake each time a book falls into the censors' hands is the right of that book to be read. Literary worth has nothing to do with that principle. We must not fudge this truth. The poor piece of work has as much right to be read − and duly judged as such − as the work of genius. Literary worth may be assessed only by critics and readers free to read the book; it is a disinterested, complex and difficult judgment that sometimes takes generations. There is a promise that future judgments by the censors will (I quote) 'more readily reflect the opinions of literary experts appointed'. The invocation of literary standards by censors as a sign of enlightenment and relaxation of strictures on the freedom of the word; above all, the reception by the public of this respected and scholarly concept as one that *could* be enthroned among censors − both are invalid. Let us never forget − and let us not let the South African public remain in ignorance of what we know: censorship may have to do with literature; but literature has nothing whatever to do with censorship.

Living in the Interregnum

(1982)[1]

By the 1980s South African fiction began to be preoccupied with thoughts of revolution in South Africa; Gordimer's eighth novel, July's People (1981)[2] was set at the future moment of revolution itself. There were perhaps good reasons for this overall concern. By this time South Africa's neighbouring countries, Mozambique, Angola and Zimbabwe, had won their independence. Inside the country the Soweto Revolt had been quelled, but it had initiated a longer-term period of political upswing. By the 1980s an independent black trade-union movement was gathering in numbers and strength. There was also renewed organisation against apartheid, both at the local level and on a broader national basis: within a year of the essay which follows here the United Democratic Front had been established, the first such mass movement, legal and active above ground, since the banning of the African National Congress and the Pan-Africanist Congress in 1960. After its own extraordinary impact the Black Consciousness movement was waning in authority, and with the renewed ideological ascendancy of the African National Congress there was again a more general commitment to 'non-racialism' in opposition to apartheid. Whereas Gordimer had attempted – and in some ways succeeded – in both her fiction and non-fiction to come to terms with the Black Consciousness challenge, the context in which her commitments could find affirmation was now once more beginning to widen.

This process was by no means straightforward, however, and as far as the following essay is concerned (originally given by Gordimer as a James Lecture at the New York Institute of the Humanities) there are two major strengths. One is the full realisation that South Africa was already in a state of revolution, and had been so for some time. The second is the awareness that this was not an unambiguous condition. What follows here must surely rank as one of the most powerful statements of what it is like to live

out the symptoms and contradictions of a state of 'interregnum':
firstly to understand them, and then to live them through. At the
same time there were signs of crisis elsewhere in the world. From her
embattled position in South Africa Gordimer used this lecture to
remark on a more global state of 'interregnum', as well as the need
for a renewed commitment to deal with it.

> *Police files are our only claim to immortality*
> Milan Kundera[3]

I live at 6,000 feet in a society whirling, stamping, swaying
with the force of revolutionary change. The vision is heady; the
image of the demonic dance — and accurate, not romantic: an
image of actions springing from emotion, knocking deliberation aside. The city is Johannesburg, the country South
Africa, and the time the last years of the colonial era in Africa.

It's inevitable that nineteenth-century colonialism should
finally come to its end there, because there it reached its
ultimate expression, open in the legalised land- and mineral-
grabbing, open in the labour exploitation of indigenous
peoples, open in the constitutionalised, institutionalised
racism that was concealed by the British under the pious
notion of uplift, the French and the Portuguese under the sly
notion of selective assimilation. An extraordinarily obdurate
crossbreed of Dutch, German, English, French in the South
African white settler population produced a bluntness that
unveiled everyone's refined white racism: the flags of European
civilisation dropped, and there it was unashamedly, the ugliest
creation of man, and they baptised the thing in the Dutch
Reformed Church, called it *apartheid*, coining the ultimate term
for every manifestation, over the ages, in many countries, of
race prejudice. Every country could see its semblances there;
and most peoples.

The sun that never set over one or other of the nineteenth-
century colonial empires of the world is going down finally in
South Africa. Since the black uprisings of the mid-seventies,
coinciding with the independence of Mozambique and Angola,
and later that of Zimbabwe, the past has begun rapidly to drop
out of sight, even for those who would have liked to go on living

in it. Historical co-ordinates don't fit life any longer; new ones, where they exist, have couplings not to the rulers, but to the ruled. It is not for nothing that I chose as an epigraph for my novel *July's People* a quotation from Gramsci: 'The old is dying, and the new cannot be born; in this interregnum there arises a great diversity of morbid symptoms.'*

In this interregnum, I and all my countrymen and women are living. Ten thousand miles from home, I speak to you out of it. I am going, quite frequently, to let events personally experienced as I was thinking towards or writing this paper interrupt theoretical flow, because this interaction – this essential disruption, this breaking in upon the existential coherence we call concept – is the very state of being I must attempt to convey. I have never before spoken publicly from so personal a point of view. Apart from the usual Joycean reasons of secrecy and cunning – to which I would add jealous hoarding of private experience for transmutation into fiction – there has been for me a peculiarly South African taboo. In the official South African consciousness, the ego is white: it has always seen all South Africa as ordered around it. Even the ego that seeks to abdicate this alienation does so in an assumption of its own salvation that in itself expresses ego and alienation. And the Western world press, itself overwhelmingly white, constantly feeds this ego from its own. Visiting journalists, parliamentarians, congressmen and congresswomen come to South Africa to ask whites what is going to happen there. They meet blacks through whites; they rarely take the time and trouble, on their own initiative, to encounter more than the man who comes into the hotel bedroom to take away the empty beer bottles. With the exception of films made clandestinely by South African political activists, black and white, about resistance events, most foreign television documentaries, while condemning the whites out of their own mouths, are nevertheless preoccupied with what will happen to whites when the apartheid regime goes. I have shunned the arrogance of interpreting my country through the private life that, as Theodor Adorno puts it, 'drags on only as an appendage of the

* [In a slightly different translation in] *Selections from the Prison Notebooks of Antonio Gramsci*, edited and translated by Quintin Hoare and Geoffrey Nowell Smith (London: Lawrence & Wishart, 1971), p. 276.

social process'* in a time and place of which I am a part. Now I am going to break the inhibition or destroy the privilege of privacy, whichever way you look at it. I have to offer you myself as my most closely observed specimen from the interregnum; yet I remain a writer, not a public speaker: nothing I say here will be as true as my fiction.

There is another reason for confession. The particular segment of South African society to which I belong, by the colour of my skin, whether I like it or not, represents a crisis that has a particular connection with the Western world, to which you in this audience belong. I think that may become self-evident before I arrive at the point of explication; it is *not*, I want to assure you, the old admitted complicity in the slave trade or the price of raw materials.

I have used the term 'segment' in defining my place in South African society because within the white section of that society – less than one fifth of the total population now, predicted to drop to one seventh by the year 2000† – there is a segment preoccupied, in the interregnum, neither by plans to run away from nor merely by ways to survive physically and economically in the black state that is coming. I cannot give you numbers for this segment, but in measure of some sort of faith in the possibility of structuring society humanly, in the possession of skills and intellect to devote to this end, there is something to offer the future. *How* to offer it is our preoccupation. Since skills, technical and intellectual, can be bought in markets other than those of the vanquished white power, although they are important as a commodity ready to hand, they do not constitute a claim on the future.

That claim rests on something else: how to offer *one's self*.

In the eyes of the black majority which will rule, whites of former South Africa will have to redefine themselves in a new collective life within new structures. From the all-white Parliament to the all-white country club and the separate 'white'

---

* 'Cultural Criticism and Society', in *Critical Sociology: Selected Readings*, (ed.) Paul Connerton (Harmondsworth: Penguin, 1976), p. 271.
† Total population 1980, 23·7 million, of which 4·5 million are white. *Survey of Race Relations in South Africa 1981*, (ed.) M. Horrell (Johannesburg: South African Institute of Race Relations, 1982), p. 52.

television channels, it is not a matter of blacks taking over white institutions, it is one of conceiving of institutions – from nursery schools to government departments – that reflect a societal structure vastly different from that built to the specifications of white power and privilege. This vast difference will be evident even if capitalism survives, since South Africa's capitalism, like South Africa's whites-only democracy, has been unlike anyone else's. For example, free enterprise among us is for whites only, since black capitalists may trade only, and with many limitations on their 'free' enterprise, in black ghettos. In cities the kind of stores and services offered will change when the life-style of the majority – black, working-class – establishes the authority of the enfranchised demand in place of the dictated demand. At present the consumer gets what the producer's racially-estimated idea of his place in life decrees to be his needs.

A more equitable distribution of wealth may be enforced by laws. The hierarchy of perception that white institutions and living habits implant throughout daily experience in every white, from childhood, can be changed only by whites themselves, from within. The weird ordering of the collective life, in South Africa, has slipped its special contact lens into the eyes of whites; we actually *see* blacks differently, which includes *not seeing*, not noticing their unnatural absence, since there are so many perfectly ordinary venues of daily life – the cinema, for instance – where blacks have never been allowed in, and so one has forgotten that they could be, might be, encountered there.

I am writing in my winter quarters, at an old deal table on a verandah in the sun; out of the corner of my eye I see a piece of junk mail, the brochure of a chain bookstore, assuring me of constantly expanding service and showing the staff of a newly opened branch – Ms So-and-So, Mr Such-and-Such, and (one black face) 'Gladys'. What a friendly, informal form of identification in an 'equal opportunity' enterprise! Gladys is seen by fellow workers, by the photographer who noted down names, and – it is assumed – readers, quite differently from the way the white workers are seen. I gaze at her as they do ... She is simply 'Gladys', the convenient handle by which she is taken up by the white world, used and put down again, like the glass the king drinks from *in Rilke's poem.* Her surname, her African name, belongs to Soweto, which her smiling white companions are less likely ever to visit than New York or London.*

The successfully fitted device in the eye of the beholder is something the average white South African is not conscious of, for apartheid is above all a habit; the unnatural seems natural – a far from banal illustration of Hannah Arendt's banality of evil. The segment of the white population to which I belong has become highly conscious of a dependency on distorted vision induced since childhood; and we are aware that with the inner eye we have 'seen too much to be innocent.'† But this kind of awareness, represented by white guilt in the 1950s, has been sent by us off into the sunset, since, as Czeslaw Milosz puts it, 'guilt, which is so highly developed in modern man ... saps his belief in the value of his own perceptions and judgments',‡ and we have need of ours. We have to believe in our ability to find new perceptions, and our ability to judge their truth. Along with weeping over what's done, we've given up rejoicing in what Günter Grass calls headbirths,§ those Athenian armchair deliveries of the future presented to blacks by whites.

Not all blacks even concede that whites can have any part in the new that cannot yet be born. An important black leader who does, Bishop Desmond Tutu,[4] defines that participation:

> what I consider to be the place of the white man in this – popularly called the liberation struggle. I am firmly non-racial and so welcome the participation of all, both black and white, in the struggle for the new South Africa which must come whatever the cost. But I want ... to state that at this stage the leadership of the struggle must be firmly in black hands. They must determine what will

---

* Rainer Maria Rilke, 'Ein Frauenschicksal' (A Woman's Fate), in *Selected Poems of Rainer Maria Rilke*, translated by C. F. MacIntyre (Berkeley and Los Angeles, Ca.: University of California Press, 1941), p. 71.

† Edmundo Desnoes, *Memories of Underdevelopment* (Harmondsworth: Penguin, 1971), p. 104.

‡ *Native Realm: A Search for Self-Definition*, translated by Catherine S. Leach (New York: Doubleday, 1968), p. 125.

§ *Headbirths, or The Germans are Dying Out*, translated by Ralph Manheim (London: Secker & Warburg; New York: Harcourt Brace Jovanovich; 1982).

be the priorities and the strategy of the struggle.

Whites unfortunately have the habit of taking over and usurping the leadership and taking the crucial decisions – largely, I suppose, because of the head start they had in education and experience . . . of this kind. The point is that however much they want to identify with blacks it is an existential fact . . . that they have not really been victims of this baneful oppression and exploitation . . . It is a divide that can't be crossed and that must give blacks a primacy in determining the course and goal of the struggle. Whites must be willing to follow.*

Blacks must learn to talk; whites must learn to listen – wrote the black South African poet Mongane Wally Serote, in the seventies.† This is the premise on which the white segment to which I belong lives its life at present. Does it sound like an abdication of the will? That is because you who live in a democracy are accustomed to exerting the right to make abstract statements of principle for which, at least, the structures of practical realisation exist; the symbolic action of the like-minded in signing a letter to a newspaper or the lobbying of Congress is a reminder of constitutional rights to be invoked. For us, Tutu's premise enjoins a rousing of the will, a desperate shaking into life of the faculty of rebellion against unjust laws that has been outlawed by the dying power, and faculties of renewal that often are rebuffed by the power that is struggling to emerge. The rider Desmond Tutu didn't add to his statement is that although white support is expected to be active, it is also expected that whites' different position in the still-standing structures of the old society will require actions that, while complementary to those of blacks, must be different from the blacks'. Whites are expected to find their own forms of struggle, which can only sometimes coincide with those of blacks.

That there can be, at least, the coincident co-operation is reassuring; that, at least, should be a straightforward form of

* Bishop Desmond Tutu, letter to *Frontline* (Johannesburg), vol. 2, no. 5 (April 1982), p. 4.
† Paraphrased from the poem 'Ofay-watcher, throbs – phase', in *Yakhal' Inkomo* (Johannesburg: Renoster, 1972), pp. 50–1.

activism. But it is not; for in this time of morbid symptoms
there are contradictions within the black liberation struggle
itself, based not only, as would be expected, on the opposing
ideological alignments of the world outside, but also on the
moral confusion of claims – on land, on peoples – from the
pre-colonial past in relation to the unitary state the majority of
blacks and the segment of whites are avowed to. So, for whites,
it is not simply a matter of follow-the-leader behind blacks; it's
taking on, as blacks do, choices to be made out of confusion,
empirically, pragmatically, ideologically, or idealistically
about the practical moralities of the struggle. This is the
condition, imposed by history, if you like, in those areas of
action where black and white participation coincides.

*I am at a public meeting at the Johannesburg City Hall one night, after
working at this paper during the day. The meeting is held under the aus-
pices of the Progressive Federal Party, the official opposition in the all-
white South African parliament. The issue is a deal being made between
the South African government and the kingdom of Swaziland whereby
three thousand square miles of South African territory and 850,000 South
African citizens, part of the Zulu 'homeland' KwaZulu, would be given to
Swaziland. The principal speakers are Chief Gatsha Buthelezi, leader of
5·5 million Zulus, Bishop Desmond Tutu, and Mr Ray Swart, a white
liberal and a leader of the Progressive Federal Party. Chief Buthelezi has
consistently refused to take so-called independence for KwaZulu, but –
although declaring himself for the banned African National Congress –
by accepting all stages of so-called self-government up to the final one, has
transgressed the non-negotiable principle of the African National Congress, a unitary South Africa. Bishop Tutu upholds the principle of a
unitary South Africa. The Progressive Federal Party's constitution provides for a federal structure in a new, non-racial South Africa, recognising
as de facto entities the 'homelands' whose creation by the apartheid government the party nevertheless opposes. Also on the platform are members of
the Black Sash, the white women's organisation that has taken a radical
stand as a white ally of the black struggle; these women support a unitary
South Africa. In the audience of about two thousand, a small number
of whites is lost among exuberant, ululating, applauding Zulus. Order
– and what's more, amicability – is kept by Buthelezi's marshals,
equipped, beneath the garb of a private militia drawn from his tribal
Inkatha movement, with Zulu muscle in place of guns.*

What is Bishop Tutu doing here? He doesn't recognise the 'homelands'.

What are the Black Sash women doing here? They don't recognise the 'homelands'.

What is the Progressive Federal Party doing — a party firmly dedicated to constitutional action only — hosting a meeting where the banned black liberation salute — and battle cry — 'Amandla! Awethu!': 'Power — to the people!' — is shaking the columns of municipal doric, and a black man's tribal army instead of the South African police is keeping the peace?

What am I doing here, applauding Gatsha Buthelezi and Ray Swart? I don't recognise the homelands nor do I support a federal South Africa.

I was there — *they* were there — because, removed from its areas of special interest (KwaZulu's 'national' concern with land and people belonging to the Zulus), the issue was yet another government device to buy off surrounding states that give shelter to South African freedom fighters, and create support for a proposed 'constellation' of southern African states gathered protectively around the present South African regime; finally, to dispossess black South Africans of their South African citizenship, thus reducing the ratio of black to white population.

Yet the glow of my stinging palms cooled; what a paradox I had accommodated in myself! Moved by a display of tribal loyalty when I believe in black unity, applauding a 'homelands' leader, above all, scandalised by the excision of part of a 'homeland' from South Africa when the 'homelands' policy is itself the destruction of the country as an entity. But these are the confusions blacks have to live with, and if I am making any claim to accompany them beyond apartheid, so must I.

The state of interregnum is a state of Hegel's disintegrated consciousness,[5] of contradictions. It is from its internal friction that energy somehow must be struck, for us whites; energy to break the vacuum of which we are subconsciously aware, for however hated and shameful the collective life of apartheid and its structures has been to us, there is, now, the unadmitted fear of being without structures. The interregnum is not only between two social orders but also between two identities, one known and discarded, the other unknown and undetermined. Whatever the human cost of the liberation struggle, whatever 'Manichaean poisons'* must be absorbed as stimulants in the interregnum, the black knows he will be at home, at last, in the future. The white who has declared himself or herself for that future, who belongs to the white segment that was never at home in white supremacy, does not know whether he will find his home at last. It is assumed, not only by racists, that this depends entirely on the willingness of blacks to let him in; but we, if we live out our situation consciously, proceeding from the Pascalian wager that the home of the white African exists, know that this depends also on our finding our way there out of the perceptual clutter of curled photographs of master and servant relationships, the 78 *rpm*s of history repeating the conditioning of the past.

A black man I may surely call my friend because we have survived a time when he did not find it possible to accept a white's friendship, and a time when I didn't think I could accept that he should decide when that time was past, said to me this year, 'Whites have to learn to struggle.' It was not an admonition but a sincere encouragement. Expressed in political terms, the course of our friendship, his words and his attitude, signify the phasing out or passing usefulness of the extreme wing of the Black Consciousness movement, with its separatism of the past ten years, and the return to the tenets of the most broadly based and prestigious of black movements, the banned African National Congress: non-racialism, belief that race oppression is part of the class struggle, and recognition that it is possible for whites to opt out of class and race privilege and identify with black liberation.

My friend was not, needless to say, referring to those whites, from Abram Fischer to Helen Joseph and Neil Aggett,[6] who have risked and in some cases lost their lives in the political struggle with apartheid. It would be comfortable to assume that he was not referring, either, to the articulate outriders of the white segment, intellectuals, writers, lawyers, students, church and civil rights progressives, who keep the whips of protest cracking. But I know he *was*, after all, addressing those

* Czeslaw Milosz, 'The Accuser', in *Bells in Winter* (New York: The Ecco Press, 1978), p. 62.

of us belonging to the outriders on whose actions the newspapers report and the secret police keep watch, as we prance back and forth ever closer to the fine line between being concerned citizens and social revolutionaries. Perhaps the encouragement was meant for us as well as the base of the segment – those in the audience but not up on the platform, young people and their parents' generation, who must look for some effective way, in the living of their own personal lives, to join the struggle for liberation from racism.

For a long time, such whites have felt that we are doing all we can, short of violence – a terrible threshold none of us is willing to cross, though aware that all this may mean is that it will be left to blacks to do so. But now blacks are asking a question to which every white must have a personal answer, on an issue that cannot be dealt with by a show of hands at a meeting or a signature to a petition; an issue that comes home and enters every family. Blacks are now asking why whites who believe apartheid is something that must be abolished, not defended, continue to submit to army call-up.

We whites have assumed that army service was an example of Czeslaw Milosz's 'powerlessness of the individual involved in a mechanism that works independently of his will.'* If you refuse military service your only options are to leave the country or go to prison. Conscientious objection is not recognised in South Africa at present; legislation may establish it in some form soon, but if this is to be, is working as an army clerk not functioning as part of the war machine?

These are reasons enough for all – except a handful of men who choose prison on religious rather than on political grounds – to get into the South African army despite their opposition to apartheid.[7] These are not reasons enough for them to do so, on the condition on which blacks can accept whites' dedication to mutual liberation. Between black and white attitudes to struggle there stands the overheard remark of a young black woman: 'I break the law because I am alive.' We whites have still to thrust the spade under the roots of our lives; for most of us, including myself, struggle is still something that has a place. But for blacks it is everywhere or nowhere.

* *Native Realm*, p. 120.

> *What is poetry which does not save nations or peoples?*
> Czeslaw Milosz[8]

I have already delineated my presence here on the scale of a minority within a minority. Now I shall reduce my claim to significance still further. A white; a dissident white; a white writer. If I were not a writer, I should not have been invited here at all, so I must presume that although the problems of a white writer are of no importance compared with the liberation of 23·5 million black people, the peculiar relation of the writer in South Africa as interpreter, both to South Africans and to the world, of a society in struggle, makes the narrow corridor I can lead you down one in which doors fly open on the tremendous happening experienced by blacks.

For longer than the first half of this century the experience of blacks in South Africa was known to the world as it was interpreted by whites. The first widely read imaginative works exploring the central fact of South African life – racism – were written in the 1920s by whites, William Plomer[9] and Sarah Gertrude Millin.[10] If blacks were the subjects but not the readers of books written about them, then neither white nor black read much of what have since become the classics of early black literature – the few works of Herbert and Rolfes Dhlomo,[11] Thomas Mofolo, and Sol Plaatje. Their moralistic essays dealt with contemporary black life, but their fiction was mainly historical, a desperate attempt to secure, in art forms of an imposed culture, an identity and history discounted and torn up by that culture.

In the 1950s urban blacks – Ezekiel Mphahlele, Lewis Nkosi, Can Themba, Bloke Modisane, following Peter Abrahams[12] – began to write in English only, and about the urban industrial experience in which black and white chafed against one another across colour barriers. The work of these black writers interested both black and white at that improvised level known as intellectual, in South Africa: 'aware' would be a more accurate term, designating awareness that the white middle-class establishment was not, as it claimed, the paradigm of South African life, and white culture was not the definitive South African culture. Somewhere at the black writers' elbows, as they wrote, was the joggle of independence coming to one colonised country after another, north of South Africa. But they wrote ironically of their lives under oppression; as victims, not fighters. And even those black writers who were political activists, such as the novelist Alex La Guma and the poet Dennis Brutus, made of their ideologically-channelled bitterness not more than the Aristotelian catharsis, creating in the reader empathy with the oppressed rather than rousing rebellion against repression.

The fiction of white writers also produced the Aristotelian effect — and included in the price of hardback or paperback a catharsis of white guilt, for writer and reader. (It was at this stage, incidentally, that reviewers abroad added their dime's worth of morbid symptoms to our own by creating 'courageous' as a criterion of literary value for South African writers ...) The subject of both black and white writers — which was the actual entities of South African life instead of those defined by separate entrances for white and black — was startlingly new and important; whatever any writer, black or white, could dare to explore there was considered ground gained for advance in the scope of all writers. There had been no iconoclastic tradition; only a single novel, William Plomer's *Turbott Wolfe*, written thirty years before, whose understanding of *what our subject really was* was still a decade ahead of our time when he phrased the total apothegm: 'The native question — it's not a question, it's an answer.'[13]

In the 1970s black writers began to give that answer — for themselves. It had been vociferous in the consciousness of resistance politics, manifest in political action — black mass organisations, the African National Congress, the Pan-Africanist Congress, and others — in the 1960s. But except at the oral folk-literature level of 'freedom' songs, it was an answer that had not come, yet, from the one source that had never been in conquered territory, not even when industrialisation conscripted where military conquest had already devastated: the territory of the subconscious, where a people's own particular way of making sense and dignity of life — the base of its culture, remains unget-at-able. Writers, and not politicians, are its spokespeople.

With the outlawing of black political organisations, the

banning of freedom songs and platform speeches, there came from blacks a changed attitude towards culture, and towards literature as verbal, easily-accessible culture. Many black writers had been in conflict – and challenged by political activists: are you going to fight or write? Now they were told, in the rhetoric of the time: there is no conflict if you make your pen our people's weapon.

The Aristotelian catharsis, relieving black self-pity and white guilt, was clearly not the mode in which black writers could give the answer black resistance required from them. The iconoclastic mode, though it had its function where race fetishists had set up their china idols in place of 'heathen' wooden ones, was too ironic and detached, other-directed. Black people had to be brought back to themselves. Black writers arrived, out of their own situation, at Brecht's discovery: their audience needed to be educated to be *astonished at the circumstances under which they functioned*.* They began to show blacks that their living conditions are their story.

South Africa does not lack its Chernyshevskys to point out that the highroad of history is not the sidewalks of fashionable white Johannesburg's suburban shopping malls any more than it was that of the Nevsky Prospect.† In the bunks of migratory labourers, the 4 a.m. queues between one-room family and factory, the drunken dreams argued round braziers, is the history of blacks' defeat by conquest, the scale of the lack of value placed on them by whites, the degradation of their own acquiescence in that value; the salvation of revolt is there, too, a match dropped by the builders of every ghetto, waiting to be struck. The difficulty, even boredom, many whites experience when reading stories or watching plays by blacks in which, as they say, 'nothing happens', is due to the fact that the experience conveyed is not 'the development of actions' but 'the representation of conditions',‡ a mode of artistic revela-

---

* Walter Benjamin, 'What is Epic Theatre?', in *Illuminations*, edited with an introduction by Hannah Arendt, translated by Harry Zohn (London: Fontana, 1973), p. 152. [Gordimer's italics.]
† Nikolai G. Chernyshevsky, *Polnoye sobraniye sochinenii [v. 10–i tomakh* (St Petersburg, 1906)], vol. 8. Paraphrased from the translated quotation, 'The highroad of History is not the sidewalk of the Nevsky Prospect', in Tibor Szamuely, *The Russian Tradition*, edited with an introduction by Robert Conquest (London: Secker & Warburg, 1974), p. 167.
‡ Benjamin, 'What is Epic Theatre?', p. 152.

tion and experience for those in whose life dramatic content is in its conditions.

This mode of writing was the beginning of the black writer's function as a revolutionary; it was also the beginning of a conception of himself differing from that of the white writer's self-image. The black writer's consciousness of himself as a writer comes now from his participation in those living conditions; in the judgment of his people, that is what makes him a writer — the authority of the experience itself, not the way he perceives it and transforms it into words. Tenets of criticism are accordingly based on the critic's participation in those same living conditions, not on his ability to judge how well the writer has achieved 'the disposition of natural material to a formal end that shall enlighten the imagination' — this definition of art by Anthony Burgess* would be regarded by many blacks as arising from premises based on white living conditions and the thought patterns these determine: an arabesque of smoke from an expensive cigar. If we have our Chernyshevskys we are short on Herzens. Literary standards and standards of human justice are hopelessly confused in the interregnum. Bad enough that in the case of white South African writers some critics at home and abroad are afraid to reject sensationalism and crass banality of execution so long as the subject of a work is 'courageous'. For black writers the syllogism of talent goes like this: all blacks are brothers; all brothers are equal; therefore you cannot be a better writer than I am. The black writer who questions the last proposition is betraying the first two.[14]

As a fellow writer, I myself find it difficult to accept, even for the cause of black liberation to which I am committed as a white South African citizen, that a black writer of imaginative power, whose craftsmanship is equal to what he has to say, must not be regarded above someone who has emerged — admirably — from political imprisonment with a scrap of paper on which there is jotted an alliterative arrangement of protest slogans. For me, the necessity for the black writer to find imaginative modes equal to his existential reality goes without question. But I cannot accept that he must deny, as proof of solidarity with his people's struggle, the torturous inner quali-

* 'Creativity', *Observer* (London), 9 May 1982, p. 27.

ties of prescience and perception that will always differentiate him from others and that make of him — a writer. I cannot accept, either, that he should have served on him, as the black writer now has, an orthodoxy — a kit of emotive phrases, an unwritten index of subjects, a typology.

The problem is that agitprop, not recognised under that or any other name, has become the first contemporary art form that many black South Africans feel they can call their own. It fits their anger; and this is taken as proof that it is an organic growth of black creation freeing itself, instead of the old shell that it is, inhabited many times by the anger of others. I know that agitprop binds the artist with the means by which it aims to free the minds of the people. I can see, now, how often it thwarts both the black writer's common purpose to master his art and revolutionary purpose to change the nature of art, create new norms and forms out of and for a people re-creating themselves. But how can my black fellow writer agree with me, even admit the conflict I set up in him by these statements? There are those who secretly believe, but few who would assert publicly, with Gabriel García Márquez: 'The writer's duty — his revolutionary duty, if you like — is to write well.'[15] The black writer in South Africa feels he has to accept the criteria of his people because in no other but the community of black deprivation is he in possession of selfhood. It is only through unreserved, exclusive identification with blacks that he can break the alienation of having been 'other' for nearly 350 years in the white-ordered society, and only through submitting to the beehive category of 'cultural worker', programmed, that he can break the alienation of the artist/élitist in the black mass of industrial workers and peasants.

And, finally, he can toss the conflict back into my lap with Camus's words: 'Is it possible . . . to be in history while still referring to values which go beyond it?'*

The black writer is 'in history' and its values threaten to force out the transcendent ones of art. The white, as writer and South African, does not know his place 'in history' at this stage, in this time.

There are two absolutes in my life. One is that racism is evil —

---

* *Carnets 1942–51*, p. 104.

human damnation in the Old Testament sense, and no compromises, as well as sacrifices, should be too great in the fight against it. The other is that a writer is a being in whose sensibility is fused what Lukács calls 'the duality of inwardness and outside world',* and he must never be asked to sunder this union. The coexistence of these absolutes often seems irreconcilable within one life, for me. In another country, another time, they would present no conflict because they would operate in unrelated parts of existence; in South Africa now they have to be co-ordinates for which the coupling must be found. The morality of life and the morality of art have broken out of their categories in social flux. If you cannot reconcile them, they cannot be kept from one another's throats, within you.

For me, Lukács's 'divinatory-intuitive grasping of the un-attained and therefore inexpressible meaning of life'† is what a writer, poorly evolved for the task as he is, is made for. As fish that swim under the weight of many dark fathoms look like any other fish but on careful examination are found to have no eyes, so writers, looking pretty much like other human beings, but moving deep under the surface of human lives, have at least some faculties of supra-observation and hyperperception not known to others. If a writer does not go down and use these — why, he's just a blind fish. *Exactly* — says the new literary orthodoxy: he doesn't see what is happening in the visible world, among the people, on the level of their action, where battle is done with racism every day. On the contrary, say I, he brings back with him the thematic life-material that underlies and motivates their actions. 'Art ... lies at the heart of all events,' Joseph Brodsky writes.‡ It is from there, in the depths of being, that the most important intuition of revolutionary faith comes: the people know what to do, before the leaders.[16] It was from that level that the yearning of black school-children for a decent education was changed into a revolt in 1976; their strength came from the deep silt of repression and the abandoned wrecks of uprisings that sank there before they

---

* *The Theory of the Novel* [as quoted by Walter Benjamin, in the translation by Harry Zohn: see 'The Storyteller', *Illuminations*, p. 99].
† Ibid. [Both here and in the previous quotation the extracts differ somewhat from the standard translation by Anna Bostock, *The Theory of the Novel* (London: Merlin Press, 1971), pp. 127, 129.]
‡ 'Homage to Yalta', in *A Part of Speech* (New York: Farrar, Straus & Giroux, 1980), p. 12.

were born. It was from that level that an action of ordinary people for their own people made a few lines low down on a newspaper page, the other day: when some migrant contract workers from one of the 'homelands' were being laid off at a factory, workers with papers of permanent residence in the 'white' area asked to be dismissed in their place, since the possession of papers meant they could at least work elsewhere, whereas the migrant workers would be sent back to the 'homelands', jobless.

'Being an "author" has been unmasked as a role that, whether conformist or not, remains inescapably responsible to a given social order.' Nowhere in the world is Susan Sontag's statement* truer than in South Africa. The white writer has to make the decision whether to remain responsible to the dying white order — and even as dissident, if he goes no further than that position, he remains *negatively* within the white order — or to declare himself positively as answerable to the order struggling to be born. And to declare himself for the latter is only the beginning; as it is for whites in a less specialised position, only more so. He has to try to find a way to reconcile the irreconcilable within himself, establish his relation to the culture of a new kind of posited community, non-racial but conceived with and led by blacks.

I have entered into this commitment with trust and a sense of discovering reality, coming alive in a new way — I believe the novels and stories I have written in the last seven or eight years reflect this — for a South Africa in which white middle-class values and mores contradict realities has long become the unreality, to me. Yet I admit that I am, indeed, determined to find my place 'in history' while still referring as a writer to the values that are beyond history. I shall never give them up.

Can the artist go through the torrent with his precious bit of talent tied up in a bundle on his head? I don't know yet. I can only report that the way to begin entering history out of a dying white regime is through setbacks, encouragements and rebuffs from others, and frequent disappointments in oneself. A necessary learning process . . .

---

* From 'Approaching Artaud', in *Under the Sign of Saturn* (New York: Farrar, Straus & Giroux, 1980), p. 14.

I take a break from writing.

I am in a neighbouring black country at a conference on Culture and Resistance.[17] *It is being held outside South Africa because exiled artists and those of us who still live and work in South Africa cannot meet at home. Some white artists have not come because, not without reason, they fear the consequences of being seen, by South African secret police spies, in the company of exiles who belong to political organisations banned in South Africa, notably the African National Congress; some are not invited because the organisers regard their work and political views as reactionary. I am dubbed the blacks' darling by some whites back home because I have been asked to give the keynote address at a session devoted to literature; but I wonder if those who think me favoured would care to take the flak I know will be coming at me from those corners of the hall where black separatists group. They are here not so much out of democratic right as of black solidarity; paradoxically, since the conference is in itself a declaration that in the conviction of participants and organisers the liberation struggle and post-apartheid culture are non-racial. There is that bond of living conditions that lassos all blacks within a loyalty containing, without constraining or resolving, bitter political differences.*

Do I think white writers should write about blacks?

The artless question from the floor disguises both a personal attack on my work and an edict publicly served upon white writers by the same orthodoxy that prescribes for blacks. In the case of whites, it proscribes the creation of black characters — and by the same token, flipped head-to-tails, with which the worth of black writers is measured: the white writer does not share the total *living conditions of blacks, therefore he must not write about them. There are some whites — not writers, I believe — in the hall who share this view. In the ensuing tense exchange I reply that there are whole areas of human experience, in work situations — on farms, in factories, in the city, for example — where black and white have been observing one another and interacting for nearly 350 years. I challenge my challenger to deny that there are things we know about each other that are never spoken, but are there to be written — and received with the amazement and consternation, on both sides, of having been found out. Within those areas of experience, limited but intensely revealing, there is every reason why white should create black and black white characters. For myself, I have created black characters in my fiction: whether I have done so successfully or not is for the reader to decide. What's certain is that there is no representation of our social reality without that strange area of our lives in which we have knowledge of one another.*

I do not acquit myself so honestly a little later, when persecution of South African writers by banning is discussed. Someone links this with the persecution of writers in the Soviet Union, and a young man leaps to reply that the percentage of writers to population is higher in the Soviet Union than in any other part of the world and that Soviet writers work 'in a trench of peace and security'.

The aptness of the bizarre image, the hell for the haven he wishes to illustrate, brings no smiles behind hands among us; beyond the odd word-substitution is, indeed, a whole arsenal of tormented contradictions that could explode the conference.

Someone says, out of silence, quietly and distinctly: 'Bullshit.'

There is silence again. I don't take the microphone and tell the young man: there is not a contrast to be drawn between the Soviet Union's treatment of writers and that of South Africa, there is a close analogy — South Africa bans and silences writers just as the Soviet Union does, although we do not have resident censors in South African publishing houses and dissident writers are not sent to mental hospitals. I am silent. I am silent because, in the debates of the interregnum, any criticism of the communist system is understood as a defence of the capitalist system which has brought forth the pact of capitalism and racism that is apartheid, with its treason trials to match Stalin's trials, its detentions of dissidents to match Soviet detentions, its banishment and brutal uprooting of communities and individual lives to match, if not surpass, the gulag. Repression in South Africa has been and is being lived through; repression elsewhere is an account in a newspaper, book, or film. The choice, for blacks, cannot be distanced into any kind of objectivity: they believe in the existence of the lash they feel. Nothing could be less *than better* than *what they have known as the 'peace and security' of capitalism.**

I was a coward and no doubt often shall be one again, in my actions and statements as a citizen of the interregnum; it is a place of shifting ground, forecast for me in the burning slag heaps of coal mines we children used to ride across with furiously pumping bicycle pedals and flying hearts, in the Transvaal town where I was born.

And now the time has come to say I believe you stand on shifting ground with me, across ten thousand miles, not

* *Star* (Johannesburg), 4 August 1982.

because I have brought it with me, but because in some strange pilgrimage through the choices of our age and their consequences the democratic left of the Western world has arrived by many planned routes and plodding detours at the same unforeseen destination. It seems to be an abandoned siding. There was consternation when, early this year, Susan Sontag had the great courage and honesty publicly to accuse herself and other American intellectuals of the left of having been afraid to condemn the repression committed by communist regimes because this was seen as an endorsement of America's war on Vietnam and collusion with brutish rightist regimes in Latin America.* This moral equivocation draws parallel with mine at the writer's congress, far away in Africa, she has given me the courage, at second hand, to confess. Riding handlebar to handlebar across the coal slag, both equivocations reveal the same fear. What is its meaning? It is fear of the abyss, of the greater interregnum of human hopes and spirit where against Sartre's socialism as the 'horizon of the world' is silhouetted the chained outline of Poland's Solidarity, and all around, in the ditches of El Salvador, in the prisons of Argentina and South Africa, in the roofless habitations of Beirut, are the victims of Western standards of humanity.

I lie and you lie not because the truth is that Western capitalism has turned out to be just and humane, after all; but because we feel we have nothing to offer, now, except the rejection of it.

Because communism since 1917 has turned out not to be just or humane either, has failed this promise even more cruelly than capitalism, have we to tell the poor and dispossessed of the world there is nothing else to be done than to turn back from the communist bosses to the capitalist bosses? In South Africa's rich capitalist state stuffed with Western finance, fifty thousand black children a year die from malnutrition and malnutrition-related diseases, while the West piously notes that communist states cannot provide their people with meat and butter. In two decades in South Africa, three million black people have been ejected from the context of their lives, forcibly removed from homes and jobs and

* Text of speech by Susan Sontag, 6 February 1982, Town Hall, New York (*Nation*, 27 February 1982, pp. 230–1).

'resettled' in arid, undeveloped areas by decree of a white government supported by Western capital. It is difficult to point out to black South Africans that the forms of Western capitalism are changing towards a broad social justice in the example of countries like Sweden, Denmark, Holland, and Austria, with their mixed welfare economies, when all black South Africans know of Western capitalism is political and economic terror. And this terror is not some relic of the colonial past; it is being financed *now* by Western democracies – concurrently with Western capitalist democracy's own evolution towards social justice.

The fact is, black South Africans and whites like myself no longer believe in the ability of Western capitalism to bring about social justice where we live. We see no evidence of that possibility in our history or our living present. Whatever the Western democracies have done for themselves, they have failed and are failing, in their great power and influence, to do for us. This is the answer to those who ask, 'Why call for an alternative left? Why not an alternative capitalism?' Show us an alternative capitalism working from without for real justice in our country. What are the conditions attached to the International Monetary Fund loan of approximately $1 billion[18] that would oblige the South African government to stop population removals, to introduce a single standard of unsegregated education for all, to reinstate millions of black South Africans deprived of citizenship?*

If the injustices of communism cannot be reformed, must we assume that those of capitalism's longer history, constantly monitored by the compassionate hand of liberalism, can be? Must we accept that the workers of the Third World may hope only to be manipulated a little for their betterment and never to attain worker self-rule because this has been defeated in Poland by those very people in power who professed to believe in it? The dictum I quoted earlier carried, I know, its supreme irony: most leaders in the communist world have betrayed the basic intuition of democracy, that 'the people know what to do'

---

* The US has a 20 per cent slice under the weighted voting system of the IMF and so outvoted all loan opponents combined. The US consequently surely has corresponding responsibility for how the money South Africa receives is spent. Is there any evidence that this responsibility is being taken up?

– which is perhaps why Susan Sontag saw communism as fascism with a human face. But I think we can, contrary to her view, 'distinguish' among communisms, and I am sure, beyond the heat of an extemporary statement, so does she. If the US and Sweden are not Botha's South Africa, was Allende's Chile East Germany, though both were in the socialist camp? We must 'distinguish' to the point where we take up the real import of the essential challenge Susan Sontag levelled – to love truth enough, to pick up the blood-dirtied, shamed cause of the left, and attempt to re-create it in accordance with what it was meant to be, not what sixty-five years of human power-perversion have made of it. If, as she rightly says, once we did not understand the nature of communist tyranny – now we do, just as we have always understood at first hand the nature of capitalist tyranny. This is not a Manichaean equation – which is god and which the devil is not a question the evidence could decide, anyway – and it does not license withdrawal and hopelessness. We have surely learned by now something of where socialism goes wrong, which of its precepts are deadly dangerous and lead, in practice, to fascist control of labour and total suppression of individual freedom. Will the witchcraft of modern times not be exorcised, eventually, by this knowledge? If fascist rule is possible within the framework of communist society, does this not mean we must apply the kind of passion that goes into armaments research to research a socialism that progressively reduces that possibility? Let the West call us traitors once again, and the East deride us as revisionists. Is it really inconceivable that socialism can ever be attained without horrors? Certainly Lech Walesa and his imprisoned followers don't find it so.

As for capitalism, whatever its reforms, its avowed self-perpetuation of advancement for the many by creation of wealth for the few does not offer any hope to fulfil the ultimate promise of equality, the *human* covenant man entered into with himself in the moment he did the impossible, stood up, a new self, on two feet instead of four. In the interregnum in which we co-exist, the American left – disillusioned by the failure of communism – needs to muster with us of the Third World – living evidence of the failure of capitalism – the cosmic obstinacy to believe in and work towards the possibility of an alternative left, a democracy without economic or military terror. If we cannot, the possibility itself will die out, for our age, and who knows when, after what even bloodier age, it will be rediscovered.

There is no forgetting how we could live if only we could find the way. We must continue to be tormented by the ideal. Its possibility must be there for peoples to attempt to put into practice, to begin over and over again, wherever in the world it has never been tried, or has failed. This is where your responsibility to the Third World meets mine. Without the will to tramp towards that possibility, no relations of whites, of the West, with the West's formerly subject peoples can ever be free of the past, because the past, for them, was the jungle of Western capitalism, not the light the missionaries thought they brought with them.

The Essential Gesture

(1984)[1]

If the previous essay is Gordimer's strongest personal and political statement on the obligations and ambiguities of 'living in the interregnum', then the one which follows here is her most powerful consideration of these issues in relation to her writing. Fundamentally, it is a meditation on responsibility. Developing the themes of 'A Writer's Freedom' and 'Relevance and Commitment', and ranging through European and Third World literature as well as South African, it is again a reflection on the writer's dual commitments: to society, and to writing itself. Holding these two in balance, it is also an attempt – perhaps finally unresolved here – to see whether they cannot ultimately come to the same thing. In order to set off these thoughts, and indirectly showing how far she had come in the interim, Gordimer returned to where we first saw her, in 'A Bolter and the Invincible Summer' ...

When I began to write at the age of nine or ten, I did so in what I have come to believe is the only real innocence – an act without responsibility. For one has only to watch very small children playing together to see how the urge to influence, exact submission, defend dominance, gives away the presence of natal human 'sin' whose punishment is the burden of responsibility. I was alone. My poem or story came out of myself I did not know how. It was directed at no one, was read by no one.

Responsibility is what awaits outside the Eden of creativity. I should never have dreamt that this most solitary and deeply marvellous of secrets – the urge *to make* with words – would become a vocation for which the world, and that life-time lodger, conscionable self-awareness, would claim the right to call me and all my kind to account. The creative act is not pure.

History evidences it. Ideology demands it. Society exacts it. The writer loses Eden, writes to be read, and comes to realise that he is answerable. The writer is *held responsible*: and the verbal phrase is ominously accurate, for the writer not only has laid upon him responsibility for various interpretations of the consequences of his work, he is 'held' before he begins by the claims of different concepts of morality – artistic, linguistic, ideological, national, political, religious – asserted upon him. He learns that his creative act was not pure even while being formed in his brain: already it carried congenital responsibility for what preceded cognition and volition: for what he represented in genetic, environmental, social and economic terms when he was born of his parents.

Roland Barthes wrote that language is a 'corpus of prescriptions and habits common to all writers of a period'.*

He also wrote that a writer's 'enterprise' – his work – is his 'essential gesture as a social being'.

Between these two statements I have found my subject, which is their tension and connection: the writer's responsibility. For language – language as the transformation of thought into written words in any language – is not only 'a' but *the* corpus common to all writers in our period. From the corpus of language, within that guild shared with fellow writers, the writer fashions his enterprise, which then becomes his 'essential gesture as a social being'. Created in the common lot of language, that essential gesture is individual; and with it the writer quits the commune of the corpus; but with it he enters the commonalty of society, the world of other beings who are not writers. He and his fellow writers are at once isolated from one another far and wide by the varying concepts, in different societies, of what the essential gesture of the writer as a social being is.

By comparison of what is expected of them, writers often have little or nothing in common. There is no responsibility arising out of the status of the writer as a social being that could call upon Saul Bellow, Kurt Vonnegut, Susan Sontag, Toni Morrison or John Berger to write on a subject that would result in their being silenced under a ban, banished to internal exile

* From *Writing Degree Zero* [in *Barthes, Selected Writings*, edited and introduced by Susan Sontag (London: Fontana, 1983), p. 31].

or detained in jail. But in the Soviet Union, South Africa, Iran, Vietnam, Taiwan, certain Latin American and other countries, this is the kind of demand that responsibility for the social significance of being a writer exacts: a double demand, the first from the oppressed to act as spokesperson for them, the second, from the state, to take punishment for that act. Conversely, it is not conceivable that a Molly Keane, or any other writer of the quaint Gothic-domestic cult presently discovered by discerning critics and readers in the United States as well as Britain, would be taken seriously in terms of the interpretations of the 'essential gesture as a social being' called forth in countries such as the Soviet Union and South Africa, if he or she lived there.

Yet those critics and readers who live safe from the realm of midnight arrests and solitary confinement that is the dark condominium of East and West have their demands upon the writer from such places, too. For them, his essential gesture as a social being is to take risks they themselves do not know if they would.

This results in some strange and unpleasant distortions in the personality of some of these safe people. Any writer from a country of conflict will bear me out. When interviewed abroad, there is often disappointment that you are there, and not in jail in your own country. And since you are not — why are you not? Aha ... does this mean you have not written the book you should have written? Can you imagine this kind of self-righteous inquisition being directed against a John Updike for not having made the trauma of America's Vietnam war the theme of his work?*

There is another tack of suspicion. The London *Daily Telegraph* reviewer of my recent book of stories said I must be exaggerating: if my country really was a place where such things happened, how was it I could write about them? And then there is the wish-fulfilment distortion, arising out of the homebody's projection of his dreams upon the exotic writer: the journalist who makes a bogus hero out of the writer who

---

* American and European societies do not demand this 'orthodoxy' of their writers, because (arguably) their values are not in a crisis of survival concentrated on a single moral issue. Which does not authorise self-appointed cultural commissars to decide whether or not writers from other countries are fulfilling their 'essential gesture' in their own societies.

knows that the pen, where he lives, is a weapon not mightier than the sword.

One thing is clear: ours is a period when few can claim the absolute value of a writer without reference to a context of responsibilities. Exile as a mode of genius no longer exists; in place of Joyce we have the fragments of works appearing in *Index on Censorship*. These are the rags of suppressed literatures, translated from a Babel of languages; the broken cries of real exiles, not those who have rejected their homeland but who have been forced out − of their language, their culture, their society. In place of Joyce we have two of the best contemporary writers in the world, Czeslaw Milosz and Milan Kundera; but both regard themselves as amputated sensibilities, not free of Poland and Czechoslovakia in the sense that Joyce was free of Ireland − whole: out in the world but still in possession of the language and culture of home. In place of Joyce we have, one might argue, at least Borges; but in his old age, and out of what he sees in his blindness as he did not when he could see, for years now he has spoken wistfully of a desire to trace the trails made by ordinary lives instead of the arcane pattern of abstract forces of which they are the finger-painting. Despite his rejection of ideologies (earning the world's inescapable and maybe accurate shove over to the ranks of the Right) even he senses on those lowered lids the responsibilities that feel out for writers so persistently in our time.

What right has society to impose responsibility upon writers and what right has the writer to resist? I want to examine not what is forbidden us by censorship − I know that story too well − but to what we are bidden. I want to consider what is expected of us by the dynamic of collective conscience and the will to liberty in various circumstances and places; whether we should respond, and if so, how we do.

'It is from the moment when I shall no longer be more than a writer that I shall cease to write.' One of the great of our period, Camus, could say that.* In theory at least, as a writer he accepted the basis of the most extreme and pressing demand of our time. The ivory tower was finally stormed; and it was not with a white flag that the writer came out, but with manifesto

* *Carnets 1942–51.*

unfurled and arms crooked to link with the elbows of the people. And it was not just as their chronicler that the compact was made; the greater value, you will note, was placed on the persona outside of 'writer': to be 'no more than a writer' was to put an end to the justification for the very existence of the persona of 'writer'. Although the aphorism in its characteristically French neatness appears to wrap up all possible meanings of its statement, it does not. Camus's decision is a hidden as well as a revealed one. It is not just that he has weighed within himself his existential value as a writer against that of other functions as a man among men, and found independently in favour of the man; the scale has been set up by a demand outside himself, by his world situation. He has, in fact, accepted its condition that the greater responsibility is to society and not to art.

Long before it was projected into that of a world war, and again after the war, Camus's *natal* situation was that of a writer in the conflict of Western world decolonisation – the moral question of race and power by which the twentieth century will be characterised along with its discovery of the satanic ultimate in power, the means of human self-annihilation. But the demand made upon him and the moral imperative it set up in himself are those of a writer anywhere where the people he lives among, or any sections of them marked out by race or colour or religion, are discriminated against and repressed. Whether or not he himself materially belongs to the oppressed makes his assumption of extraliterary responsibility less or more 'natural', but does not alter much the problem of the conflict between integrities.

Loyalty is an emotion, integrity a conviction adhered to out of moral values. Therefore I speak here not of loyalties but integrities, in my recognition of society's right to make demands on the writer as equal to that of the writer's commitment to his artistic vision; the source of conflict is what demands are made and how they should be met.

The closest to reconciliation that I know of comes in my own country, South Africa, among some black writers. It certainly cannot be said to have occurred in two of the most important African writers outside South Africa, Chinua Achebe and Wole Soyinka.[2] They became 'more than writers' in answer to their country's — Nigeria's — crisis of civil war; but in no sense did the demand develop their creativity. On the contrary, both sacrificed for some years the energy of their creativity to the demands of activism, which included, for Soyinka, imprisonment. The same might be said of Ernesto Cardenal.[3] But it is out of being 'more than a writer' that many black men and women in South Africa *begin* to write. All the obstacles and diffidences — lack of education, of a tradition of written literary expression, even of the chance to form the everyday habit of reading that germinates a writer's gift — are overcome by the imperative to give expression to a majority not silent, but whose deeds and whose proud and angry volubility against suffering have not been given the eloquence of the written word. For these writers, there is no opposition of inner and outer demands. At the same time as they are writing, they are political activists in the concrete sense, teaching, proselytising, organising. When they are detained without trial it may be for what they have written, but when they are tried and convicted of crimes of conscience it is for what they have done as 'more than a writer'. 'Africa, my beginning ... Africa my end' — these lines of the epic poem written by Ingoapele Madingoane* epitomise this synthesis of creativity and social responsibility; what moves him, and the way it moves him, are perfectly at one with his society's demands. Without those demands he is not a poet.

The Marxist critic Ernst Fischer reaches anterior to my interpretation of this response with his proposition that 'an artist who belonged to a coherent society [here, read preconquest South Africa] and to a class that was not an impediment to progress [here, read not yet infected by white bourgeois aspirations] did not feel it any loss of artistic freedom if a certain range of subjects was prescribed to him' since such subjects were imposed 'usually by tendencies and traditions deeply rooted in the people.'† Of course, this may provide, in general, a sinister pretext for a government to invoke certain tendencies and traditions to suit its purpose of proscribing writers' themes, but applied to black writers in South Africa,

---

* *Africa My Beginning* (Johannesburg: Ravan Press, 1979; London: Rex Collings, 1980).

† Ernst Fischer, *The Necessity of Art: A Marxist Approach*, translated by Anna Bostock (Harmondsworth: Penguin, 1963), p. 47.

history evidences the likely truth of the proposition. Their tendency and tradition for more than three hundred years has been to free themselves of white domination.

Art is on the side of the oppressed. Think before you shudder at the simplistic dictum and its heretical definition of the freedom of art. For if art is freedom of the spirit, how can it exist within the oppressors? And there is some evidence that it ceases to. What writer of any literary worth defends fascism, totalitarianism, racism, in an age when these are still pandemic? Ezra Pound is dead. In Poland, where are the poets who sing the epic of the men who have broken Solidarity? In South Africa, where are the writers who produce brilliant defences of apartheid?

It remains difficult to dissect the tissue between those for whom writing is a revolutionary activity no different from and to be practised concurrently with running a political trade union or making a false passport for someone on the run, and those who interpret their society's demand to be 'more than a writer' as something that may yet be fulfilled through the nature of their writing itself. Whether this latter interpretation is possible depends on the society within which the writer functions. Even 'only' to write may be to be 'more than a writer' for one such as Milan Kundera, who goes on writing what he sees and knows from within his situation – his country under repression – until a ban on publishing his books strips him of his 'essential gesture' of being a writer at all. Like one of his own characters, he must clean windows or sell tickets in a cinema booth for a living. That, ironically, is what being 'more than a writer' would come down to for him, if he were to have opted to stay on in his country – something I don't think Camus quite visualised. There are South Africans who have found themselves in the same position – for example, the poet Don Mattera,[4] who for seven years was banned from writing, publishing, and even from reading his work in public. But in a country of total repression of the majority, like South Africa, where literature is nevertheless only half-suppressed because the greater part of that black majority is kept semi-literate and cannot be affected by books, there is – just – the possibility for a writer to be 'only' a writer, in terms of activity, and yet 'more than a writer' in terms of fulfilling the demands of his society. An honourable category has been found for him. As 'cultural worker' in the race/class struggle he still may be seen to serve, even if he won't march towards the tear gas and bullets.

In this context, long before the term 'cultural worker' was taken over from the vocabulary of other revolutions, black writers had to accept the social responsibility white ones didn't have to — that of being the only historians of events among their people; Dhlomo, Plaatje, Mofolo created characters who brought to life and preserved events either unrecorded by white historians or recorded purely from the point of view of white conquest.*[5] From this beginning there has been a logical intensification of the demands of social responsibility, as over decades discrimination and repression set into law and institution, and resistance became a liberation struggle. This process culminated during the black uprising of 1976, calling forth poetry and prose in an impetus of events not yet exhausted or fully explored by writers. The uprising began as a revolt of youth and it brought to writers a new consciousness — bold, incantatory, messianically reckless. It also placed new demands upon them in the essential gesture that bound them to a people springing about on the balls of their feet before dawn-streaks of freedom and the threat of death. Private emotions were inevitably outlawed by political activists who had no time for any; black writers were expected to prove their blackness *as a revolutionary condition* by submitting to an unwritten orthodoxy of interpretation and representation in their work. I stress unwritten because there was no Writers' Union to be expelled from. But there was a company of political leaders, intellectuals, and the new category of the alert young, shaming others with their physical and mental bravery, to ostracise a book of poems or prose if it were found to be irrelevant to the formal creation of an image of people anonymously, often spontaneously heroic.

* See H. I. E. Dhlomo, 'Valley of a Thousand Hills' [reprinted in his *Collected Works*, (eds) N. Visser and T. Couzens (Johannesburg: Ravan Press, 1985)]; Sol. T. Plaatje, *Mhudi* (Lovedale: Lovedale Press [1930]), edited by Stephen Gray, introduction by Tim Couzens (London: Heinemann; Washington D.C.: Three Continents Press, 1978), *Native Life in South Africa* (1916; Johannesburg: Ravan Press, 1982; London: Longman, 1987), and *The Boer War Diary of Sol. T. Plaatje*, (ed.) J. L. Comaroff (Johannesburg: Macmillan, 1973); Thomas Mofolo, *Chaka: An Historical Romance* (1931; London and New York: Oxford University Press, 1967), new translation by Daniel P. Kunene (London: Heinemann, 1981).

Some of my friends among black writers have insisted that this 'imposition' of orthodoxy is a white interpretation; that the impulse came from within to discard the lantern of artistic truth that reveals human worth through human ambiguity, and to see by the flames of burning vehicles only the strong, thick lines that draw heroes. To gain his freedom the writer must give up his freedom. Whether the impulse came from within, without, or both, for the black South African writer it became an imperative to attempt that salvation. It remains so; but in the 1980s many black writers of quality have come into conflict with the demand from without — responsibility as orthodoxy — and have begun to negotiate the right to their own, inner interpretation of the essential gesture by which they are part of the black struggle.* The black writer's revolutionary responsibility may be posited by him as the discovery, in his own words, of the revolutionary spirit that rescues for the present — and for the post-revolutionary future — that nobility in ordinary men and women to be found only among their doubts, culpabilities, shortcomings: their courage-in-spite-of.

To whom are South African writers answerable in their essential gesture if they are not in the historical and existential situation of blacks, and if (axiomatic for them in varying degrees) they are alienated from their 'own', the historical and existential situation of whites? Only a section of blacks places any demands upon white writers at all; that grouping within radical blacks which grants integrity to whites who declare themselves for the black freedom struggle. To be one of these writers is firstly to be presented with a political responsibility if not an actual orthodoxy: the white writer's task as 'cultural worker' is to raise the consciousness of white people, who, unlike himself, have not woken up. It is a responsibility at once minor, in comparison with that placed upon the black writer as composer of battle hymns, and yet forbidding if one compares the honour and welcome that await the black writer, from blacks, and the branding as traitor, or, at best, turned backside of indifference, that awaits the white, from the white estab-

---

* Among the most recent examples: Njabulo Ndebele, *Fools* (Johannesburg: Ravan Press, 1983; London: Longman, 1986), Ahmed Essop, *The Emperor* (Johannesburg: Ravan Press, 1984), and Es'kia Mphahlele, *Afrika my Music* (Johannesburg: Ravan Press, 1984).

lishment. With fortunate irony, however, it is a responsibility which the white writer already has taken on, for himself, if the other responsibility – to his creative integrity – keeps him scrupulous in writing about what he knows to be true whether whites like to hear it or not: for the majority of his readers are white. He brings some influence to bear on whites, though not on the white-dominated government; he may influence those individuals who are already coming-to bewilderedly out of the trip of power, and those who gain courage from reading the open expression of their own suppressed rebellion. I doubt whether the white writer, even if giving expression to the same themes as blacks, has much social use in inspiriting blacks, or is needed to. Sharing the life of the black ghettoes is the primary qualification the white writer lacks, so far as populist appreciation is concerned. But black writers do share with white the same kind of influence on those whites who read them; and so the categories that the state would keep apart get mixed through literature – an unforeseen 'essential gesture' of writers in their social responsibility in a divided country.

The white writer who has declared himself answerable to the oppressed people is not expected by them to be 'more than a writer', since his historical position is not seen as allowing him to be central to the black struggle. But a few writers have challenged this definition by taking upon themselves exactly the same revolutionary responsibilities as black writers such as Alex La Guma, Dennis Brutus and Mongane Serote,[6] who make no distinction between the tasks of underground activity and writing a story or poem. Like Brutus, the white writers Breyten Breytenbach and Jeremy Cronin were tried and imprisoned for accepting the necessity they saw for being 'more than a writer'.[7] Their interpretation of a writer's responsibility, in their country and situation, remains a challenge, particularly to those who disagree with their actions while sharing with them the politics of opposition to repression. There is no moral authority like that of sacrifice.

In South Africa the ivory tower is bulldozed anew with every black man's home destroyed to make way for a white man's. Yet there are positions between the bulldozed ivory tower and the maximum security prison. The one who sees his responsibility in being 'only a writer' has still to decide whether this means he can fulfil his essential gesture to society only by ready-packaging his creativity to the dimensions of a social realism *those who will free him of his situation* have the authority to ask of him, or whether he may be able to do so by work George Steiner defines as 'scrupulously argued, not declaimed ... informed, at each node and articulation of proposal, with a just sense of the complex, contradictory nature of historical evidence'.* The great mentor of Russian revolutionary writers of the nineteenth century, Belinsky, advises: 'Do not worry about the incarnation of ideas. If you are a poet, your works will contain them without your knowledge – they will be both moral and national if you follow your inspiration freely.'† Octavio Paz, speaking from Mexico for the needs of the Third World, sees a fundamental function as social critic for the writer who is 'only a writer'. It is a responsibility that goes back to source: the corpus of language from which the writer arises. 'Social criticism begins with grammar and the re-establishing of meanings.'‡ This was the responsibility taken up in the post-Nazi era by Heinrich Böll and Günter Grass, and is presently being fulfilled by South African writers, black and white, in exposing the real meaning of the South African government's vocabulary of racist euphemisms – such terms as 'separate development', 'resettlement', 'national states', and its grammar of a racist legislature, with segregated chambers for whites, so-called coloureds and Indians, and no representation whatever for the majority of South Africans, those classified as black.

If the writer accepts the social realist demand, from without, will he be distorting, paradoxically, the very ability he has to offer the creation of a new society? If he accepts the other, self-imposed responsibility, how far into the immediate needs of his society will he reach? Will hungry people find revelation in the ideas his work contains 'without his knowledge'? The

* George Steiner, review of E. M. Cioran, *Drawn and Quartered, New Yorker*, 16 April 1984, p. 156.
† Vissarion Belinsky, 1810–48. The quote is from my notebook: unable to locate source.
‡ Octavio Paz, 'Development and other mirages', from *The Other Mexico: Critique of the Pyramid*, translated by Lysander Kemp (New York: Grove Press, 1972), p. 48.

one certainty, in South Africa as a specific historical situation, is that there is no opting out of the two choices. Outside is a culture in sterile decay, its achievements culminating in the lines of tin toilets set up in the veld for people 'resettled' by force. Whether a writer is black or white, in South Africa the essential gesture by which he enters the brotherhood of man — which is the only definition of society that has any permanent validity — is a revolutionary gesture.

'Has God ever expressed his opinion?' — Flaubert, writing to George Sand.[8] 'I believe that great art is scientific and impersonal . . . I want to have neither hate, nor pity, nor anger. The impartiality of description would then become equal to the majesty of the law.'

Nearly a century passed before the *nouveau roman* writers attempted this kind of majesty, taking over from another medium the mode of still-life. The work aspired to be the object-in-itself, although made up of elements — words, images — that can never be lifted from the 'partiality' of countless connotations. The writers went as far as it is possible to go from any societal demand. They had tried so hard that their vision became fixed on Virginia Woolf's mark on the wall — and as an end, not a beginning. Yet the anti-movement seems to have been, after all, a negative variation on a kind of social responsibility some writers have assumed at least since the beginning of the modern movement: to transform the world by style. This was and is something that could not serve as the writer's essential gesture in countries such as South Africa and Nicaragua, but it has had its possibilities and sometimes proves its validity where complacency, indifference, accidie, and not conflict, threaten the human spirit. To transform the world by style was the iconoclastic essential gesture tried out by the Symbolists and Dadaists; but whatever social transformation (in shaping a new consciousness) they might have served in breaking old forms was horribly superseded by different means: Europe, the Far, Middle and Near East, Asia, Latin America and Africa overturned by wars; millions of human beings wandering without the basic structure of a roof.

The Symbolists' and Dadaists' successors, in what Susan

Sontag terms 'the cultural revolution that refuses to be political' have among them their '... spiritual adventurers, social pariahs determined to disestablish themselves ... not to be morally useful to the community' – the essential gesture withheld by Céline and Kerouac.* Responsibility reaches out into the manifesto, however, and claims the 'seers' of this revolution. Through a transformation by style – depersonalised laconicism of the word almost to the Word – Samuel Beckett takes on as his essential gesture a responsibility direct to human destiny, and not to any local cell of humanity. This is the assumption of a messenger of the gods rather than a cultural worker. It is a disestablishment from the temporal; yet some kind of final statement exacted by the temporal. Is Beckett the freest writer in the world, or is he the most responsible of all?

Kafka was also a seer, one who sought to transform consciousness by style, and who was making his essential gesture to human destiny rather than the European fragment of it to which he belonged. But he was unconscious of his desperate signal. He believed that the act of writing was one of detachment that moved writers 'with everything we possess, to the moon.'† He was unaware of the terrifyingly impersonal, apocalyptic, prophetic nature of his vision in that ante-room to his parents' bedroom in Prague. Beckett, on the contrary, has been signalled to and consciously responded. The summons came from his time. His place – not Warsaw, San Salvador, Soweto – has nothing specific to ask of him. And unlike Joyce, he can never be in exile wherever he chooses to live, because he has chosen to be answerable to the twentieth-century human condition which has its camp everywhere, or nowhere – whichever way you see Vladimir, Estragon, Pozzo and Lucky.

Writers who accept a professional responsibility in the transformation of society are always seeking ways of doing so that

---

* Susan Sontag, 'Approaching Artaud', in *Under the Sign of Saturn*, p. 15: '... authors ... recognised by their effort to disestablish themselves, by their will not to be morally useful to the community, by their inclination to present themselves not as social critics but as seers, spiritual adventurers, and social pariahs'.
† Letter to Max Brod, quoted in Ronald Hayman, *K: A Biography of Kafka* (London: Weidenfeld & Nicolson, 1981), p. 237.

their societies could not ever imagine, let alone demand: asking
of themselves means that will plunge like a drill to release the
great primal spout of creativity, drench the censors, cleanse the
statute books of their pornography of racist and sexist laws,
hose down religious differences, extinguish napalm bombs and
flame-throwers, wash away pollution from land, sea and air,
and bring out human beings into the occasional summer fount
of naked joy. Each has his own dowsing twig, held over heart
and brain. Michel Tournier sees writers' responsibilities as to
'disrupt the establishment in exact proportion to their creativity'. This is a bold global responsibility, though more Orphic
and terrestrial than Beckett's. It also could be taken as an
admittance that this is *all* writers can do; for creativity comes
from within, it cannot be produced by will or dictate if it is not
there, although it can be crushed by dictate. Tournier's — this
apparently fantastical and uncommitted writer's — own creativity is nevertheless so close to the people that he respects as a
marvel — and makes it so for his readers — the daily history of
their lives as revealed in city trash dumps.* And he is so
fundamentally engaged by what alienates human beings that
he imagines for everyone the restoration of wholeness (the
totality which revolutionary art seeks to create for alienated
man) in a form of Being that both sexes experience as one —
something closer to a classless society than to a sexually
hermaphroditic curiosity.

The *transformation of experience* remains the writer's basic
essential gesture; the lifting out of a limited category something
that reveals its full meaning and significance only when the
writer's imagination has expanded it. This has never been
more evident than in the context of extreme experiences of
sustained personal horror that are central to the period of
twentieth-century writers. The English critic John Bayley has
written of Anna Akhmatova:

> A violently laconic couplet at the end of the sections of
> *Requiem* records her husband dead, her son in prison ... It
> is as good an instance as any of the power of great poetry
> to generalise and speak for the human predicament in

* *Gemini*, translated by Anne Carter (London: Collins; Garden City, N.Y.: Doubleday; 1981).

extremity, for in fact she had probably never loved Gumilev, from whom she had lived apart for years, and her son had been brought up by his grandmother. But the sentiment {of the poem} was not for herself but for 'her people', with whom she was at that time so totally united in suffering.*

Writers in South Africa who are 'only writers' are sometimes reproached by those, black and white, who are in practical revolutionary terms 'more than writers', for writing of events as if they themselves had been at the heart of action, endurance and suffering. So far as black writers are concerned, even though the humiliations and deprivations of daily life under apartheid enjoin them, many of them were no more among the children under fire from the police in the seventies, or are among the students and miners shot, tear-gassed and beaten in the eighties, or are living as freedom fighters in the bush, than Akhmatova was a heart-broken wife or a mother separated from a son she had nurtured. Given these circumstances, their claim to generalise and speak for a human predicament in extremity comes from the lesser or greater extent of their *ability to do so*; and the development of that ability is their responsibility towards those with whom they are united by this extrapolation of suffering and resistance. White writers who are 'only writers' are open to related reproach for 'stealing the lives of blacks' as good material. Their claim to this 'material' is the same as the black writers' at an important existential remove nobody would discount. Their essential gesture can be fulfilled only in the integrity Chekhov demanded: 'to describe a situation so truthfully ... that the reader can no longer evade it.'†

The writer is eternally in search of entelechy in his relation to his society. Everywhere in the world, he needs to be left alone and at the same time to have a vital connection with others; needs artistic freedom and knows it cannot exist without its wider context; feels the two presences within – creative self-absorption and conscionable awareness – and

* John Bayley, review of *Akhmatova: A Poetic Pilgrimage* by Amanda Haight, *Observer* (London), 31 October 1976, p. 29.
† From Isaiah Berlin, *Russian Thinkers* (London: The Hogarth Press, 1978), p. 303.

must resolve whether these are locked in death-struggle, or are really foetuses in a twinship of fecundity. Will the world let him, and will he know how to be the ideal of the writer as a social being, Walter Benjamin's story-teller, the one 'who could let the wick of his life be consumed completely by the gentle flame of his story'?*

* 'The Story-Teller', in *Illuminations*, pp. 108–9.

Letter from Johannesburg, 1985[1]

As the 1980s progressed, political conditions in South Africa intensified to a degree previously unknown. In 1983 there was a referendum on the introduction of a tricameral Parliament, now to include — separately — Indians and so-called 'coloureds' as well as whites. It was after this further elaboration of the myriad ways of apartheid, as well as the continued denial of the aspirations of the black majority, that a renewed wave of uprisings broke out. In September 1984 the Vaal 'triangle' near Johannesburg erupted in revolt. On 21 March 1985 — twenty-five years to the day after Sharpeville — there was another round of police shooting, this time at Uitenhage in the Eastern Cape, where twenty died and at least twenty-seven were injured. Riots spread speedily and spontaneously elsewhere in the townships and appeared to be beyond the control of the police; as the military moved in it seemed South Africa was in a state of civil war. It was in these circumstances that on 21 July 1985 the second State of Emergency since 1960 was declared. And it was in these circumstances, in much the same way as in 1976, that Gordimer wrote her second 'letter from Johannesburg'.

Dear —,

What is it you need to know about us that you cannot read as plain reportage, I wonder?

Well, maybe there is an indication in the ambiguity of the pronoun 'us'. When I, as a white English-speaking South African, employ it in this context, of whom do I speak? Of whom do you understand me to be speaking? For you ask about the 'position that non-Afrikaners find themselves in after the declaration of the State of Emergency in South Africa', and doubtless you would assume it is from that position that I respond because I am white, English-speaking etc. But your question at once reveals that an old misconception is still current abroad: the Afrikaners are the baddies and the English-speakers the goodies among whites in our country; all Afrikaners support the state of emergency and the sadistic police and army actions that led up to it, and all English-speakers would implode apartheid tomorrow if it were possible to prevail against the Afrikaner army that mans the Afrikaner fortress. This surprises me because anyone who follows the reports of foreign press correspondents in South Africa must be aware that in November 1983 the then Prime Minister, Mr P. W. Botha, received an overwhelming 'yes' vote for his new constitution with its tricameral parliament for whites, Indians, and so-called coloureds, and total exclusion of the black majority. The referendum held was open to whites only, Afrikaans and English-speaking; Mr Botha could not have received a mandate if the English-speakers had voted 'no'. 'Yes' they said, voting along with Mr Botha's supporters in the National Party. 'Yes' they said, 15·5 million black people shall have no say in the central government of South Africa.

And 'yes' said the Reagan government, entering into constructive engagement with a policy destructive of justice and human dignity, while mumbling obeisance to abhorrence of apartheid like those lapsed believers who cross themselves when entering church.

There is no such special position as 'one in which non-Afrikaners find themselves' now, nor has there been for a very long time. The categories do not fall so neatly into place. The actual division among whites falls between those – the majority – Afrikaner and English-speaking who support, whether directly or circuitously, the new constitution as a valid move towards 'accommodating black aspirations' (let us not invoke justice), and those – the minority – English-speaking and Afrikaner who oppose the constitution as irremediably unjust and unjustifiable. There are fewer Afrikaners than English-speakers in the latter category, but the support of English-speakers in the former represents a majority in their language group. When blacks speak about the 'Boere' these days, the term has become a generic rather than an ethnic one: it is likely to refer to a mode of behaviour, an attitude of mind, a *position* in which the nomenclature encompasses all whites who voluntarily and knowingly collaborate in oppression of blacks. Not all Afrikaners are 'Boere', and many English-speakers with pedigrees dating back to the 1820 Settlers are . . .

States of mind and ways of life under crisis would be expected more or less to follow the lines of division, and I believe that states of mind do. Everywhere I go I sense a relaxation of the facial muscles among whites who had appeared to be tasting the ashes of the good life when Soweto was on fire in the week before the state of emergency was declared. Approval of the state's action is not often explicit in my company because it is known that I belong to the minority-within-the-white-minority that opposes the constitution as a new order of oppression in contempt of justice, and sees the state of emergency as an act of desperation: a demonstration of the failure of the government's atrocious 'new deal' only a few months after it was instituted. The general feeling among whites is that fear has been staved off – at least for a while. The police dogs are guarding the gates of paradise.* Keep away from roads that pass where the blacks and the police/army are contained in their vortex of violence, and life can go on as usual. One can turn one's attention to matters that affect one directly and can be dealt with without bloodying one's hands: lobbying all over the world against disinvestment and sports boycotts – an area where sophisticated people understand one another in economic and leisure self-interests; for many, the only brotherhood that transcends nation and race. There is a physical and mental cordoning-off of 'areas of unrest'. The police and army take care of the first, and that extraordinary sense of whiteness, of having always been different, always favoured, always shielded from the vulnerabilities of poverty and powerlessness, takes care of the second. We whites in South Africa present an updated version of the tale of the Emperor's clothes; we are not aware of our nakedness – ethical, moral, and fatal – clothed as we are in our own skin. This morning on the radio the news of the withdrawal of more foreign diplomats from South Africa, and the continuing threat of the withdrawal by foreign banks, was followed by a burst of

---

* Paraphrased from the song by the South African David Kramer, '*Hekke van Paradise*': *En ek vra jou mos,/ Ek vra jou mos,/ Ek vra jou mos so* nice,/ *Hoekom blaf daai honde by die hekke van* Paradise?' (And I ask you . . . so 'nice',/ Why are those dogs barking at the gates of Paradise?)

pop-music defiance by the state-owned South African Broadcasting Corporation, on behalf of Afrikaner and English-speaking whites. *Allies*, yelled a disco idol, *We're allies, with our backs against the w-a-ll* ...

As for the less worldly among the white majority, they express openly their approval of government violence in the last few months, and there is a group that believes there has not been enough of it. 'The government should shoot the lot.' This remark was offered to my friend the photographer David Goldblatt, in all crazy seriousness, not as a manner of speaking: there are whites in whose subconscious the power of the gun in a white man's hand is magical (like his skin?) and could wipe out an entire population nearly four times as large as that of the whites. This, in bizarre historical twinship, is the obverse of the belief of the mid-nineteenth-century Xhosa prophetess Nongqause, who told her people that by following her instructions they could cause all those who wore trousers (the white men) to be swept away by a whirlwind ...

It is not true that the South African government is bent on genocide, as some black demagogues have averred (the black man is too useful for that); but it is true that the unconscious will to genocide is there, in some whites. So is belief in the old biblical justification for apartheid that has been embarrassedly repudiated by even the Dutch Reformed Church. Over lunch on his father's Transvaal farm recently, I met a handsome young Afrikaner on leave from military service. Grace was said; when the young man lifted his bowed head he began an exposition of biblical justification that was all his own, I think: blacks are the descendants of Cain and a curse on humankind. I did not rise to the bait; but my eyes must have betrayed that I could scarcely believe my ears. When, among the women of the family, I was being shown their new acquisition, a pristine white dishwasher that had replaced the black maid, he took the opportunity to fire at me: 'Yes, it's a good white kaffir girl.'

During the weeks that led up to the state of emergency, the Eastern Cape black townships had become ungovernable. Violence was horrific in the vicinity of Grahamstown. The white town of Grahamstown is the English 1820 Settlers' Association[2] show-piece answer to the Afrikaner Voortrekker Monument at Pretoria; here soldiers and armoured vehicles had taken the place of visitors to the town's annual cultural festival. Most whites in South Africa were in a state of anguish: over the outcome of the New Zealand government's determination to stop a rugby tour of South Africa by its national team. It was only when Soweto became a hell to which Johannesburg's black workers returned each night as best they could (buses would not venture farther than Soweto boundaries) that white faces in Johannesburg became strained.

But the state of mind of the minority-within-the-white-minority did not have to wait for any declaration to be aware of an emergency beyond rugby fields. People like Bishop Tutu, Reverend Beyers Naudé, Reverend Allan Boesak,[3] and Sheena Duncan of the Black Sash – a women's organisation that has done more than any other source to expose the appalling forced removals of black rural people – had been warning for months that an uprising was inevitable: built into the new constitution as its own consequence. The government was arresting trade union leaders and leaders of the non-racial United Democratic Front. Just as, abroad, one may mutter abhorrence of apartheid and go on funding it morally and materially, so the government continued (as it continues) to reiterate a litany of dedication to consultation and change while arresting almost every black leader with any claim to be consulted about change. On the minority side of the dividing line between white and white, a new organisation had grown in urgent response to the use of army recruits against the people of the black township of Sebokeng last October. Resistance to conscription was suddenly no longer some fringe defection on religious grounds by a handful of Seventh Day Adventists, but a wave of revulsion against 'defending one's country' by maiming, killing, and breaking into the humble homes of black people. In this horrifying domestic context, the End Conscription Campaign held a three-day gathering in Johannesburg where a large crowd of young men and their families debated the moral issues of conscientious objection and defined their position not as pacifist but as a refusal to defend apartheid. I gave a reading there of poetry by South African writers, black and white, in whose work, like that of playwrights, lately, this has been the theme. The subject has to be handled gingerly, whether in poetry or platform prose; it is a treasonable offence, in South Africa, to incite anyone to refuse military service. The ECC is not yet a mass movement, and maybe will not be, but the government is sufficiently alarmed by it to have detained several members.[4]

Again, there is a strange historical twinship. Even after 1960 when the South African revolution may be said to have begun, the sons of liberal and left-wing families docilely accepted, *force majeure*, the obligation to do military service, if with a sense of resentment and shame. At the same time, whites who support black liberation have long wondered why blacks have not turned significantly against the informers and collaborators among their own people. Now, young whites have at last found the courage to fulfil the chief provision blacks demand of them if they are to prove their commitment to the black cause: to refuse to fight to protect racism; while young blacks themselves have reached the stage of desperation that leads them to hunt down and destroy those who are their own people in terms of skin but not loyalty. Both developments – the first positive, the second tragic – are the direct result of the new constitution. The blacks were not consulted about it, rejected it, and are now in a continuous stage of rebellion out of bottomless frustration at finding themselves finally cast out, in civic and even physical terms, from their own country. The government deals with this rebellion by sending in white soldiers to terrorise them into temporary submission; young whites are confronted with the loathsome 'duty' it was surely always clear racism eventually would demand.

For years, when one asked blacks why they allowed black police to raid and arrest them, they would answer: 'Our brothers have to do what whites tell them. We are all victims together.' Now, black youths are confronted with what surely always was clear would be the ultimate distortion of their lives by apartheid: brothers, co-opted as police informers and City Fathers by white power, becoming enemies.

Many of us who belong to the minority-within-the-white-minority already were accustomed, before the state of emergency, to using the telephone for the kind of call not made outside thriller movies in Europe and America. When the South African Defence Force raided the capital of one of our neighbouring countries, Botswana, earlier this year, we feared for the lives of friends living in exile there. For some days, we could piece together their fate only by exchanging guarded word-of-mouth news. For my fellow writer, Sipho Sepamla,[5] the news was bad; he travelled across the border to Botswana to the funeral of a relative murdered in the raid, and we were nervous about his doing so, since the brutal raid — which resulted in indiscriminate killing, so that even children died — was purportedly against African National Congress revolutionaries, and the demonstration of any connection with even random victims could rub off as guilt by association. With the beginning of the state of emergency there came mass arrests, and severe penalties for revealing without authority the identity of any detainee.[6] The names we know are confined to those permitted by the police to be published. Who can say how many others there are? So our ominous kind of morning gossip has increased — and there remains the fear that the individual one calls may not answer because he or she has been taken.

Some of us have friends among those who are the accused in the treason trials, mainly trade unionists and leaders of the United Democratic Front, in session or about to commence. I telephoned my old friend, Cassim Saloojee, a social worker, and an office-bearer in the United Democratic Front. He is at home on bail after many weeks of detention before being charged formally with treason. One discovers, these days, that genuine cheerfulness exists, and it is a by-product of courage. He has only one complaint, which is expressed in a way that catches me out: 'I've been spending my time watching pornographic films.' And with my tactfully unshockable laugh, I remember that active resistance to apartheid is political pornography in South Africa. The state has seized video cassettes of public meetings made by the United Democratic Front as records of their activities. For the purposes of their defence, the accused must study what may now be used as evidence against them. 'Ninety hours of viewing . . .'

The case is *sub judice*, so I suppose I cannot give here my version of whether the particular meetings I attended (the UDF is a non-racial, non-violent and legally-constituted movement) could possibly be construed as violent and treasonous, but I hope that among all that footage there is at least recorded the time when the crowd in a Johannesburg hall heard that there was police harassment of some supporters in the foyer, and from the platform Cassim Saloojee succeeded in preventing the crowd from streaming out to seek a confrontation that doubtless would have resulted in police violence.

While writing this letter I have had a call from a young white student at the University of the Witwatersrand, down the road, who himself is a veteran of detention, and whose brother is now in detention for the second time. At last, after more than two weeks, his parents have managed to get permission to visit his brother in prison – like well over a thousand others, he has not been charged. The parents are founder members of the well-established Detainees' Parents' Support Committee, a title and status that indicate the enduring state of mind, stoic but unintimidatedly active on the part of all prisoners of conscience black and white, whether or not in the family, that prevails among white people like these. Their son has called to ask me to take part in a panel discussion on South African culture to be held by the students' Academic Freedom Committee. Irrelevant while we are in a state of emergency? Concurrently with engagement in the political struggle for the end of apartheid, there exists an awareness of the need for a new conception of culture, particularly among whites. Young people like these are aware that a *change of consciousness*, of the white sense of self, has to be achieved along with a change of regime, if, when blacks do sit down to consult with whites, there is to be anything to talk about. The arts in South Africa sometimes do bear relation to the real entities of South African life in the way that the euphemisms and evasions of white politics do not.

These are the *states of mind* of the majority of white South Africans, and of the minority within the white population. In the first, the preoccupations of the second are no more than newspaper stories you, too, read thousands of miles away: so long as the Casspir armoured monsters[7] patrol the black townships and even mass funerals are banned, the majority feel safe, since there is no possibility that they may be imprisoned for a too-active sense of justice, or find any member of their families or their friends in detention, on trial, or in danger of losing a life in right-wing terrorist attacks. Nor is there any possibility that one of their lawyers might be gunned down, as was a member of a treason trial defence team outside her home a few nights ago.

The *conditions of life*, for whites, are a different matter. Even those few whites who have members of their families in prison themselves continue to wake up every morning as I do, to the song of weaver birds and mechanical-sounding whirr of crested barbets in a white suburb. Soweto is only eight miles from my house; if I did not have friends living there, I should not be aware of the battles of stones against guns and tear-gas that are going on in its streets, for images on a TV screen come by satellite as easily from the other side of the world as from eight miles away, and may be comprehended as equally distanced from the viewer. How is it possible that the winter sun is shining, the randy doves are announcing spring, the domestic workers from the backyards are placing bets on the numbers game, Fah-Fee, with the Chinese runner, as usual every afternoon? In terms of *ways of life*, conditions of daily living are sinisterly much the same for all whites, those who manage to ignore the crisis in our country, and those for whom it is the determining state of mind. Some go to protest meetings, others play golf. All of us go home to quiet streets, outings to the theatre and cinema, good meals and secure shelter for the night, while in the black townships thousands of children no longer go to school, fathers and sons disappear into police vans or lie shot in the dark streets, social gatherings are around coffins and social intercourse is confined to mourning.

The night the State of Emergency was declared I was at a party held at an alternative education centre, the Open School, in the downtown area where banks and the glass palaces of mining companies run down into Indian stores and black bus queues. The School is directed by Colin and Dolphine Smuts (black, despite their Afrikaans surname) for black youths and children who study drama, painting, dance and music there – subjects not offered by government 'bantu' education.[8] The occasion was a celebration: the School, which had been in danger of closure for lack of funds, had received a Ford Foundation grant. Colin had not known until the evening began whether the new ban on gatherings might not be served on the celebration; Dolphine had gone ahead and prepared food. There were polite speeches, music, drumming, and the declamatory performance of poetry that has been part of resistance rhetoric since young people began to compose in prison in 1976, and which sets such gatherings apart from their counterparts in other countries. Soweto was sealed off by military roadblocks. Yet the black guests had come through somehow, thoroughly frisked in the 'elegantly casual' clothes all, black and white, wear to honour this kind of occasion. I asked a couple I had not met before what it was like to be in Soweto now, looking at them in the inhibited, slightly awed way one tries not to reveal to people who have emerged alive from some unimaginable ordeal. The man took a bite from a leg of chicken and washed it down with his drink. 'In your street, one day it's all right. The next day, you can cross the street when a Casspir comes round the corner, and you'll die. It's like Beirut.'

Yes, if you want to know what it's like here, it's more like Beirut than he knew. I remember a film I once saw, where the camera moved from destruction and its hateful cacophony in the streets to a villa where people were lunching on a terrace, and there were birds and flowers. That's what it's like. I also remember something said by a character in a novel I wrote ten years ago. 'How long can we go on getting away scot free?'[9]

Sincerely,
Nadine Gordimer.

Notes

Though my sources are not often given in these notes, I have found the following reference and narrative works extremely helpful: T. Karis and G. M. Carter (eds), *From Protest to Challenge: A Documentary History of African Politics in South Africa 1882–1964*, 4 vols (Stanford, Ca.: Hoover Institution Press, 1972–7); the annual *Survey of Race Relations in South Africa, 1951–84*, compiled by M. Horrell et al. (Johannesburg: South African Institute of Race Relations); H. M. Zell, C. Bundy and V. Coulon (eds), *A New Reader's Guide to African Literature*, 2nd rev. and exp. edn (London: Heinemann, 1983); Colin Legum (ed.), *Africa: A Handbook*, rev. and enl. edn (London: Anthony Blond, 1965); David Birmingham and Phyllis M. Martin (eds), *History of Central Africa*, vol. 2 (London and New York: Longman, 1983); Christopher Hibbert, *Africa Explored* (London: Allen Lane, 1982; New York: Norton, 1983); and Peter Forbath, *The River Congo* (London: Secker & Warburg, 1977).

Introduction

1 This was 'The Quest for Seen Gold', less a short story than a fable, published in the children's section of the *Sunday Express* (Johannesburg), 13 June 1937, p. 38.

2 A shorter volume, in German, has already appeared: Nadine Gordimer, *Leben im Interregnum: Essays zu Politik und Literatur*, edited and introduced by Stephen Clingman (Frankfurt: S. Fischer Verlag, 1987).

3 For all titles otherwise unspecified in the introduction or these notes, see the essays in this volume.

4 Here I cannot help using a phrase I have used elsewhere in relation to Gordimer's fiction: see Stephen Clingman,

The Novels of Nadine Gordimer: History from the Inside (London and Boston: Allen & Unwin; Johannesburg: Ravan Press; 1986).

5 See 'A Bolter and the Invincible Summer'.

6 See 'A Writer's Freedom'.

7 See 'Relevance and Commitment'.

8 See 'Letter from Johannesburg, 1985'.

9 See 'Relevance and Commitment'.

10 See 'Living in the Interregnum'.

11 See 'Selecting My Stories'.

12 From a personal interview on her travel writing conducted with Nadine Gordimer especially for this publication, Johannesburg, March 1987.

13 Ibid.

14 Ibid.

15 *A Guest of Honour* (London: Jonathan Cape; New York: Viking; 1971).

16 *A Sport of Nature* (London: Jonathan Cape; New York: Knopf; Cape Town and Johannesburg: David Philip/Taurus; 1987).

17 Nevertheless, those with a special interest in this should consult the original published versions, given wherever possible for each essay. Even in these, however, there is frequently some difference from the original typescripts, which, by and large, have been given authority.

A Bolter and the Invincible Summer

1 First published in *London Magazine*, vol. 3 no. 2 (May 1963), pp. 58–65.

2 See general Introduction, p. 1 and n.1. Gordimer continued to publish in the *Sunday Express* for over a year.

3 Paul Kruger, President of the South African Republic before and during the Anglo-Boer War of 1899–1902, and enduring symbol in South Africa of a proud Afrikaner nationalism.

4 'Come Again Tomorrow', *Forum*, 18 November 1939, p. 14.

5 Pauline Smith, the South African writer, best known for *The Little Karroo* (London: Jonathan Cape, 1925; Cape

Town: Balkema, 1981), and *The Beadle* (London: Jonathan Cape, 1926; Cape Town: Balkema, 1981).

6 The famous story by Tolstoy (1884).

7 By William Plomer, in *The Child of Queen Victoria* (London: Jonathan Cape, 1933).

8 See Albert Camus, 'The Road to Tipasa', in his *Lyrical and Critical Essays*, selected and translated by Philip Thody (London: Hamish Hamilton, 1967), p. 131: 'There lay in me an unconquerable summer.' This was no doubt seen elsewhere and earlier by Gordimer in the translation she gives here.

9 'The Defeated', in *The South African Saturday Book*, compiled by Eric Rosenthal and arranged by Richard F. Robinow (London and Cape Town: Hutchinson [1948]), pp. 169–82.

10 *Face to Face* (Johannesburg: Silver Leaf Books, 1949).

11 *The Soft Voice of the Serpent* (London: Gollancz; New York: Simon & Schuster; 1953), to be followed soon after by Gordimer's first novel, *The Lying Days* (London: Gollancz; New York: Simon & Schuster; 1953).

Where Do Whites Fit In?

1 First published in *Twentieth Century*, vol. 155 no. 986 (April 1959), pp. 326–31.

2 *A World of Strangers* (London: Gollancz; New York: Simon & Schuster; 1958).

3 Seretse Khama was the first President of Botswana (the ex-Protectorate of Bechuanaland) when it became independent in September 1966. As youthful heir to the Ngwato chieftainship under the regency of his uncle, Tshekedi Khama, he had married a white woman, Ruth Williams, in England after the war. This precipitated a long and complicated chain of events whereby Khama had to fight against both his uncle's and colonial antipathy to the marriage, was exiled (as was his uncle), finally returned and won the Presidency. See also 'Pula!', p. 200.

Chief Luthuli

1 First published in *Atlantic Monthly*, vol. 203 no. 4 (April 1959), pp. 34–9. The spelling of Luthuli's surname has varied, and it appears he himself preferred the alternative, 'Lutuli'. However, Gordimer's spelling in this essay was the predominant one at the time, and so it has been retained here.

2 These were named informally after General J. B. M. Hertzog, Prime Minister of the day, and so-called 'father of modern Afrikaner nationalism'. Gordimer's account of the Bills is substantially correct.

3 The 1853 Constitution, which granted representative government to the Cape Colony, entitled adult male British subjects to vote, irrespective of race, but subject to certain economic qualifications. It was from this that the specially protected position, as regards the franchise, of blacks and 'coloureds' in the Cape Province emanated. This was entrenched under the Act of Union in 1910; but this is what the Hertzog Bills began to undo.

4 One of the foundation stones of modern apartheid, the Natives' Land Act (1913) scheduled some 7·5 per cent of South Africa's land for black occupation, at the same time prohibiting blacks (except in the Cape) from buying land outside these areas without official consent. Together with a prohibition on share-cropping on white farms, the overall effect was to deprive blacks of any relative independence, and drive them into wage-employment in white-owned agriculture and industry. For a compelling account of the effects of the Natives' Land Act by a writer who figures prominently in these essays, see Sol. T. Plaatje, *Native Life in South Africa* (1916; Johannesburg: Ravan Press, 1982; London: Longman, 1987).

5 Field Marshal Jan Christiaan Smuts, leader of the United Party, and Prime Minister of South Africa during and immediately after the Second World War. The 'bogus paternalism' referred to was Smuts's policy of 'trusteeship', posited as a kind of guardianship by whites towards blacks until such time as the latter could assume proper 'civilised' status. Smuts drafted the original

declaration of aims in the preamble to the United
Nations Charter, with its commitment to 'fundamental
human rights'; in the South African context, however, it
was clear he intended this to apply only to whites.

6 The Bantu Authorities Act (1951) provided for local
self-government for blacks at a 'tribal' level. In 1959 this
was elaborated on by the Promotion of Bantu Self-
Government Act, which envisaged self-government for
blacks in the Reserves. All this was based on land set
aside by the Natives' Land Act (1913) and the Native
Trust and Land Act (1936); and this was the basis of the
so-called black 'homelands' policy of the 1970s and
1980s.

7 This was the famous Defiance Campaign, against unjust
laws, of 1952–3. Embodying the multi-racial principles of
the African National Congress and its allies (as Gordimer
indicates), the campaign still stands as an historic and
symbolic event in South Africa.

8 This statement by Luthuli is also reprinted under the title
'The Road to Freedom is Via the Cross', in *From Protest to
Challenge*, (eds) Karis and Carter, vol. 2, pp. 486–9.

9 Sophiatown was a township on the western side of Johannesburg. Being a freehold area, it was one of the few
urban locations where blacks could own land in South
Africa. Yet, existing right next to white Johannesburg,
ethnically mixed and with a vibrant social and cultural
life (see the introduction to 'One Man Living Through
It'), it was anathema to the apartheid government. From
1954 on it was destroyed methodically, its inhabitants
removed to the ironically named Meadowlands in
Soweto, ánd an all white suburb, equally ironically
named 'Triomf' ('Triumph'), erected in its place.

10 Ultimately the Treason Trial was to last four years,
though by 1959 there were only thirty remaining defendants. It ended on 29 March 1961, before the defence had
been required to complete its concluding argument, with
an acquittal for all.

11 The Liberal Party was formed in May 1953; among its
founders (and later its leader) was the South African
author Alan Paton, most famous for his *Cry, the Beloved*

Country (London: Jonathan Cape; New York: Scribner; 1948).

12 For Africanism, see the introduction to 'Where Do Whites Fit In?' Africanism, as articulated by its most significant founding figure, Anton Lembede, was a philosophy of strict African nationalism strongly opposed to collaboration with whites on an inter-racial basis. As Gordimer notes, in 1959 the Africanists seceded from the African National Congress to form the Pan-Africanist Congress under Robert Sobukwe.

Great Problems in the Street

1 First published in *I Will Still Be Moved*, (ed.) Marion Friedmann (London: Arthur Barker, 1963), pp. 117–22.

2 Friedrich Nietzsche: 'The great problems are to be encountered in the street'. From *Daybreak: Thoughts on the Prejudices of Morality*, translated by R. J. Hollingdale, introduction by Michael Tanner (Cambridge: Cambridge University Press, 1982), aphorism 127, p. 78. Gordimer's own source for this is uncertain.

3 Nelson Mandela, acknowledged leader of the African National Congress in South Africa, though he has been in prison continuously since the 1960s. A founder member of the Congress Youth League in 1943, volunteer-in-chief during the Defiance Campaign and a Treason Trialist, in 1961 he went underground for some 17 months, and was sentenced to 5 years imprisonment in 1962. In 1964 he was first accused in the Rivonia Trial (see 'Why Did Bram Fischer Choose Jail?') and was sentenced, along with most of the others, to life imprisonment on Robben Island.

4 Oliver Tambo, leader of the African National Congress in exile since 1960. Also a founder of the Congress Youth League, and closely associated with Mandela in the 1950s, Tambo became Acting President-General of the ANC on the death of Luthuli in 1967.

5 Gangathura Mohambry 'Monty' Naicker. Banned in the 1950s and a Treason Trialist, he was twice President of the South African Indian Congress.

6 South African Congress of Democrats (SACOD): formed in

1953 as a white grouping within the Congress Alliance, along with the African National Congress, the South African Indian Congress, the South African Coloured People's Organisation, and (later) the South African Congress of Trade Unions.

7   This became the General Law Amendment Act (1962), commonly called the Sabotage Act because it was expressly designed to counter the spate of sabotage which had begun since the State of Emergency. This was the first legislation in South Africa to allow for detention without trial (initially up to 12 days), and it also had implications as regards censorship (see Gordimer's following essay).

8   A multi-racial women's organisation, this was also one of the key bodies of the 1950s. In 1956 it organised a demonstration of twenty thousand women in Pretoria, against the extension of the pass laws to women.

Censored, Banned, Gagged

1   First published in *Encounter*, vol. 20 no. 6 (June 1963), pp. 59–63.

2   This is no longer entirely the case: see Gordimer's remarks on alternative publishing (in English and Afrikaans) since the 1970s in 'The Unkillable Word'.

3   See above, 'Great Problems in the Street', n. 7.

4   South African poet and political activist, in exile since 1966. The work Gordimer would have had in mind at this time was *Sirens, Knuckles, Boots* (Ibadan: Mbari, 1963), published while Brutus was in prison.

5   South African novelist and political activist. The work Gordimer would have had in mind at this time was *A Walk in the Night* (Ibadan: Mbari, 1962; London: Heinemann; Evanston, Il.: Northwestern University Press; 1967). In exile since 1966, La Guma died in Cuba in 1985.

6   Specific works by authors mentioned here: Peter Abrahams, *Tell Freedom* (London: Faber; New York: Knopf; 1954); Ezekiel Mphahlele, *The African Image* (London: Faber; New York: Praeger; 1962); Alfred Hutchinson, *The Road to Ghana* (London: Gollancz, 1960); Todd Matshikiza, *Chocolates for my Wife* (London: Hodder & Stoughton,

1963; Cape Town: David Philip, 1982). By this time all these authors were in exile (see introduction to 'One Man Living Through It').

Why Did Bram Fischer Choose Jail?

1 First published in the *New York Times Magazine*, 14 August 1966, pp. 30–1, 80–1, 84.

2 Published in the same year as this essay, *The Late Bourgeois World* (London: Jonathan Cape; New York: Viking; 1966).

3 The other was 'The Fischer Case', *London Magazine*, March 1966, pp. 21–30.

4 *Burger's Daughter* (London: Jonathan Cape; New York: Viking; 1979).

5 Suppression of Communism Act (1950): one of the first and most wide-ranging repressive measures enacted by the National Party government after 1948. In face of it the Communist Party of South Africa disbanded, only to reconstitute itself clandestinely some years later as the South African Communist Party.

6 See above, 'Chief Luthuli', n. 6. Based on the areas allotted as tribal reserves under the Promotion of Bantu Self-Government Act (1959), 'Bantustans' was the semi-official term for the black territories which were supposed to find 'self-government' at some future stage. See 'A Vision of Two Blood-Red Suns', p. 226.

7 Also a foundation stone of apartheid, this refers historically to the reservation of certain categories of work — usually skilled — for whites, and others — usually unskilled — for blacks. Along with this have gone enormous differentials in wages paid to blacks as compared to whites, thereby substantially entrenching the class structures of apartheid.

8 This would refer primarily to the Group Areas Act (1950), which provided for strict residential and other segregation between the different race and colour groupings, and under which huge numbers of people — usually black, 'coloured' or Indian — have been removed from areas long inhabited, and 'resettled' elsewhere.

9 This refers to the predominantly Dutch origins of the Afrikaners in South Africa (although the phrasing here is slightly unusual). Later this sort of terminology reverted, with pejorative overtones, to what the Afrikaners have called themselves historically, i.e. 'Boers' (farmers). This has relevance for 'Censors and Unconfessed History', n. 6 below on *Burger's Daughter*; and for 'Letter from Johannesburg, 1985'.

10 This refers to those years of the Treason Trial when thirty defendants remained (see 'Chief Luthuli', n. 10 above). However, Fischer was a member of the defence team throughout the trial, from 1957 until its end.

11 This was the Rivonia Trial, at which Nelson Mandela was the first accused (see 'Great Problems', n. 3 above). The 'High Command' was that of *Umkhonto we Sizwe*, offshoot of the African National Congress and associated movements, which organised the turn to sabotage after the events of 1960.

12 See 'Great Problems', n. 3 above. This was from 1961–2, when Mandela travelled through East and North Africa, and also worked at Rivonia and elsewhere.

13 Tragically, it turned out to be Fischer's: he was released from jail only shortly before he died of cancer in 1975. In *Burger's Daughter* Gordimer poignantly acknowledged the irony, where these exact sentiments, having been voiced by one of the characters immediately after Lionel Burger's fictional trial, are then remembered some time after his death by his daughter, Rosa Burger, in conversation with the same character (p. 154).

One Man Living Through It

1 First published in *The Classic*, vol. 2 no. 1 (1966), pp. 11–16. Reprinted in *The World of Nat Nakasa*, (ed.) E. Patel (Johannesburg: Ravan Press, 1985), pp. xx–xxvi.

2 Themba died in Swaziland in 1968. Besides Nakasa, other deaths by suicide at this time were of the poets Ingrid Jonker and, in 1970, Arthur Nortje.

3 For this and other selected pieces by Nakasa, see Patel (ed.), *The World of Nat Nakasa*.

Speak Out: The Necessity for Protest

1 The sixth E. G. Malherbe Academic Freedom Lecture, delivered at the University of Natal, 11 August 1971. First published by the Academic Freedom Committee, Students' Representative Council, University of Natal, Durban, 1971. The title of this address was inspired by Günter Grass's *Speak Out!*, translated by Ralph Manheim, introduced by Michael Harrington (London: Secker & Warburg; New York: Harcourt, Brace & World; 1969).

2 Formed as the Women's Defence of the Constitution League in May 1955, and known as the Black Sash for the black sashes the women wore in protest at the demise of the constitution when the Cape 'coloureds' were removed from the common voters' roll at that time. Since then a major force for protest and action against apartheid.

3 The Christian Institute of Southern Africa – a non-racial organisation of churchmen opposed to apartheid. Founded in 1963, by the early 1970s it had become radicalised by the Black Consciousness ethos; it was ultimately banned in October 1977.

4 M. K. Gandhi, *Satyagraha in South Africa*, rev. 2nd edn, translated by Valji Govindji Desai (1928; Ahmedabad: Navajivan Publishing House, 1960), p. 431.

5 'A Kind of Survivor', in *Language and Silence* (Penguin: Harmondsworth, 1969), p. 131.

6 Early in 1968 the Council of the University of Cape Town appointed Archie Mafeje to a post in the Department of Social Anthropology. This was rescinded after the Council received a letter of threat, on racial grounds, from the Minister of National Education. Despite strong protests from students in Cape Town and elsewhere, Mafeje was never reinstated.

7 In October 1969 Winnie Mandela and 21 others were charged under the Suppression of Communism Act. In February 1970 the prosecution was withdrawn and all 22 were discharged. Before leaving Court, however, they were rearrested and detained under the Terrorism Act. A second trial – now of 20 accused – began in June 1970; the charges, however, were dismissed, and all were dis-

charged again, the Appeal Court upholding this decision. Strong protest against the arbitrary arrests was voiced at the English-language universities during this time.

8   Heinke, President of the Students' Representative Council at the University of the Witwatersrand, was an American citizen. In 1971 his temporary residence permit was not extended, in effect forcing him to leave the country.

9   Famous for publicising the disastrous removals of black communities in South Africa, Desmond was the author of *The Discarded People: an Account of Resettlement in South Africa* (Johannesburg: Christian Institute of South Africa, 1970; Harmondsworth: Penguin, 1971), for which Gordimer wrote the Foreword. See her further remarks on Desmond in this essay.

10 'A Kind of Survivor', p. 133.

11 Trevor Huddleston, C. R., was from 1943 priest-in-charge of the Community of the Resurrection's mission in Sophiatown, and from 1949–55 principal of St Peter's School in Johannesburg. Identified by many with the spirit of Sophiatown, he has remained an outspoken opponent of apartheid, and currently is President of the Anti-Apartheid movement in Britain.

12 South Africa's national animal is the Springbok; hence its representative sporting teams are called the 'Springboks'.

13 In 1965 the Johannesburg newspaper the *Rand Daily Mail* published reports on South African prisons, based on the revelations of Harold Strachan, a political prisoner who had just been released, as well as other sources. Laurence Gandar, the editor of the paper, as well as Benjamin Pogrund, the reporter concerned, were charged with publishing false information on prisons without taking reasonable steps to verify it. They were both ultimately found guilty, though sworn statements had been taken from their informants for the reports.

14 Formed in 1959 as a breakaway from the United Party, the Progressive Party has represented the only real parliamentary opposition to apartheid since that time. Due to various mergers it has gone through successive name changes: the Progressive-Reform Party, and the Progress-

ive Federal Party; these will appear at different stages in these essays. Helen Suzman, representing the Progressive Party continuously since 1959, has maintained a remarkable record on human rights in South Africa.

15 One of the most renowned of white opponents of apartheid. A founder member of the Congress of Democrats in 1953, national secretary of the Federation of South African Women, and a Treason Trialist, she was thereafter restricted by a series of bans. However, as Gordimer notes, she has never stopped 'speaking out' whenever possible.

16 From 'The Pinprick Speech', in *Speak Out!* (Harcourt, Brace and World edn), p. 88.

17 This refers to the period of so-called 'détente', when the Nationalist government of Prime Minister B. J. Vorster attempted to set up some kind of 'dialogue' with the countries mentioned. Gordimer had recently visited three of them: see 'Madagascar' and 'Merci Dieu, It Changes'.

18 This is a statement probably made under the impress of the relatively inchoate developments of the time. Later it would become clear that most of the homeland leaders did not have anything in mind very different from the South African government; and SASO would later by no means have identified itself with the 'homelands'.

19 For an in-depth study of Gandhi in South Africa, see Maureen Swan, *Gandhi: The South African Experience* (Johannesburg: Ravan Press, 1985).

20 See Sartre, *Anti-Semite and Jew*, translated by George J. Becker (New York: Schocken, 1965), p. 95: 'Certain ... Jews have allowed themselves to be poisoned by the stereotype that others have of them, and they live in fear that their acts will correspond to this stereotype.'

21 Majeke [Dora Taylor], *The Role of the Missionaries in Conquest* [Johannesburg: Society of Young Africa, 1952], p. 26.

22 'The Future of Liberalism', from *Irish Essays and Others*. reprinted in *English Literature and Irish Politics*, vol. 9 of *The Complete Prose Works of Matthew Arnold*, (ed.) R. H. Super (Ann Arbor: University of Michigan Press, 1973), p. 140.

23 Frantz Fanon, *Black Skin, White Masks*, translated by C. L. Markmann (New York: Grove Press, 1967), p. 226.

A Writer's Freedom

1 Address, given at the Durban Indian Teachers' Conference, December 1975. First published in *New Classic*, no. 2 (1975), pp. 11–16.

2 Gordimer's source: 'Die Büchverbrennung', translated by H. R. Hays as 'The Burning of the Books', in Bertolt Brecht, *Selected Poems* (New York: Grove Press, 1959), p. 125.

3 Chinua Achebe, famous for his set of novels beginning with *Things Fall Apart* (London: Heinemann, 1958; New York: McDowell, Obolensky, 1959), was involved with the Biafran cause during the Nigerian Civil War, and was in exile in the United States at the time of this address. Gordimer reviewed his collection of essays, *Morning Yet on Creation Day* (London: Heinemann, 1975) in the *Times Literary Supplement*, 17 October 1975, p. 1227.

4 Breyten Breytenbach, most brilliant Afrikaans writer of the *Sestiger* ('Sixties') generation, which for the first time began to challenge Afrikaner culture in a dramatic way. While living in Paris he married a Vietnamese woman; this was illegal under the South African Prohibition of Mixed Marriages Act, which was why he needed special dispensation to return with his wife. His book about the visit was *'n Seisoen in die Paradys*, first published in Afrikaans under the pseudonym of B. B. Lasarus (Johannesburg: Perskor, 1976), and later under Breytenbach's own name as *A Season in Paradise*, translated by Rike Vaughan, introduction by André Brink (New York: Persea, 1980; London: Faber, 1985). See 'The Essential Gesture', n. 7 below.

5 From Ivan Turgenev, 'Apropos of Fathers and Sons', in *Turgenev's Literary Reminiscences and Autobiographical Fragments*, translated with an introduction by David Magarshack, and an essay by Edmund Wilson (London: Faber, 1958), pp. 170–1.

6 From Turgenev's introduction to the collected edition of

his novels, quoted by Magarshack in his introduction, ibid, p. 82.

7 'Apropos of Fathers and Sons', p. 176.

Selecting My Stories

1 Originally published as the Introduction to Gordimer's *Selected Stories* (London: Jonathan Cape, 1975; New York: Viking, 1976).

2 William Plomer, from the Preface to his *Four Countries* (London: Jonathan Cape, 1949), p. 7.

3 Octavio Paz, 'The Conquest and Colonialism', in *The Labyrinth of Solitude: Life and Thought in Mexico*, translated by Lysander Kemp (New York: Grove Press, 1961), p. 114.

4 For this and all other stories by Gordimer mentioned here, see her *Selected Stories*.

Letter from Johannesburg, 1976

1 First published as 'Letter from South Africa', *New York Review of Books*, vol. 23 no. 20 (9 December 1976), pp. 3–4, 6, 8, 10.

2 Tom Lodge, *Black Politics in South Africa* (London: Longman, 1983), p. 330.

3 Rhodesia (now Zimbabwe) had declared itself independent from Britain unilaterally in November 1965. The United States' Secretary of State was visiting Southern Africa at the time of this essay in order to facilitate a negotiated settlement with the liberation movements. It failed; Ian Smith, Prime Minister of Rhodesia, attempted his own internal settlement which also failed; and Zimbabwe finally became fully independent in April 1980.

4 From *Equiano's Travels* (*The Interesting Narrative of the Life of Olaudah Equiano or Gustavus Vassa the African, Written by Himself*) (1789), edited and abridged by Paul Edwards (London: Heinemann, 1967), p. 73.

5 Gandhi, *Satyagraha in South Africa*, loc. cit.

6 Chief Minister of KwaZulu, Buthelezi has consistently refused to accept 'independence' for his 'homeland'.

However, because of his position as a 'homeland' leader, and because of his dealings with the South African government, his position has remained a profoundly ambiguous one: see Shula Marks, *The Ambiguities of Dependence in South Africa* (Johannesburg: Ravan Press; Baltimore, Md: Johns Hopkins University Press; 1986), ch. 4.

7   One-time member of the Afrikaner *Broederbond* (see 'Censors and Unconfessed History', n. 4 below), and a Moderator of the Dutch Reformed Church (see 'The Unkillable Word', n. 8 below) in the Transvaal, through a change of conscience Naudé became founder and first Director of the Christian Institute (see 'Speak Out', n. 3 above). When the Institute was banned in October 1977, Naudé was too, to have his restrictions lifted only in September 1984.

8   These were the institutions of local urban government for blacks, though they were widely suspected of collaboration with the state, and generally elected on very low polls. In 1976 most of the members of the Soweto Urban Bantu Council resigned.

9   Walter Sisulu and Govan Mbeki are both long-standing leaders within the African National Congress; both were sentenced to life imprisonment at the Rivonia Trial, though Mbeki was released in late 1987. Mandela and Sisulu are no longer on Robben Island, having been transferred with a few others to Pollsmoor Prison near Cape Town in April 1982. Robert Sobukwe, President of the Pan-Africanist Congress, was sentenced to three years' imprisonment in the wake of the Sharpeville massacre (see introduction to 'Great Problems in the Street'). Shortly before the end of his sentence, Parliament passed a General Law Amendment Act enabling the Minister of Justice to prolong indefinitely the detention of any political prisoner. Sobukwe was the first and only person to be detained (repeatedly) under this law. Released from Robben Island finally in 1969, he was restricted to the town of Kimberley where he died in 1978.

10   See Frantz Fanon, *Black Skin, White Masks*.

11   For Gordimer's response to the Transkei after its 'independence', see 'A Vision of Two Blood-Red Suns'.

12   Gordimer's paragraph here reflects the flux of the time, with the African National Congress – because of its 'non-racial' stance – opposed to the Black Consciousness movement, and vice versa; both of them opposed to Buthelezi (during the Soweto Revolt there were clashes between the students and followers of Buthelezi's Zulu-nationalist *Inkatha Yenkululeko Yesizwe* movement); and the general feeling that everyone was on the side of black liberation.

Relevance and Commitment

1   Address first given at a Conference on the State of Art in South Africa, University of Cape Town, July 1979. Also at the Radcliffe Forum, Harvard University, October 1979, and as the Neil Gunn Fellowship Address, Edinburgh 1981. Published in a slightly different version as 'Apprentices of Freedom', *New Society*, 24–31 December 1981, pp. ii–v.

2   André Pieyre de Mandiargues, *The Margin*, translated by Richard Howard (London: Calder & Boyars, 1969), p. 208.

3   Steve Biko: acknowledged leader of the Black Consciousness movement in South Africa, he died in 1977 in extremely dubious circumstances after having been kept naked and manacled in police custody.

4   Hector Petersen was the first schoolchild to be shot on 16 June 1976 at the start of the Soweto Revolt.

5   For Sol. T. Plaatje's greatest literary achievement in English, see his novel *Mhudi* (Lovedale: Lovedale Press [1930]); (ed.) Stephen Gray, introduction by Tim Couzens (London: Heinemann; Washington D.C.: Three Continents Press; 1978). See also 'Chief Luthuli', n. 4 above.

6   See Thomas Mofolo, *Chaka: An Historical Romance* (1931; London & New York: Oxford University Press, 1967); new translation by Daniel P. Kunene (London: Heinemann, 1981).

Egypt Revisited

1 Original typescript, under title 'A View of the Nile', dated December 1958. First published as 'Egypt Revisited', *National and English Review*, vol. 152 no. 911 (January 1959), pp. 47–53.

2 This refers to the union of Egypt and Syria under the title of the United Arab Republic, in February 1958. Eventually Syria withdrew in September 1961.

3 In the context of a crisis in Anglo-Egyptian relations and internal political structures, the Free Officers seized power in Egypt in July 1952. They were led by Colonel Nasser, though General Neguib was used as a figurehead. After a protracted power struggle Nasser ousted Neguib in 1954.

4 This of course refers to the invasion of Egypt by Britain, France and Israel in October and November 1956, after Nasser nationalised the Suez Canal. As Gordimer suggests, the result of this was something of a moral and diplomatic victory for Egypt.

5 After the Suez invasion, in 1957 Nasser began to nationalise foreign commercial interests and capital. This would have been going on during Gordimer's visit.

6 The conflict, which as Gordimer suggests was of international proportions, was over the funding of the Aswan Dam, which would extend enormously Egypt's electrical power and irrigation potential. Initial Western financing was withdrawn, partly in response to Egypt's 'nonaligned' policy; it was after this that Nasser nationalised the Suez Canal. In October 1956 the USSR offered to provide the funding for the Dam, which eventually came to a sum far greater than Western sources had put forward.

The Congo River

1 This essay was composed from two original typescripts, 'Towards the Heart of Darkness' and 'Africa 1960: The Great Period' (both dated 1960), and was first published as 'The Congo River', *Holiday*, vol. 29 no. 5 (May 1961),

pp. 74–103. Gordimer's original trip was in February 1960, some months before the Belgian Congo's independence, but the essay reflects additions made later for its first publication.

2   Henry Morton Stanley – who made his fame by finding Dr Livingstone in 1871 – undertook a number of journeys along the Congo River, travelling in both directions. The one Gordimer is referring to here lasted from 1879–84, when Stanley was building stations along the river on contract to Léopold II of Belgium, and establishing what later became the latter's private colony.

3   In brief, the initial sequence of events was as follows. The Congo achieved its independence on 30 June 1960. Five days later there was a revolt by the *Force Publique* soldiers against their officers (not one of the army officers at the time of independence was African) and social breakdown in various centres resulted. There was a flight of European state employees, and on 11 July the wealthiest province, Shaba (Katanga), seceded, with the backing of local European mining interests; a United Nations peace-keeping force was called in days later. Though some riots had already taken place when she undertook her trip, Gordimer missed being in the worst of all of this only by a matter of months.

4   Together with other French territories in West and Equatorial Africa, the Congo Republic also gained its independence in 1960.

5   Indeed, Livingstone's conviction, on finding the Lualaba in 1867, was that it was the source of the Nile.

6   Leader of the *Mouvement National Congolais*, Lumumba was the first Prime Minister of the newly independent state. In the breakdown after independence he was dismissed by President Kasavubu (see following note) in September 1960. Later arrested, he escaped and was recaptured attempting to reach his followers who had established themselves in Kisangani (Stanleyville). He was then handed over in custody to the Shaba regime, where he was murdered in January 1961. Kisangani remained a centre of Lumumbist opposition.

7   Joseph Kasavubu, leader of the *Alliance des Ba-Kongo*

(ABAKO), became first President of the country in a shared national government with Lumumba when the first election results were not thoroughly decisive. After the travails of the first five years of independence, Kasavubu was finally overthrown in 1965 in an army coup led by General Mobutu (now President Mobutu Sese Seko).

8 This was on Stanley's expedition of 1886–9 to rescue Emin Pasha, the Governor of Equatoria in the Sudan, who had apparently been abandoned after the fall of Khartoum. Stanley also traversed the area around Lakes Albert and Edward, the Semliki Plain and the Ruwenzori Mountains – where Gordimer was covering some of this same ground approximately seventy years later. See H. M. Stanley, *In Darkest Africa, or The Quest, Rescue and Retreat of Emin, Governor of Equatoria* (London: Sampson Low, Marston, Searle and Rivington; New York: Scribner; 1890).

9 Independence was given to the two areas making up this territory separately, as the states of Rwanda and Burundi in 1962.

10 To be followed in August 1960 by Kasai, a diamond-mining region.

11 At this stage also set to become a republic, in May 1961.

12 Tshombe's Shaba regime was finally subdued in January 1963, and Tshombe exiled. In mid-1964, in conditions of continuing breakdown, he was brought into central government, ostensibly in order to reconcile opposing groups, though in practice his solution was brutal and bloody. His struggle for power with Kasavubu in 1965 set the scene for the Mobutu coup, and he was exiled once again. Finally he was abducted in 1967 and taken to Algeria, where he died in prison in 1969.

13 The Conference was held in January 1960.

Madagascar

1 Gordimer visited Madagascar in July–August 1969. I have found no previous publication of this essay.

2 The Malagasy Republic was proclaimed independent on 26 June 1960. The *Communauté*, providing for autonomous republics within the general orbit of French control, was

established in 1958. When it became possible to take full independence and still remain within the Community, most of the former French colonies chose this option.

3   The uprising, which began in March 1947, was quelled extremely ruthlessly; over the course of more than a year the death toll was at least eleven thousand (the official French figure, though other estimates ranged far higher). For a book precipitated by the revolt, which has had some significance for Gordimer's fiction (and which is mentioned by her in 'Relevance and Commitment'), see O. Mannoni, *Prospero and Caliban: The Psychology of Colonisation*, translated by Pamela Powesland (London: Methuen; New York: Praeger; 1956).

4   Léopold Sédar Senghor, one of the greatest of Africa's poets, and President of Senegal from 1960 until his retirement in 1980. One of the founders and most committed proponents of the *négritude* movement, as mentioned by Gordimer in 'Speak Out: The Necessity for Protest'.

5   See Virginia Thompson and Richard Adloff, *The Malagasy Republic: Madagascar Today* (Stanford, Ca.: Stanford University Press, 1965), p. 184. This book has been a source for editorial information as well.

6   Ibid., p. 184.

Pula!

1   Original typescript 1970; first published in a slightly different version as 'Pula', *London Magazine*, vol. 12 no. 6 (February/March 1973), pp. 90–103.

2   Though Botswana did not recognise the Smith regime after Rhodesia's unilateral declaration of independence in 1965 (see 'Letter from Johannesburg, 1976', n. 3), it had to recognise Rhodesia's continued administration of the railway which passed through its territory. See Richard Dale, 'Botswana', in *Southern Africa in Perspective: Essays in Regional Politics*, (eds) C. P. Potholm and R. Dale (New York: Free Press, 1972), p. 120.

3   From 1885–95 the administrative capital of the Bechuanaland Protectorate was in Vryburg, in the northern Cape. Thereafter it moved north along the Line of Rail to

an enclave known as the Imperial Reserve on the outskirts of Mafeking. In 1965, the year in which the Protectorate achieved self-government, the capital finally moved north again to Gaborone. Ibid., p. 111.

4 See 'Where Do Whites Fit In?', n. 3 above.

5 'Kraal' is, precisely, an African enclosure for cattle, but the term is often used loosely for a human settlement.

6 This refers to the central character of Ernest Hemingway's story 'The Short Happy Life of Francis Macomber', first published in book form in *The Fifth Column and the First Forty-Nine Stories* (New York: Scribner, 1938; London: Jonathan Cape, 1939).

7 This was Livingstone's first significant exploratory trip, when he was still a member of the London Missionary Society, and working in the northern Cape and Bechuanaland.

Merci Dieu, It Changes

1 Original typescript 1971. First published as 'The Life of Accra, the Flowers of Abidjan: A West African Diary', *Atlantic*, vol. 228 no. 5 (November 1971), pp. 85–9.

2 Gordimer is referring here to the coup which overthrew Kwame Nkrumah in February 1966. Leader of the Convention Peoples' Party and Prime Minister since 1951, Nkrumah led Ghana to independence in 1957. However, his increasingly authoritarian rule towards the end of his regime as well as Ghana's economic decline led to disaffection, and while he was out of the country as part of a peace-making mission in response to the war in Vietnam, the coup took place. Nkrumah returned to Guinea, and remained there until he died in April 1972 in Rumania, where he was being treated for cancer. He was buried in Accra. For Nkrumah, see Basil Davidson, *Black Star: A View of the Life and Times of Kwame Nkrumah* (London: Allen Lane, 1973; New York: Praeger, 1974).

3 Nkrumah's title, 'Osagyefo', literally meant 'victor in war', though it was widely publicised as meaning 'redeemer'. Ibid., p. 192.

4 Born in 1868, author of *The Souls of Black Folk* (1903),

and founder of the National Association for the Advancement of Colored People, DuBois was an inspirational figure for Pan-Africanists. At the 1945 Pan-African Congress in Manchester, which Nkrumah attended, DuBois presided. In 1961 he moved to Ghana at Nkrumah's invitation, where he died in 1963. However, his remains did not lie 'forever' where Gordimer saw his grave; in 1986 they were reinterred in a memorial tomb in the house where he spent his last years, now established as the W. E. B. DuBois Memorial Centre for Pan-African Culture.

5 Dr Busia, a long-standing opponent of Nkrumah, won the election of 1969 when the military regime handed over power to civilian rule. However, in 1972 he was himself overthrown in a coup, led by Colonel Acheompong. It was at this stage that Nkrumah was buried in Accra.

6 Along with most of the other French colonies in West and Equatorial Africa, Ivory Coast became independent in 1960.

7 Born in 1905, a Deputy to the French Assembly in 1945, first President of the *Rassemblement Démocratique Africaine* of French West Africa, Houphoët-Boigny is still President of Ivory Coast in 1988.

8 See 'Speak Out: The Necessity for Protest', p. 98, and n. 17. Ivory Coast, under Houphoët-Boigny, was one of Vorster's most receptive targets for 'dialogue'.

A Vision of Two Blood-Red Suns

1 Original typescript dated 1977. First published as 'Transkei: A Vision of Two Blood-Red Suns', *Geo*, no. 4 (April 1978), pp. 8–42.

2 For the origins of this dispensation, see 'Chief Luthuli', notes 4, 6, above.

3 The Transkei gained its 'independence' on 26 October 1976. See 'Letter from Johannesburg, 1976', p. 128.

4 See Govan Mbeki, *South Africa: The Peasants' Revolt* (1964; London: International Defence and Aid Fund, 1984), p. 67. For Mbeki see 'Letter from Johannesburg, 1976', n. 9 above.

5   Of course this vision was also arising elsewhere. The South African Native National Congress (later the African National Congress), formed in 1912, implicitly and explicitly proclaimed it.

6   For the Cape franchise in the nineteenth century, see 'Chief Luthuli', n. 3 above.

7   This was the Glen Grey Act, establishing a council system in the Glen Grey district of the Transkei, while excluding landed property in the district as a criterion for the Cape franchise. Providing also for taxation on the basis of individual land tenure, one of its main effects was to cater to white labour requirements, especially on the mines (where Rhodes of course had a major interest), by making it necessary for Transkeian men to work as migrant labourers in order to survive.

8   See Mbeki, *The Peasants' Revolt*, p. 25.

9   Under a provision requiring a two-thirds majority at a joint sitting of both Houses of Parliament to effect any change.

10 The white franchise was extended under the Women's Enfranchisement Act (1930) and the Franchise Laws Amendment Act (1931); for Hertzog's laws of 1936 see Gordimer's account in 'Chief Luthuli', p. 42.

11 This was under the provisions of the Bantu Authorities Act (1951) (see 'Chief Luthuli', n. 6 above). The concept of 'tribal authority', though historically cognate to Sekgoma Khama's position mentioned by Gordimer in 'Pula!', has taken on far more manipulative implications in South Africa.

12 This would have been the squatter camp of Crossroads, now internationally famous.

13 Here Gordimer was responding to claims made at the time; it is not clear now, however, to what extent they remain true.

The Unkillable Word

1   Address given at the CNA Award Dinner, 17 April 1980. First published as 'Censorship and the Word', *The Bloody Horse*, no. 1 (September-October 1980), pp. 20–4.

2 For the immediately following details on censorship I am particularly grateful to Gilbert Marcus of the Centre for Applied Legal Studies, University of the Witwatersrand.

3 Nadine Gordimer et al., *What Happened to Burger's Daughter, or How South African Censorship Works* (Johannesburg: Taurus, 1980), pp. 1–2. Much of my account of *Burger's Daughter* here has been taken from this booklet Gordimer and others produced on the banning and unbanning of her novel.

4 *A Dry White Season* (London: W. H. Allen, 1979; New York: Morrow, 1980).

5 *Magersfontein, O Magersfontein!* (Cape Town: Human & Rousseau, 1976). English translation by Ninon Roets (Wynberg, South Africa: Hutchinson Group, 1983).

6 *Vaderland* (Johannesburg), 18 April 1980, p. 2.

7 The Hon. J. H. Snyman, Chairman of the Publications Appeal Board when *Burger's Daughter* was unbanned. The fact that this was the Board's decision did not prevent him from slurring the novel for its supposed 'crudity' and 'profanity'. His nick-name, 'Lammie', means 'little lamb' in Afrikaans.

8 The largest and most powerful of the Afrikaner churches, historically the Dutch Reformed Church has had a direct role in promoting and institutionalising apartheid in church and state, and attempting to justify it theologically.

9 The foremost national prize awarded in Afrikaans literature. Named after the same J. B. M. Hertzog whose 1936 Bills so affected Albert Luthuli (see 'Chief Luthuli', n. 2 above); an indication of how closely culture and politics are linked in South Africa.

10 Named after Thomas Mofolo and William Plomer, Nadine Gordimer played a role in setting it up.

11 For *Waiting for Leila* (Johannesburg: Ravan Press, 1981).

12 Brother of B. J. Vorster (Prime Minister from 1966 to 1978 and State President until 1979), Koot Vorster served as both Moderator and Assessor of the Dutch Reformed Church General Synod between 1970 and 1978.

13 President of the so-called 'independent homeland' of Bophutatswana.

14 This refers to D. J. Opperman's volume of poetry *Komas uit 'n Bamboestok* ('Comas from a Bamboo-shoot') (Cape Town: Human & Rousseau, 1979), for which he won the Afrikaans section of the CNA Prize in 1980.

15 *Sounds of a Cowhide Drum*, introduction by Nadine Gordimer (Johannesburg: Renoster, 1971; London and New York: Oxford University Press, 1972).

16 *Call Me Not a Man* (Johannesburg: Ravan Press, 1979; London: Rex Collings, 1980 and Longman, 1981). Also see 'Censors and Unconfessed History', n. 5 below.

17 Published by Ravan Press in Johannesburg, *Staffrider* became a primary journal of the black literary explosion which accompanied the Soweto Revolt. Its title refers to the black passengers who, because trains are so full, dangle from doors and windows on their rides into and out of Johannesburg.

18 *Éste es el canto de lo que pasa y de lo que será*: from 'Song to the Red Army on Its Arrival at the Gates of Prussia', the concluding poem to the third volume, 'Third Residence' (1935–45), of Neruda's *Residence on Earth*, translated by Donald D. Walsh (1973; London: Souvenir Press, 1976), p. 359; unitalicised in the original.

Censors and Unconfessed History

1 Address at a Conference on Censorship, University of Cape Town, 24 April 1980. First published as 'New Forms of Strategy – No Change of Heart', in *Critical Arts*, vol. 1 no. 2 (June 1980), pp. 27–33.

2 This happened soon after, when the Directorate won an appeal against the ban on *Forced Landing*, (ed.) Mothobi Mutloatse (Johannesburg: Ravan Press, 1980) in August 1980. An earlier appeal by the Directorate against the banning of the Ghanaian writer Ayi Kwei Armah's *Two Thousand Seasons* (1973; London: Heinemann; Chicago: Third World Press; 1979) failed, though a second appeal succeeded in 1983. This from Gilbert Marcus, 'Blacks Treated More Severely', *Index on Censorship*, vol. 13 no. 6 (December 1984), pp. 17–18.

3 State vs Moroney (1978).

4 The *Broederbond* ('Brotherhood'): a tightly-knit society of Afrikaner males, core of the Afrikaner nationalist movement, and responsible to a considerable extent for the rise of Afrikaner political and economic power since the 1930s.

5 *Call Me Not a Man* was declared 'undesirable' on 9 April 1979; this decision was rescinded only on 15 March 1985.

6 *Burger's Daughter*, p. 11. These remarks in the novel are made by Rosa Burger's friends attempting to sympathise with her after the police have detained her mother, but as Gordimer pointed out in *What Happened to Burger's Daughter*, p. 23, the censors did not pick up here the contextual irony that Rosa herself, as well as her parents, was an Afrikaner. For the real-life equivalent of this, see Bram Fischer's speech from the dock in 'Why Did Bram Fischer Choose Jail?', p. 74.

7 Miriam Tlali, *Muriel at Metropolitan* (Johannesburg: Ravan Press, 1979), p. 12.

8 See Barthes, *Mythologies*, translated by Annette Lavers (London: Jonathan Cape; New York: Hill & Wang; 1972), especially the final essay, 'Myth Today', for the 'naturalisation' of social and historical relationships in contemporary myth.

9 The Immorality Amendment Act (1950) extended the existing prohibition on sexual relations between whites and Africans to those between whites and all 'non-whites'.

10 It would be interesting to know whether this term derived from the concept of the 'implied reader' specified by German 'reception theory' from the early 1970s onwards: see Wolfgang Iser, *Der implizite Leser* (Munich: W. Fink, 1972). If so it might be a good example of a South African administrative pattern: adapting conceptual developments elsewhere to its own repressive ends.

11 One of the first major pieces of legislation enacted by the National Party after 1948 was the Population Registration Act (1950) under which all South Africans had to be classified racially. To this end a Race Classification Board was set up to adjudicate in cases of doubt, and two of the tests used – usually to distinguish so-called 'coloureds' from whites – were the inspection of finger nails and

seeing whether a pencil would stick in the victim's hair (tight curls supposedly being a sign of race in these cases).

12 Quoted by Steiner, 'To Civilize Our Gentlemen', in *Language and Silence*, p. 90.

Living in the Interregnum

1 Given as the William James Lecture, New York University Institute of the Humanities, 14 October 1982. First published in a slightly different version, *New York Review of Books*, vol. 29 nos. 21 and 22 (20 January 1983), pp. 21–2, 24–9.

2 *July's People* (London: Jonathan Cape; New York: Viking; Johannesburg: Ravan Press; 1981).

3 *The Book of Laughter and Forgetting*, translated by Michael Henry Heim (Harmondsworth: Penguin, 1981), p. 87.

4 In 1984 the second South African to win the Nobel Prize for Peace.

5 Gordimer's source for this was Lionel Trilling, *Sincerity and Authenticity* (London: Oxford University Press, 1972), p. 114. See her footnote, 'Relevance and Commitment', p. 136.

6 Dr Neil Aggett, Transvaal organiser of the African Food and Canning Workers' Union, was detained on 27 November 1981, and died in detention on 5 February 1982. Though the inquest brought evidence of extraordinary brutality and torture during his detention, the magistrate found his death not caused by any act or omission on the part of the police.

7 This is something which changed as the decade progressed. For Gordimer's remarks on the growth of a small, but significant resistance to army service among whites, see her 'Letter from Johannesburg, 1985'.

8 From 'Dedication', *Selected Poems* (New York: The Ecco Press, 1980), p. 45.

9 William Plomer, *Turbott Wolfe* (London: The Hogarth Press, 1925; New York: Harcourt, Brace & Co., 1926; reprint, Johannesburg: Donker, 1980).

10 Sarah Gertrude Millin, *God's Step-Children* (London:

Constable; New York: Boni & Liveright; 1924); reprint, introduced by Tony Voss (Johannesburg: Donker, 1986).

11 The Dhlomo brothers are among the major black South African writers of this century, though their legacy has been largely ignored until recently. Rolfes Dhlomo wrote mainly in Zulu, but for his one novel in English, see R. R. R. Dhlomo, *An African Tragedy* (Lovedale: Lovedale Press, [1928]). For Herbert Dhlomo, see H. I. E. Dhlomo, *Collected Works*, (eds.) N. Visser and T. Couzens (Johannesburg: Ravan Press, 1985).

12 For representative works of the time by these writers, see Mphahlele, *Down Second Avenue* (1959; London: Faber; New York: Doubleday; 1971); Nkosi, *Home and Exile* (1965; London and New York: Longman, 1983); Themba, *The Will to Die* (London: Heinemann, 1972; Cape Town: David Philip, 1982), and *The World of Can Themba*, (ed.) E. Patel (Johannesburg: Ravan Press, 1985); Modisane, *Blame Me On History* (London: Thames & Hudson; New York: Dutton; 1963; Johannesburg: Donker, 1986); Abrahams, *Mine Boy* (1946; New York: Macmillan, 1970; London: Heinemann, 1976). See also 'Censored, Banned, Gagged', n. 6, above, and introduction to 'One Man Living Through It'.

13 Paraphrased from *Turbott Wolfe* (1925), p. 122; (1980), p. 65.

14 Again, this is something which has changed to some extent since Gordimer gave this lecture. For her account of a renewal of aesthetic preoccupations in black writing in the mid-1980s, see 'The Essential Gesture'.

15 In *Fragrance of Guava*, Plinio Apuleyo Mendoza in conversation with Gabriel García Márquez, translated by Ann Wright (London: Verso, 1983), p. 59.

16 This thought, deriving from Rosa Luxemburg, forms a significant motif in *Burger's Daughter*.

17 Held in Gaborone, Botswana, July 1982. Gordimer gave a version of 'Relevance and Commitment' at this conference.

18 This was a loan given to South Africa by the IMF in 1982. With regard to Gordimer's remarks which follow,

after the outcry over the loan the United States imposed restrictions on money going to South Africa via the IMF.

The Essential Gesture

1 Originally given as the Tanner Lecture on Human Values, University of Michigan, 12 October 1984. Published in *The Tanner Lectures on Human Values*, (ed.) Sterling M. McMurrin (Salt Lake City, Utah: University of Utah Press; Cambridge: Cambridge University Press; 1985), and in a slightly different version, *Granta*, no. 15 (Spring 1985), pp. 135–51.

2 Wole Soyinka, the Nigerian playwright, poet and novelist, and winner in 1986 of the Nobel Prize for Literature. In 1967, during the Nigerian Civil War, Soyinka was arrested for alleged pro-Biafran activities, and imprisoned for two years; his account of this experience is recorded in *The Man Died* (London: Rex Collings; New York: Harper & Row; 1972). For Achebe see 'A Writer's Freedom', n. 3 above.

3 Trappist monk, ordained Catholic priest, poet and Sandinista revolutionary, Cardenal became Nicaragua's Minister of Culture after the revolution.

4 See Don Mattera, *Azanian Love Song* (Johannesburg: Skotaville, 1983).

5 This is no longer true, as a new school of South African historians has begun to recover black history in a more authentic and searching way. Two of the writers Gordimer mentions have themselves been the subjects of major biographies: see Brian Willan, *Sol. Plaatje: A Biography* (London: Longman; Berkeley, Ca.: University of California Press; Johannesburg: Ravan Press; 1984), and Tim Couzens, *The New African: A Study of the Life and Work of H. I. E. Dhlomo* (Johannesburg: Ravan Press, 1985).

6 Poet of the 1970s, and latterly extraordinary novelist: see *To Every Birth Its Blood* (Johannesburg: Ravan Press, 1981; London: Heinemann, 1983).

7 After his 1972 visit (see 'A Writer's Freedom', n. 4 above), Breyten Breytenbach made one more return to South Africa, this time with even more dramatic results. Travel-

ling under an assumed name, he had come to set up an underground liberation organisation; however, he was trailed the whole way by the police and arrested as he was about to leave the country. Sentenced to nine years' imprisonment, he was released with two years' remission in 1982. Jeremy Cronin (one of the university lecturers on trial Gordimer mentions in 'Letter from Johannesburg, 1976') was sentenced to seven years' imprisonment for African National Congress activities. His volume of poetry, *Inside* (Johannesburg: Ravan Press, 1983; London: Jonathan Cape, 1987), speaks directly from these prison years.

8 Three-quarters of Gordimer's full quotation here comes from letters to Sand dated 5–6 December 1866, 15–16 December 1866, and 10 August 1868, in *The Letters of Gustave Flaubert 1857–1880*, selected, edited and translated by Francis Steegmuller (Cambridge, Ma. and London: Harvard University Press, 1982), pp. 94, 95, 118.

Letter from Johannesburg, 1985

1 Previously unpublished in this original version. Published in a different form as 'Guarding "The Gates of Paradise"', *New York Times Magazine*, 8 September 1985, pp. 34–8, 105–8.

2 An organisation which commemorates the landing and heritage of the 1820 Settlers – the beginnings of large-scale British colonial settlement in South Africa. The Voortrekker Monument, erected in Pretoria in 1938, commemorates the Dutch Voortrekkers, who left the Cape in the 1830s after the abolition of slavery by the British.

3 President of the World Alliance of Reformed Churches at the time of this letter. It was following a call by Allan Boesak for progressive forces to unite in resistance to the government's constitutional plans that the United Democratic Front was formed in August 1983.

4 This attack on the ECC intensified during yet a *further* State of Emergency declared in June 1986, when many more of its members were detained.

5 A poet of the 1970s generation, and more recently novelist on the Soweto Revolt – see *A Ride on the Whirlwind* (Johannesburg: Donker, 1981; London: Heinemann; New York: Readers International; 1984).

6 Again, this was something that worsened in the following State of Emergency, when it became illegal, initially, to reveal the names of any detainees at all.

7 These were the successors to the 'hippo' cars of 1976, mentioned in 'The Unkillable Word'.

8 A reference to the education offered blacks since the Bantu Education Act of 1953. This, according to the then Minister of Native Affairs (and later Prime Minister), Verwoerd, would equip blacks to fill 'certain forms of labour' only.

9 The character is Mehring, in Gordimer's sixth novel, *The Conservationist* (London: Jonathan Cape, 1974; New York: Viking, 1975), p. 42.

Index

FOR THE BEST IN PAPERBACKS, LOOK FOR THE

In every corner of the world, on every subject under the sun, Penguin represents quality and variety – the very best in publishing today.

For complete information about books available from Penguin – including Pelicans, Puffins, Peregrines and Penguin Classics – and how to order them, write to us at the appropriate address below. Please note that for copyright reasons the selection of books varies from country to country.

In the United Kingdom: Please write to *Dept E.P., Penguin Books Ltd, Harmondsworth, Middlesex, UB7 0DA*

If you have any difficulty in obtaining a title, please send your order with the correct money, plus ten per cent for postage and packaging, to *PO Box No 11, West Drayton, Middlesex*

In the United States: Please write to *Dept BA, Penguin, 299 Murray Hill Parkway, East Rutherford, New Jersey 07073*

In Canada: Please write to *Penguin Books Canada Ltd, 2801 John Street, Markham, Ontario L3R 1B4*

In Australia: Please write to the *Marketing Department, Penguin Books Australia Ltd, P.O. Box 257, Ringwood, Victoria 3134*

In New Zealand: Please write to the *Marketing Department, Penguin Books (NZ) Ltd, Private Bag, Takapuna, Auckland 9*

In India: Please write to *Penguin Overseas Ltd, 706 Eros Apartments, 56 Nehru Place, New Delhi, 110019*

In Holland: Please write to *Penguin Books Nederland B.V., Postbus 195, NL–1380AD Weesp, Netherlands*

In Germany: Please write to *Penguin Books Ltd, Friedrichstrasse 10–12, D–6000 Frankfurt Main 1, Federal Republic of Germany*

In Spain: Please write to *Longman Penguin España, Calle San Nicolas 15, E–28013 Madrid, Spain*

In France: Please write to *Penguin Books Ltd, 39 Rue de Montmorency, F-75003, Paris, France*

In Japan: Please write to *Longman Penguin Japan Co Ltd, Yamaguchi Building, 2–12–9 Kanda Jimbocho, Chiyoda-Ku, Tokyo 101, Japan*